"Hillary Rodham Clinton has been a global thought leader throughout the past-quarter century in many roles—a high-profile First Lady, elected U.S. Senator, and activist Secretary of State. Yet why is she such a complex figure arousing mixed emotions? In *The Global Hillary*, Sharma and his colleagues could not be more timely in offering a better understanding of this complex American leader."

—*Harold Takooshian, PhD, Professor of Psychology, Fordham University;*
Former President, Division of International Psychology,
American Psychological Association

"*The Global Hillary* presents a multifaceted assessment of Hillary Clinton as an international leader and defender of the rights of women and children. It is indispensable reading for all those who want to understand her powerful impact on global society."

—*Uwe P. Gielen, Founder and Director, Institute for International and*
Cross-Cultural Psychology, St. Francis College

"If you want depth of coverage, no matter what your own political bent, and you want to learn what Hillary Clinton has done for women and girls, how she has pushed economic development, and the impact she has made globally, Sharma's book *The Global Hillary* provides the answers. Journalist, academic and a Harvard trained psychologist, Sharma combines theory of leadership, political science and social psychology. He has woven a textured picture of Hillary Clinton that makes her a humanist and a politician. Biographical chapters compare Hillary Clinton with Eleanor Roosevelt, her feminist role model, and Sarah Palin, her polar opposite. Sharma has brought together exciting writers to present history and the leadership style of Hillary Clinton in different parts of the world, such as Europe, China, Japan, Afghanistan, Africa and the Middle East. Intelligent readers and policy wonks will find this book an important and resourceful guide."

—*Dr. Leonard Davidman, PhD, Past-President,*
New York State Psychological Association; President,
New York City Psychologists; Assistant Professor of Psychiatry
and Behavioral Sciences, New York Medical College

"A rare collection of insights into Hillary Clinton's leadership style, *The Global Hillary* examines one of the most influential women of our time and her historic role as a champion for women's rights and gender equality worldwide."

—*Alyse Nelson, President & CEO, Vital Voices Global Partnership*

THE GLOBAL HILLARY

Is there a linkage between "smart power" and Hillary Clinton's leadership style? Can she advance American leadership and women's development worldwide? *The Global Hillary* addresses these questions and many others.

Bringing together two key aspects of Clinton's ongoing career—her advocacy for international women's rights and the mission to foster democratic development around the world—*The Global Hillary* critically analyzes Clinton's role as a transformative leader of global influence. Essays in this collection provide insight into Clinton's leadership style, particularly her use of American "smart power" in foreign policy, while examining her impact on the continuing worldwide struggle for women's rights. Using international perspectives on the historical and cultural contexts of Clinton's leadership, this book also looks toward the future of women's political leadership in the 21st century, with special attention to the prospect of electing a woman to the United States presidency.

Dinesh Sharma is an Associate Research Professor at the Institute for Global Cultural Studies, SUNY Binghamton. His current teaching work is focused on human rights, globalization, leadership and the UN. In addition, Sharma teaches about global leadership and the UN at Fordham University at Lincoln Center, and has authored and edited several books, including *The Global Obama* and *Barack Obama in Hawai'i and Indonesia*.

LEADERSHIP: Research and Practice Series
A James MacGregor Burns Academy of Leadership Collaboration

SERIES EDITORS
Georgia Sorenson, PhD, Møller Leadership Scholar and Møller By-Fellow, Churchill College, University of Cambridge, founder of the James MacGregor Academy of Leadership at the University of Maryland, and co-founder of the International Leadership Association.

Ronald E. Riggio, PhD, Henry R. Kravis Professor of Leadership and Organizational Psychology and former director of the Kravis Leadership Institute at Claremont McKenna College.

THE GLOBAL HILLARY

Women's Political Leadership in
Cultural Contexts

Edited by Dinesh Sharma

Routledge
Taylor & Francis Group

NEW YORK AND LONDON

First published 2016
by Routledge
711 Third Avenue, New York, NY 10017

and by Routledge
2 Park Square, Milton Park, Abingdon, Oxon, OX14 4RN

Routledge is an imprint of the Taylor & Francis Group, an informa business

© 2016 Taylor & Francis

Library of Congress Cataloging in Publication Data
A catalog record for this book has been requested

ISBN: 978-1-138-82973-2 (hbk)
ISBN: 978-1-138-82974-9 (pbk)
ISBN: 978-1-315-73761-4 (ebk)

Typeset in Bembo
by diacriTech, Chennai

Printed and bound in the United States of America by Publishers Graphics, LLC on sustainably sourced paper.

To call woman the weaker sex is a libel.
—Mahatma Gandhi, *Young India* (1930)

The battle for the individual rights of women is one of long standing and none of us should countenance anything which undermines it.
—Eleanor Roosevelt, "My Day" (1941)

Dedicated to three strong women, my Daughter, Wife and Mother
Anoushka Sharma
Ruby Sharma
Krishna Sharma

CONTENTS

SERIES EDITORS' FOREWORD

Talk about timely. This remarkable look at the global impact of Hillary Clinton's leadership and political agenda by noted international scholars is much anticipated and sorely needed. Much like his previous book, *The Global Obama,* Dinesh Sharma has brought a strong selection of thinkers and policy people together in this balanced book to shed light on the apparent complexity of America's foremost political feminist icon.

The polarizing media focus over three decades has produced the picture of a complex politician, but as Sharma's book makes clear, Clinton's leitmotif, whether you agree with it or not, has always been crystal clear. As early as her undergraduate days, as noted women's studies scholar and psychologist Florence Denmark and her co-authors detail in this book, Rodham Clinton has championed women and children, both as an end in itself and as a means of economic and transformational world development. As the first lady, she gave a landmark speech on women's rights in China and led the fight for equal rights for women. ("Women's rights are human rights"). She has championed women's right to education, health, and political participation both in the United States and abroad. But her passion is not merely rhetorical, but crafted into a lifetime of activism and deliberate social change. As an activist secretary of state, travelling more miles than any other secretary, she melded women's empowerment and development with democracy as central concerns of US foreign policy.

James MacGregor Burns and Georgia Sorenson (full disclosure), writing about the troika of political power in the Clinton White House (Clinton, Gore, Rodman Clinton) saw Rodham Clinton as the most gifted of the three leaders—potentially a transforming leader. While *Global Hillary* offers no apotheosis—Rodham Clinton's use of military might and soft power is nuanced and controversial. But her considered strategy of lifting the power and economic potential of women and girls as a means to human transformation makes this look at the sui generis "Hillary Doctrine" exactly what is needed to understand what really motivates and informs Hillary Rodham Clinton's decades of public work.

Georgia Sorenson
Ronald E. Riggio

PROLOGUE

The Hillary Doctrine is Smart Power

Dinesh Sharma

As we think of power in the 21st century, we want to get away from the idea that power's always zero sum—my gain is your loss and vice versa. Power can also be positive sum, where your gain can be my gain.

—Joseph Nye[1]

Both love and democracy depend on voice—having a voice and also the resonance that makes it possible to speak and be heard.

—Carol Gilligan[2]

I attended the same high school as Hillary Rodham Clinton. In the mid-1970s when my parents decided to uproot from India to the US, we were one of the few Indian-American families in Des Plaines, Illinois, a town adjacent to Park Ridge, where Hillary Rodham had spent most of her childhood. Situated in the northwest suburbs of Chicago—originally Ojibwa, Potawatomi and Chippewa Native American settlements between the city of Chicago and the Des Plaines River—these towns were inhabited by European settlers after the War of 1812, the Second War of American Independence. Early waves of migrants arrived in 1833, mostly families from New England and New York, and French and German immigrants. The railroad connected Des Plaines and Park Ridge to the city of Chicago in the late 1850s. With the gentrification of the suburbs, almost a century later, the population of the small towns had nearly doubled. When the Rodham family moved to Park Ridge in 1950, it was inhabited by approximately 16,000 residents.

The inflow of Asian immigrants into major American cities through the 1970s was a direct result of the changes in the US immigration laws. During the

1980s and 90s, Indian-Americans gradually settled into the cities and suburbs of the major metropolitan areas like Chicago, New York and San Francisco; the population of Des Plaines is now 13% Asian American and Park Ridge is 4%, with the majority being Caucasian and minority Hispanic residents.

As one of a handful of Asian students at Maine East High School in the late 1970s, where the young Hillary Rodham was a precocious student in the 1960s and ran for class president, little did I know I was taking significant steps in the mainstream of cultural life. My gateway into the US couldn't have been more American; the original arches from the first McDonald's franchise started by Ray Kroc, now turned into a museum, still stand on Lee Street five minutes from our old duplex on Potter Road. My high school may have been the crucible for shaping cultural icons, including the subject of this book, the former first lady and potentially the first woman president of the US.

Other notable personalities include the actor Harrison Ford, who has represented timeless characters such as the archaeologist Indiana Jones in *Raiders of the Lost Ark* and space traveler Han Solo in *Star Wars*. Clearly, my immigrant roots reflect a typical story, the changing yet constant rhythm of American life. America is still the mythic land of opportunity and never ending skyscrapers and highways, where almost anything is possible.

As we look in the rearview mirror in order to look ahead, this book about Hillary Clinton's global image—former First Lady, US Senator and Secretary of State—is as much about the changing nature of American life as it is about the American narrative that has remained fixed. America still represents a revolutionary idea; a nation founded by a band of rebellious brothers on the principles of freedom and equality. Americans are still holding out the promise of liberty, a torch held high for the rest of the world, trying to shape the world in their own image.

When we examine Hillary Clinton's global ambitions, we also see her domestic challenges in a better light. Fighting for better jobs in a globalized economy through the Asian pivot and securing better pay for women in a world where American women make .79 cents on the dollar, she represents the fight for economic justice. Fighting for improved infrastructure in a world that is rapidly catching up with America and calling for investment in early education for young children to support better life outcomes, she advocates for America's scientific and competitive DNA. In all of these domestic fights, we see Hillary's vision of a global America, reaching out to welcome the world beyond our shores as part of a global community that is ever more interconnected and interdependent.

What is the role of American leadership in the 21st century? We address this question in the book. Hillary Clinton offers a "smart power" approach to global politics through engagement of both "hard" military power and "soft" cultural power. This approach is very different from the "America First" strategy and the "Isolationist" policies offered by the candidates on the right. Unlike her colleagues on the left, who call for "disengagement" from world affairs, Hillary Clinton cautions us that Americans must remain engaged and intervene whenever necessary to protect our global interests. At the start of the 2016 election cycle, she seemed most experienced and poised in terms of foreign policy credentials and a moderate centrist on key domestic issues; yet, there was trouble ahead on the campaign trail.

At the start of primary elections in February 2016, on a bitterly cold winter day, I travelled through the Granite State, New Hampshire, to look for the trail Hillary Clinton had blazed. She was retreading the same path she had traversed only eight years ago. As the first woman candidate who could possibly reach the nomination against the flank of male politicians on both sides of the aisle, including more than a dozen Republicans and a handful of Democrats, she was close to breaking the old glass ceiling into millions of pieces. Yet, there was 'something wrong with Kansas.' At rallies, I could observe the absence of young women voters in Concord, Henniker, Portsmouth and Keen.

Hillary was snapping the heels of her ruby red slippers, but the young women were not coming out for her in large enough numbers. As she lost the New Hampshire primary election by 22 points, the irony was profoundly troubling. The woman politician who has championed the rights of women and young girls worldwide throughout her professional life and authored the so-called "Hillary Doctrine," which places women's rights and violence against women as an important national security concern, may not be able to inspire the younger generation of women.

The younger women were threatening to derail Hillary's potential run for the highest office in the land by succumbing to inducements from her opponent, Senator Bernie Sanders from Vermont, who has promised 'free college,' 'free healthcare,' and '$15 minimum wage' while threatening to cut big-banks down to size and tax the millionaires and billionaires.

Archetypal feminists from an earlier era were brought out to confront the missing young women voters. Madeline Albright said at a rally in Concord, "There's a special place in hell for women who don't help each other."[3] Gloria Steinem chimed in on another late night show, "When you're young, you're thinking: 'Where are the boys?' The boys are with Bernie."[4] The confrontational strategy with the younger voters seemed to have backfired.

The younger women could not care less about traditional feminism; the first, second and third waves of the women's movement do not hold the same value for them. Having embraced the new-found freedoms to vote with their own minds and bodies, the younger twenty-something and thirty-something women—the polls were evidently clear—were voting for Bernie Sanders over the first viable woman presidential candidate. They didn't think feminism has anything to do with their voting behavior. The young people had already moved on with the social change that older women were still trying to inculcate in the population and among the elected officials.

In Iowa, women under thirty voted for Sanders with overwhelming numbers (84% vs. 14%) and women under forty-five voted along similar lines (58% vs. 37%).

In New Hampshire, the gender break down was also significant for women under thirty (79% vs. 20%) and under forty-five (66% vs. 16%). In Michigan, voters under thirty voted for Sanders (81% vs. 19%) and voters under forty-five did the same (53% vs. 42%).[5]

The older women who fought for the rights of women for a half-century felt somewhat disheartened. There hasn't been a woman president in the 240 years since America's founding, and this historical lag may not disappear easily. We are currently in the midst of the aging of America, now ironically represented as 'the gender gap' between younger and older women.

With the Democratic primary election dragging on much longer than predicted, it was clear we were looking at not only a generational election, but also the aging of American society where the voters under 45 years of age have markedly different notions of income inequality and fairness. Democratic socialism may no longer carry the taint that it did during the Cold War for the younger generation of voters. Conversely, on the Republican side we witnessed a populist Trump uprising, where the older, middle class, somewhat less-educated voters felt they were losing their country to the waves of new immigrants, and social and demographic changes sweeping the country.

It was evident at the political rallies I attended in New Hampshire, New York, Pennsylvania, Ohio and California that America was in the midst of an aging demographic shift. Many of the candidates themselves reflected this fact. On both sides, the leading candidates in the 2016 race were sporting their credentials as grandparents, now running for office in their late 60s and 70s. They were invariably speaking to the concerns of the older age voters whether it was healthcare, prescription medication, retirement savings or taxing the millionaires and billionaires.

President Obama with his youthful vigor, sprinting to the podium at many of the political rallies when he ran for office in 2008 and 2012, may have forestalled the reckoning, but now the impending crisis of the aging population was upon the nation. How could we balance the high cost of healthcare and other social entitlement programs against the low growth economy? How could we keep America competitive when the rest of the world is catching up with the West in terms of development, economy and innovation? These secular trends required new thinking as Americans tried to shape the 21st century. While the Democratic candidates offered a continuation and radical extension of Obama's progressive agenda by pulling the country to the extreme left, the Republican candidates seemed to be a huge panoply of protest candidates vehemently dead-set against everything the Obama agenda represented. They wanted to drag the country to the extreme right and keep the politics from veering further left towards a radically progressive agenda.

The electorate was sagging from the weight of the two opposite polls, displaying a high degree of willingness to vote in larger numbers, evidenced by the populist rage both on the right and left. According to Pew Research, "Through the first 12 primaries of 2016, combined Republican turnout has been 17.3% of eligible voters—the highest of any year since at least 1980. Democratic turnout so far is 11.7%—the highest since 1992, with the notable exception of the extraordinarily high turnout in 2008."[6] Overwhelmingly, the voters were dissatisfied with the direction of the country, where more than two-thirds were feeling that the country was heading in the wrong direction (67% vs. 29%).[7] According to predictions, the voting-age population that turned out in 2012 and 2008 (53.6% and 56.9%) may be overwhelmed by the electorate in 2016 general election.[8]

Democrats were counting on the growing diversity of the American electorate, while the Republicans were counting on the majority Caucasian voters feeling disengaged from and disenchanted with the political process. The divide between the older 20th century America and newly emerging 21st century America couldn't have been more stark.

The US Census has predicted America will be an ethnically-diverse nation by 2044, a blended nation of mixed races and ethnicities.[9] This trend is already creeping into the make-up of the candidates and their electorate. It is precisely within the long-term demographic and economic trends that the driving fear and anxieties of the populace were gaining traction.

At this point, we know that the CEO pay has increased more than 250% in the past thirty years for the Fortune 500 companies, dominated by Caucasian male executives. There is a significant underrepresentation of women and minorities in the upper rungs of the corporate positions and corporate boards. During the same period, federal wages and the wages of middle class Americans have remained stagnant, even while corporate profits have soared and S&P 500 has garnered greater than 100% returns. Finally, these trends are further complicated by the demographic shifts in the US population and the rise of majority-minority states, where the growing minority population has threatened to rattle the power balance in the border states from Florida to California. Exacerbated by globalization and the outsourcing of jobs, the transfer of wealth to the top 1%, the so-called plutocrats, has generated a lot of rage among the working class and middle class voters. Thus, the recent finding that middle-class, middle-aged Caucasian men and women are at greater risk of mortality due to suicide, drug addiction to painkillers, and other chronic psychological ailments seems to be part and parcel of a cultural syndrome ailing the American dream.[10]

The political candidates on the right and left were offering piecemeal solutions to these social problems. The candidates on the right were adept at channeling the anger and fear of the voters who feel they are being left behind, while the progressive left wanted to level the playing field and curtail the power of the plutocrats on Wall Street. The only candidate that seemed to have a 360-degree view or a complete and rational understanding of the woes that are ailing America was Hillary Rodham Clinton, largely because of the positions she has held in and outside of government.

Hillary Clinton was projecting herself as the candidate of continuity, maintaining the legacy of the first Black President and leading to interesting dynamics on the domestic and foreign policy front. Hillary Clinton was willing to push further, go out on a limb not only to defend Obama's record but also to defend her husband, Bill Clinton, and his two economically vibrant administrations. Within this shifting context, this edited collection examines the potential of Hillary Clinton to bring serious national security credentials to the job of keeping America safe as Commander-in-Chief. Using the idea of "smart power"—that is, deploying America's cultural and military might—Hillary Clinton had already outlined what America needed to do around the world. It remained to be seen whether the American people were willing to accept her message. In the midst of all the political hoopla, nobody seemed to be discussing the Hillary Doctrine, one of the key achievements of her tenure as Secretary of State.

The linkage between women's development and violence against women as a national security issue has not been explicitly coupled by the US government in the manner that Hillary Clinton has done it. This axiomatic linkage is in essence the Hillary Doctrine, which states that the subjugation of women leads to the deterioration of human conditions, and in order to improve the social and developmental conditions around the world, we should invest in improving the conditions of women. Consistent with the postwar liberalism championed by Eleanor Roosevelt, the torch is now carried by Hillary Clinton.[11]

The diverse set of essays in this book deal with this linkage in an explicit as well as tacit manner. We don't debate the significant correlation or causal relationship between women's development and societal development. Rather, we demonstrate ethnographically and journalistically how Hillary Clinton's career has been dedicated to this profound and singular conviction and policy mission. We also demonstrate in most of the essays that the Hillary Doctrine is at the heart of her smart power approach offered as a candidate, with a potential to offer great dividends both in terms of humanitarian goals—soft power—and national security objectives—hard power.

This doctrine was outlined by Hillary Clinton in her book, *Hard Choices*:

> It was no coincidence that the places where women's lives were most undervalued largely lined up with the parts of the world most plagued by instability, conflict, extremism, and poverty. .... 'Women's issues' had long been relegated to the margins of U.S. foreign policy and international diplomacy, considered at best a nice thing to work on but hardly a necessity. I became convinced that, in fact, this was a cause that cut to the heart of our national security.[12]

The essays in this book are a dedication to the spirit of this principle. Based on a significant collection of social science evidence[13] and corporate data trends[14], this book demonstrates that the Hillary Doctrine is indeed central to smart power and the US population may be ready—due to internal demographic changes and the forces of globalization—to make a quantum leap forward in nominating and electing a woman president. This can only enhance America's global image, improve the lives of girls and women around the world, and propel America into the 21st century.

References

1 Nye, J. (2010). Global power shifts, *TED Talk*, Oct; last accessed on April 22, 2016; www.ted.com/talks/joseph_nye_on_global_power_shifts/transcript?language=en

2 Gilligan, C. (2003). *The Birth of Pleasure: A New Map of Love*. New York: Random House, p 233.

3 Neidig, H. (2016). Albright: 'Special place in hell for women who don't help each other', *The Hill*, Feb 6; last accessed on April 22, 2016; http://thehill.com/blogs/ballot-box/268501-albright-theres-a-special-place-in-hell-for-women-who-dont-help-each-other

4 Schapiro, R. (2016). Gloria Steinem, feminist icon, says young women support Bernie Sanders to meet 'boys'—then apologizes, *New York Daily News*, Feb 8; last accessed on April 22, 2016; www.nydailynews.com/news/politics/gloria-steinem-young-women-support-sanders-meet-boys-article-1.2522753

5 Brownstein, R. (2016). The great democratic age gap, *The Atlantic*, Feb 2; last accessed on April 18, 2016; www.theatlantic.com/politics/archive/2016/02/the-great-democratic-age-gap/459570/

6 Desilver, D. (2016). So far the turnout in the primaries rivals the 2008 elections, *Pew Research*, March 8; last accessed on April 18, 2016; www.pewresearch.org/fact-tank/2016/03/08/so-far-turnout-in-this-years-primaries-rivals-2008-record/

7 Real Clear Politics (2016). Direction of country; last accessed on April 18, 2016; www.realclearpolitics.com/epolls/other/direction_of_country-902.html

8 Desilver, D. (2015). US voter turnout trails most developed countries, *Pew Research*, May 6; last accessed on April 18, 2016; www.pewresearch.org/fact-tank/2015/05/06/u-s-voter-turnout-trails-most-developed-countries/

9 US Census. (2015). New census bureau report analyzes US population projections, March 3; last accessed on April 18, 2016; www.census.gov/newsroom/press-releases/2015/cb15-tps16.html

10 Squires, D. and Blumenthal, D. (2016). Mortality trends among working-age whites: The untold story, *The Commonwealth Fund*, January 29; last accessed on April 18, 2016; www.commonwealthfund.org/publications/issue-briefs/2016/jan/mortality-trends-among-middle-aged-whites

11 Black, A. (1996). Casting her own shadow: Eleanor Roosevelt and the shaping of postwar liberalism. New York: Columbia University Press.

12 Clinton, H. (2015). *Hard Choices*, New York: Simon and Schuster, p. 469.

13 King, E. and Winthrop, R. (2015). Today's challenges for girls' education, *Brookings*, June 25; last accessed on April 18, 2016; www.brookings.edu/research/papers/2015/06/22-challenges-for-girls-education-king-winthrop

14 EY. (2016). Women. Fast forward; last accessed on April 18, 2016; www.ey.com/Publication/vwLUAssets/ey-women-fast-forward-thought-leadership/$FILE/ey-women-fast-forward-thought-leadership.pdf

1

THE GLOBAL HILLARY

Smart Power and the Making of a Woman President

Dinesh Sharma

The United States is the oldest constitutional democracy in the world, but it has not succeeding in electing a woman as the head of state. As one of the few advanced democracies with a developed economy that granted women the right to vote approximately a century ago, why has the US not succeeded in placing a woman in the executive office?[1]

This is only one of the questions we grapple with in this book.

While the recent survey and polling data suggests that Americans are ready to elect a qualified woman president, the idea of the first American woman president remains only a potentiality, not yet fully realized, even though the trend may be strong enough that it may happen in 2016.[2] Women voters have always taken on the idea of the first woman president much more seriously, but now American men may be accepting the idea gradually.[3] However, it remains to be seen whether in a crowded field of male candidates, Americans will gravitate toward a qualified woman candidate to lead the country on the basis of equality, qualifications, and experience.

What are the sociocultural and political factors for this historical lag? In the era of globalization, where women's rights and incomes are increasingly on the rise, isn't it a cultural and economic imperative that one of the foremost democratic nations lead the way in women's political leadership? The women's movement around the world has generated mixed results as tracked by the Millennium Development Goals (MDG),[4] while there has been a retrenchment along traditional lines. Will American leadership remain strong in the 21st century or will it face a global backlash?

Globalization has accelerated to far-flung places in the world, where women's right to education, health and political participation has gained more credence, oftentimes pushed by the United States Development Agency and the State Department.[5] Hillary Clinton, the former First Lady and the former Secretary of State, has championed these causes through her long and complicated career.

As a young lawyer at Yale, she gave voice to the concerns of children and women. As the First Lady, she gave a landmark speech on women's rights in China and led the fight for equal rights for women. At the State Department, she has melded development with democracy as central concerns of US foreign policy.

With Hillary Clinton's political rise to the presidency, we may have seen the emergence of women's rights as central to political discourse in the US and around the world. Women's rights have indeed become human rights, to paraphrase Hillary Clinton's landmark speech in Beijing more than two decades ago.[6] What was the impact of that speech? We will examine this question in the book.

Thus, this book deals with the nexus of women, development and democracy—as a post-Enlightenment, postmodern, and global feminist project of the West—by focusing on the political leadership of one of the best-known women politicians the United States has produced in recent times. While in this book we will compare Hillary with other leading women politicians around the world and draw parallels with important historical figures in the women's rights movement, we are principally interested in examining the role Hillary Clinton—as First Lady, Senator, and Secretary of State—has played as a transformational figure in bridging women's development with democratic institutions in the developing and developed societies. This is clearly one of her lasting legacies, independent of any political fortunes she may have won or lost in American politics.

The triumvirate purpose of this book is to examine 1) America's "smart power" through the life and work of Hillary Clinton; 2) offer a perspective on globalization by examining the American agenda for women's development as a democratic project around the world; and 3) offer a way forward for women's political leadership in the 21st century. In essence, this book is about America's smart power or cultural capital, wielded through development aid, assistance, and peace-building measures, as seen through the beneficial effects of foreign policy on behalf of women and children.

We achieve the aim of this book by offering contextual or ethnographic perspectives on women's development[7] and on the global image of Hillary Clinton from five different continents. In other words, this book offers a perspective on America's global leadership on behalf of half of the world's population by examining the causes and projects Hillary Clinton has championed throughout her career.

This book was conceived as the complementary volume to the earlier edited book *The Global Obama*, which examined the rise of the first Black and multicultural head of state of any Western democracy.[8] Here, we undertake a similar project by examining the movement for women's rights through the political rise of Hillary Clinton, who by all accounts has had a stellar career even before running for the highest office in the country. As she is running for the office of the US President again, this book will be a timely addition to the growing literature on her political biography.

While there are many books on her years in the White House as the First Lady and few on her career as a Senator and Secretary of State, there are no books to date that examine her life's mission for women's rights within the context of globalization, on the one hand, and America's leadership in fostering development and democracy around the world, on the other.

Thus, this book will specifically demonstrate how Hillary Clinton has shaped the debate around women's participation in the political economy as a central concern of her purview around the world. The various chapters in this book reveal the underbelly of US power, as a counterbalance to US military force, where American security forces and diplomats play a critical role as peacekeepers and policemen of the world.

Adventures in Global Feminism

Today, the term *feminism* evokes the original social movement at the turn of the 20th century. Along with the civil rights movement in the mid-twentieth century and the movement for marriage equality more recently, the struggles for minority rights have turned a corner. As many of the social movements of previous century have fulfilled most, if not all, of their original mission and purpose, are we entering a new territory or a different phase of post-feminist activism?[9]

Given the US elected and reelected the first Black president—Barack H. Obama—someone who truly is a social progressive, is the US political system now primed to elect the first woman president?[10] Some historians have argued that the recent electoral history reflects the earlier generations when minorities and women fought for the right to vote.[11] Will history repeat or possibly rhyme itself?

From abolition to the suffrage movement, from the Equal Rights Amendment to post-feminism, we have followed this trajectory before in an earlier era. Does the US now stand a better chance of electing a woman president in the age of Obama, who has pushed several progressive causes forward from protection of the environment to women's reproductive health? Are we in fact seeing the worldwide convergence of several social progressive causes that might help elevate a woman politician to the highest office in the land?

These are difficult questions to answer, but from the perspective of emerging global feminism and as social scientists, journalists, psychologists, and historians, we will be able to address these issues effectively. Relying on a combination of ethnographic and journalistic reporting styles, we will provide worldwide coverage and in-depth analysis on Hillary Clinton as a global leader, diplomat, and presidential candidate.

Smart Power and the Melding Development, Democracy, and Diplomacy

Women are to nature as men are to culture. This used to be an old truism in the history of anthropology, sociology, and the social sciences.[12] Many anthropologists went to study exotic cultures to examine the domestication of women as part of the social and cultural organization. This truism no longer holds, as many traditional cultures have embraced modernization and development, and there is an upsurge in the rights of women and girls. Women's roles are no longer simply aligned with what is sanctioned by natural constraints or social structures and patriarchy.[13] Hillary Clinton, along with an army of development aid workers, has been a proponent of this change around the world, otherwise known as a key part of America's smart power strategy.

The book will focus on smart power, examining two human developmental themes that run through Hillary's work: 1) Policies for girl's education, health, and well-being; and 2) women's rights and participation in the political economy. Hillary Clinton announced recently that as part of the Clinton Global Initiative, she has undertaken a review of the progress towards women's rights since the Beijing speech starting almost twenty years ago.[14] We believe this would be an ideal opportunity for us to review the progress in this book. How successful has been the strategy to meld soft power with smart power? We will explore this topic in the book (see Chapter 5 by Professor Assie-Lumumba).

Foreign Policy for the 21st Century

There is nothing foreign about foreign policy, as many of the domestic issues—such as education, innovation, and security—impinge on the US image abroad.[15] As a "rock star diplomat," Hillary Clinton significantly improved the US image abroad, but her foreign policy legacy is still being debated (see Chapter 8 on Afghanistan and Chapter 9 on the Middle East).[16]

On the foreign policy front, we will assess her diplomatic and global impact in the various continents and countries she has covered. From China, India, and Myanmar to Cape Town, her celebrity status is evident in Asia and Africa to Latin America. Yet, her long-term impact on the policy changes remains unclear.

Did she improve the peace process in the Middle East? How successful was she in advancing the Asian pivot after announcing it as a grand strategy? Did she help steer the right course in North Africa during the Arab Spring? These are some of the toughest questions we can tackle in the international relations arena at this turning point in history.[17]

Main Themes

There are no existing books that have examined Hillary Clinton's global presence as a leader within a cultural and historical context, on the one hand, and foreign policy implications for women's development and the sustainability of American power, on the other. This is a unique book that examines Hillary Clinton as a global politician and statesman, who has advanced women's development, democracy, and political leadership into the 21st century. We cover Hillary Clinton's candidacy from a variety of angles that are politically and culturally relevant to America and the world.

Hillary and American Exceptionalism

Many Americans believe they are part of an exceptional nation, which is unde-niably true, but they may not be aware that America suffers from an exceptional lag of women politicians in the public life. What are the reasons for this lag of exceptional women in politics?

The United States is an exceptional nation in many ways: "Its political culture, history, and electoral system create a unique mixture of principles, attitudes, practices, and institutions that are qualitatively different from those found in other democratic countries," argue Gregory Striech and Robynn Kuhlmann in Chapter 2. Americans rightly believe they live in the land of opportunity, where mobility, equality, and freedom are the drivers of everyday democracy. "However, this same mixture of principles, attitudes, practices, and institutions also make the US exceptional not because it leads but because it lags," especially, when we look at the paucity of women politicians, according to Striech and Kuhlmann.

In many other cultures—from advanced democracies in Europe to developing nations in Asia and Africa—women have been elected in higher percentages to their national governments and as heads of state as prime minister or president. This trend is evident in newly emerging economies, such as, Indonesia, as well as mature economies, such as the UK (also see Chapter 7 by Don Morrison on France and Germany).[18]

Thus, from a political science perspective Striech and Kuhlmann conclude, "Paradoxically, upward political mobility for women has been blocked due to the very same cultural attitudes that set it apart as unique. In short, for women candidates in the US, upward political mobility and opportunity are blocked by cultural phenomena such as gender stereotyping and religious traditionalism as well as institutional practices that fail to recruit, nominate, and elect women to state and national legislative bodies. And because women are not recruited or nominated by party leaders, this reinforces the cultural assumption that women do not have what it takes to hold the highest elected office of the land."

Hillary Clinton can resoundingly put American exceptionalism on the right course again, argue Morrison, Striech, Kuhlmann, and Denmark in this book. Clinton's experience, brand recognition, and fundraising capabilities will be put through the test. She will contend with the deeply entrenched cultural attitudes and practices that place women candidates at an inferior position. Clinton, who has served as Secretary of State and a US Senator, must contend with the stereotypes that she is "not tough enough" or "not decisive" or "not trustworthy" because of her gender and privileged position as the former First Lady. While many Americans say they are willing to vote for a qualified woman for president, the idea of the first woman president still makes many Americans uncertain, anxious, and scared.

While highlighting the core principles of the American founding—opportunity and equality—at the heart of American exceptionalism, Clinton can take on the system and argue for the need for cultural change, as suggested in Chapter 7 by Don Morrison while locating Hillary's soft power in France and Germany. However, she must make the case that what makes the US exceptional is not only these principles but the ability to embrace change and dismantle discriminatory barriers. She can position herself as the embodiment of American exceptionalism, representing upward mobility and opportunity for women candidates.

On foreign policy, she must position herself as a strong leader who is willing to make "hard choices" in contrast to the bellicose posturing of her opponents. If she embodies the exception to the rule and truly exemplifies American exceptionalism, she can make history again.

Hillary's Activism

Many of the Hillary supporters admire her for the fight she has led for women's causes, the 18 million cracks she created in the glass ceiling in 2008 democratic primaries. Florence Denmark, a well-known women's studies professor and the former president of the American Psychological Association, highlights Clinton's pivotal turning points—her student life at Wellesley College, her activities as First Lady of the United States, and up to the recent day. From a young age, she had a keen intellect and was very outspoken and assertive. Hillary fought within the system for the things she believed in, including women's rights and correcting social injustice, argues Denmark.

Denmark draws inspiration from Hillary's remarks, "My mother and my grandmothers could never have lived my life; my father and my grandfathers could never have imagined it. But they bestowed on me the promise of America, which made my life and my choices possible."[19] For Denmark, in Chapter 3, Hillary represents the American progressive spirit in all its contradictions and complexities.

Hillary and the Beijing Speech

In this book, we examine in depth the speech she made on the rights of women from a global African perspective, presented in Chapter 5. We trace the impact of her speech on the status of women in the UN and find that the trail she has left behind for women's rights is exemplary and will continue to offer dividends to future generations worldwide. More than two decades after the Beijing Conference, the new mission for gender equality has been aligned with the SDG 2030: "We envisage a world where all women and girls have equal opportunities and rights by 2030. Step It Up asks governments to make national commitments that will close the gender equality gap—from laws and policies to national action plans and adequate investment. NOW is the time to Step It Up!"[20]

The celebration of Beijing +20 has coincided with the most consequential campaign of Hillary Clinton's career. If she were to become the first woman to lead the most powerful nation in the world, it would be a new day for women's development worldwide, argues Professor Assie-Lumumba. Factors that made Beijing speech necessary are still relevant today, dealing with the "glass ceiling" in the US and overseas.

The Beijing Conference back in 1995 resonated with women struggling for structural change toward gender and holistic equality locally, nationally, and globally. Those in the struggle for gender equality are from a wide political spectrum in terms of views on nation-states and global affairs and their contradictions. Yet, the call for structural change still resonates. Nevertheless, Clinton's intelligence and stamina are consistent with what is needed to actualize at least one of the resolutions of the Beijing Platform for Action and the Beijing Declaration: Women's political empowerment everywhere, including in the most powerful country in the world, argues Professor Assie-Lumumba.

Hillary and Palin

When we compare Hillary's appeal closer at home to women across the political aisle, with the other female candidates to run in a general election, namely Sarah Palin, we find a deep chasm that divides the American electorate. Many in the lower 48 states were shocked at how Sarah Palin was selected as the US vice presidential candidate for a major political party. However, Alaskans were just as taken aback by how such an "out-of-touch" liberal East Coast elite as Hillary Clinton could possibly represent their national interest, according to Grant Rich. Alaska is not New York State, and in many ways it is special, and unique as a non-contiguous state that joined the American Union before Hawaii.

Alaskans who identify with Sarah Palin feel excited and happy by her local passions about dog mushing or snow-machines. However, "when Katie Couric or Tina Fey put Palin under pressure, and caused her embarrassment, for many Alaskans, this seemed like a personal attack on Alaska and the Alaskan way of life," according to Grant Rich. Such gut reactions to politics are in keeping with behavioral research, such as, the research on moral and political psychology which suggests that politics is as much about emotions as it is about rational policy making.

For many Alaskans, the fact that Hillary Clinton has traveled millions of miles for her country as Secretary of State counts for far less than the fact that Sarah Palin comes from Wasilla, the duct tape capital of the world. When Palin jokes about John Kerry as an "elitist loon" (2009, p. 181) it connects with many Alaskans, who don't understand the value of a French-speaking politician for global diplomacy.

Research in social psychology and neuroscience clearly suggests that we like things and people that are similar to us as individuals and in terms of group affiliations. We instinctively gravitate towards the familiar—are persuaded by those we perceive to be similar to ourselves—and are willing to go the extra mile for them. This psychological concept is simple, and at base, well supported by the evidence. When Palin and Clinton are viewed through this lens, as women representatives of their polarizing groups, their reception among disparate electorate and voting blocs largely vanishes. Are you with us or against us? During election time, this fundamental question assumes greater importance, driven by gut instincts, feelings, emotions, likes and preferences, rather than policy directives.

Hillary and the Arab Spring

We revisit her leadership style in some of the controversial policies of the Obama administration in a chapter by Kenneth Christie at Royal Roads University, Canada. He comments on the Arab Spring and the Benghazi incident. Hillary Clinton has come across as a normative figure in the run up to the US presidential campaign, which has seen the dramatic rise of anti-establishment candidates. The next election will be fascinating to watch particularly if Donald Trump succeeds in taking the Republican nomination.

In the Democratic primary elections, Hillary Clinton has publicly distanced herself from some of Obama's policies. Is this due to the politics of the presidential campaign? The Obama administration's attempts to mollify the Islamic world have largely proved difficult to manage. "The war on terror has continued and his use of drones in conflict has been widely criticized by friends and foe alike. Hillary wants to provide some distance for the share of the blame," according to Kenneth Christie.

Today, the Middle East has witnessed the greatest humanitarian crisis. This affects the US policy on a daily basis. Clinton has been vocal about her disagreement with the Obama administration's characterization of foreign policy as "Don't do stupid stuff." Clinton played down this approach this approach in an interview in the Atlantic magazine, arguing "Great nations need organizing principles and don't do stupid stuff' is not an organizing principle." In *Hard Choices*, published in 2014, she also outlined that at the boiling point of the Arab Spring she wanted to see Mubarak, the Egyptian president, set-up a mechanism for his transition and pick a successor, but her plan was overruled by the Obama administration.

Hillary Clinton envisioned an assertive role or "hawkish" stance for the US in Syria and against ISIS, but Secretaries of State don't dictate foreign policy entirely. "Clinton's lack of a grand strategy in many ways could be attributed to her job. And that was to implement Barack Obama's ideas," suggests Christie.

Hillary Clinton's smart power strategies—including gender issues in the developing world, empowering girls and women, supporting public health campaigns, and opening Mynamar, among others—delivered solid progress. "Her lack of strategy and insight into the Arab uprisings, however, were problematic and may have exacerbated the situation. Clinton was a realist that wanted more but was frustrated because of the administration's control over policy," argues Christie.

Some political commentators have argued that foreign policy is a liability for Hillary Clinton. The fact that she has more foreign policy experience than any of the other potential candidates may turn into a potentially higher risk. According to Kenneth Christie, the crises of the Arab Spring have not disappeared, ISIS remains powerful, and threats in Syria, Iraq, Turkey and Middle East continue to challenge American foreign policy. The Benghazi incident may continue to pose political challenges.

"The Arab Spring has certainly not met any stated goals of US foreign policy, such as, the promotion of democracy, human rights, and the empowerment of women in the Middle East," according to Christie. Jihadism has continued, the Islamic state in Syria and Iraq has remained a threat, and democratic movement has backtracked. The Arab Spring has become a winter, with humanitarian crisis from the population displacement all over the Middle East and overflowing into Europe and North America.

Hillary Clinton is an advocate of smart power, a realist who understands the limits of American power. In her recent interview in the *Atlantic magazine* she stated, "We've also learned about the limits of our power to spread freedom and democracy. That's one of the big lessons of Iraq. But we've also learned about the importance of our power, our influence, and our values appropriately deployed and explained."

Hillary and Afghanistan

Have the Clintons been able to understand South Asia better than other administrations? Prakhar Sharma answers this question in the affirmative. Will this transfer into Hillary's vision for South Asia? In 1999, First Lady Hillary Clinton spoke out against the egregious treatment of Afghan women at the hands of the Taliban. She became among the few members of the Clinton White House to openly condemn the Taliban. Since then, the relationship between Hillary Clinton and Afghanistan has evolved from championing the rights of Afghan women to active engagement in the country's political evolution.

As a Senator, Hillary Clinton visited Afghanistan on several occasions to understand the progress in the war. In the 2008 campaign, she called for renewed focus on Afghanistan, specifically advocating for more American troops. When she became the Secretary of State in the Obama administration, she supported the troop surge in Afghanistan, against the reasoned skepticism of Vice President Biden, Rahm Emanuel, General Jones and Richard Holbrooke. However, despite the limited troop surge, the war did not end.

The evolution of politics in Afghanistan steadfastly refused to adhere to a script, according to Sharma. Hillary's ambitious attempts to get the Taliban to the negotiation table also met with frustration from both Washington and Kabul. This chapter briefly presents a history of Hillary Clinton's engagement in Afghanistan. Three questions merit attention. Can Hillary sustain US engagement in Afghanistan in face of mixed results and unfavorable domestic public opinion for such engagement? Can she ensure a role for the United States in bringing a negotiated end to the Afghan war? And, can she develop and implement a regional framework for stability in Afghanistan? We examine these question in this book. Prakhar Sharma concludes if anyone can resolve these issues it is most likely Hillary Clinton.

Hillary and Mideast peace

We examine the prospects of a rapprochement with Israel under Hillary Clinton. Will she be able to break through the tense relations with PM Netanyahu? The Israeli-Palestinian conflict would seem to be intractable. Most Israelis and

Palestinians themselves, as well as worldwide observers, anecdotally report they believe the problem will never end.

Ellen Fleischman, a New York–based psychologist who also has family in Israel, argues, "Yet the British left India, and India became an independent democracy, with a continually growing middle class. The Soviet Union fell, as did the Berlin Wall. Peace came to Northern Ireland. Apartheid ended in South Africa. Sadat signed a peace agreement with Begin through Jimmy Carter's mediation. The outcome of that extended Camp David retreat was uncertain to the last minute, however. The talks were about to break down many times during those days. It was only through sheer persistence and luck that the agreement was realized."

Fleischman believes peaceful resolution of the Israeli/Palestinian conflict will occur when that happy confluence of factors arises and the conflict will become history. The horror of war is not only visited upon the victims but also the perpetrators: post-traumatic stress disorder can destroy lives; suicide rates are astronomically high among veterans and victims; and people report high degree of insecurity and uncertainty. Will people lay aside their enmity for the benefit of their children?

At some point in the future, we may look fondly at Hillary Clinton's approach, attempting to persuade the opposing parties to step into each other's shoes. We will herald her, and Obama before her, as having foresight and perspicacity, suggests Fleischman. It would be nothing more than encouraging to develop empathy for the neighbor, who was seen as an enemy but was after all no different than ourselves.

Hillary in Asia

Finally, we examine Hillary's presence in Asia by looking at her biographical appeal with the Japanese public, who have consumed her books over the years. Trying to obtain a different perspective on her pivot to Asia, when the Japanese read Clinton's new book, *Hard Choices*, they may feel better again. "The feelings of being slighted in *Living History* have been mostly compensated for in this new book," argues Professor Senaha at Haikodo University. Clinton describes Japan and its people as her first priority, with special memories of feeling confidence and intimacy with the Japanese people.

Clinton's revisionism of Japan and its people appears more personal rather than political. She discusses the importance of Japan as an ally, but recalls it "like a good old friend she has known for a long time." She devotes sixteen pages to Japan in *Hard Choices* from her first visit to the country with her husband in 1993, the economy of the "Lost Decade," and to the recent Asian pivot. Clinton discusses her official visit as the US Secretary of State in 2009 and her first town hall meeting at the University of Tokyo.

As a feminist politician, Clinton described her gratitude at meeting with Japanese women, including the first women astronauts, Chiaki Mukai and Naoko Yamazaki, and praised Prime Minister Shinzo Abe's announcement of increasing women's economic participation called "womenomics." Clinton's detailed description of the Asian pivot outlines three approaches in the region: 1) broadening the relationship with China, 2) strengthening the US treaty alliances in order to provide a counterbalance to China's growing power, or 3) harmonizing the regional multilateral organizations. Her decision to use "smart power" to meld all three approaches and choose Japan as the first key destination was critical to the Asian pivot.

Senaha argues, Clinton's second memoir may become popular in Japan and regain Japanese trust. *Living History* was difficult book for the Japanese to pick up and read, but *Hard Choices* may be seen in Japanese hands regularly. During the years that span the two biographies, Clinton has developed a unique voice and writing style, with passionate language and a multifaceted vision. Her literary voice remains rare and hard to classify.

In this book, we see the mind of a leading woman politician in full gear, wrestling with and solving some of the hardest problems that the world faces today. We see her unique gifts as a policy maker—willingness to take on complex problems and solve them with a humanist and feminist perspective, as well as with a hard-nosed realist perspective when it comes to world events. Armed with the years of experience as First Lady, Senator and Secretary of State (and as a mother and grandmother), she offers a "smart power" approach for dealing with the global challenges, which may arguably be the cornerstone of "the Hillary doctrine" that propels her forward in the upcoming elections. This doctrine—which puts women's rights and development at the center of America's foreign policy and diplomacy—reflects not only her formative education and work experience, but her latest forays into globalization, counterterrorism, and nation-building. Based on these chapters, it can be concluded that the uses of smart power as seen through Clinton's lifelong career may offer a significant way forward for other women politicians coming up in a traditionally male-dominated field.

References

1 Falk, Erika. (2010). *Women for President: Media Bias in Nine Campaigns*. Chicago, IL: University of Illinois Press.
2 Gray, E., Carter, J. and Auletta, K. (2015). 56% Of People Think We'll Have a Female President in the Next Decade, *Huffington Post,* Nov 16; last accessed on Feb 25, 2016; http://presidentialgenderwatch.org/polls/a-woman-president/
3 The Shriver Report. (2015). A Woman's Nation, Apr 10; last accessed on Feb 25, 2016; http://awomansnation.org/twenty-first-century-man-poll/
4 SUNY Levin Project. (2015). *Women and Globalization Project, Globalization* 101; Last accessed Feb 25, 2016; www.globalization101.org/uploads/File/Women/Women.pdf

5 Naples, Nancy and Desai, Manisha. (2002). *Women's Activism and Globalization.* New York: Routledge; Trask, Bahira Sherif (2013). *Women, Work and Globalization.* New York: Routledge.

6 Peters, Julie and Wolper, Andrea. (1995). *Women's Rights, Human Rights.* New York: Psychology Press.

7 Browner, Carole and Sargent, Carolyn. (2011). *Reproduction, Globalization and the State.* Durham, NC: Duke University Press.

8 Sharma, Dinesh and Gielen, Uwe (2014). *The Global Obama: Crossroads of Leadership in the 21st Century.* New York: Routledge.

9 Gamble, Sarah. (2008). *Routledge Companion to Feminism and Post-Feminism.* New York: Routledge.

10 Clift, Eleanor and Brazaitis, Tom. (2003). *Madam President.* New York: Taylor Francis.

11 White House, Celebrating Women's Equality Day, www.whitehouse.gov/ blog/2013/08/26/celebrating-women-s-equality-day; Buchanan, Paul. (2010). *The American Women's Right Movement, 1600–2008.* Boston, MA: Branden Books.

12 Rosaldo, Michelle and Lamphere, Louise. (1974). *Women, Culture and Society.* Palo Alto, CA: Stanford University Press.

13 Nussbaum, Martha and Glover, Jonathan. (2001). *Women, Culture and Development.* New York: Oxford Press.

14 Lerer, Lisa. (2013). Hillary Clinton Plans Global Review of Women's Rights, Sep 25; last accessed on April 30, 2016; www.bloomberg.com/news/2013-09-25/hillary-clinton-plans-global-review-of-women-s-rights.html

15 Iyer, Mayura. (2013). There Is Nothing Foreign about Foreign Policy Anymore, Feb 20; last accessed on April 30, 2016; www.policymic.com/articles/27060/secretary-of-state-john-kerry-there-is-nothing-foreign-about-foreign-policy-anymore

16 Ghattas, Kim. (2012). *The Secretary: A Journey with Hillary Clinton.* New York: Times Books.

17 Glasser, Susan. (2013). Was Hillary Clinton a Good Secretary of State? *Politico,* Dec 8; last accessed on April 30, 2016; www.politico.com/magazine/story/2013/12/was-hillary-clinton-a-good-secretary-of-state-john-kerry-2016-100766.html

18 The World Bank. (2015). Proportions of seats held by women in national parliaments; last accessed on Feb 26, 2015; http://data.worldbank.org/indicator/ SG.GEN.PARL.ZS

19 Clinton, H. (2003). *Living History.* New York: Simon and Schuster.

20 UN Women. (2015). Step it up for gender equality, Sep 27; last accessed on Feb 26, 2016; http://beijing20.unwomen.org/en/step-it-up Copyright © 2016 by the United Nations Entity for Gender Equality and the Empowerment of Women (UN Women). All worldwide rights reserved.

2

SEE HILLARY RUN

Hillary Clinton, American Exceptionalism and Exceptions to the Rule

Gregory W. Streich and Robynn Kuhlmann

Americans like to think of the United States as "#1." Textbooks, politicians, and pundits are keen to offer Americans a narrative in which the United States is the "exceptional" nation in world history and contemporary global affairs. Ask an average American *why* they think the U.S. is exceptional and they are likely to say that the U.S. is a model of liberty, justice, and democracy; it is a nation of laws, not of men; it is the richest nation on earth with the most dynamic and innovative economy; it is the sole military superpower in the 21st century; and, it has a culture—from Hollywood to Broadway—that sets a standard for others to admire, imitate, and consume. Moreover, they might add that the U.S. is a nation of "firsts," from inventing rock and roll to discovering the cure for polio. It was, after all, the first nation to put a man on the moon. However, if the U.S. is such an exceptional nation, why has it not yet elected its first Madam President? Indeed, why are women under-represented in state and national legislatures when compared to other countries? To be sure, many other countries—from Argentina to Pakistan—*have* elected a woman as their nation's head of government (as president or prime minister), and many have a higher percentage of women in their national legislatures. Does this mean the U.S. is *not* as exceptional as it claims to be? Or, put differently, is the U.S. "exceptional" not because it *leads* but because it *lags*?

To answer these questions, this chapter examines American Exceptionalism and gender representation in the U.S. by focusing on Hillary Clinton as a potential first female president of the United States. In the first part, we examine the extent to which American voters are willing to vote for a qualified female presidential candidate. Due to gender stereotyping, Hillary Clinton will face barriers that her male counterparts will not. Second, we examine the concept of American Exceptionalism to highlight how scholars, politicians, and average Americans describe what makes the U.S. a unique and exceptional nation. While American Exceptionalism is a deeply held cultural belief, it is also a "double-edged sword" (Lipset 1997), and this sheds light on the paradox that what makes the U.S. unique simultaneously helps explain why the U.S. has not yet elected a Madam President. Third, we discuss some of Hillary Clinton's views on the topic of American Exceptionalism. And fourth, we highlight some unique historical and institutional forces that provide additional explanations as to why other countries surpass the U.S. when it comes to the number of women elected to political office. Historically, women do not have a long track record of political representation in the U.S. —either at the state or national levels—and this prevents many Americans from envisioning a female president. And institutionally, the way in which the electoral system is designed is friendly to newcomers such as well-funded individuals without much political experience. As we shall demonstrate, the U.S. is, paradoxically, an exceptional nation in part because it is the exception to the rule when it comes to electing a female head of state.

Public Opinion and a Female President

According to recent public opinion polls, Americans are indeed willing to elect a Madam President. With Hillary Clinton positioned as a frontrunner for the Democratic nomination in 2016, "71% of the public say it would not matter if a presidential candidate is a woman; 19% say they would be *more likely* to vote for a female candidate, while 9% would be *less likely*" (Pew 2014a: 3). While 24% of women and 14% of men say they would be *more* likely to support a female candidate, large majorities of both women and men say a candidate's gender would not matter. Among Democrats, 40% of liberal Democrats would be more likely to support a female presidential candidate compared to only 23% of conservative and moderate Democrats. By contrast, 74% of Republicans say a candidate's gender would not matter, while 15% of Republicans would be *less likely*—and another 10% of Republicans would be *more likely*—to vote for a female presidential candidate (Pew 2014a: 3). Additionally, Gallup has found that 95% of Americans—including 97% of Democrats, 96% of Independents, and 92% of Republicans—would vote for a well-qualified candidate who "happened to be a woman," while 5% would not (Jones 2012). With numbers like those, it seems as if a female candidate—especially one with Hillary Clinton's résumé—can indeed run a successful campaign for the presidency.

However, despite this apparent willingness to support a female presidential candidate, there are two barriers lurking underneath these polling numbers. First, in the post-9/11 era, voters are less confident in women to handle national security- and defense-related issues, and this translates into less support for a female presidential candidate. Even though the U.S. has now had three women serve as secretary of state (Madeline Albright, Condoleezza Rice, and Hillary Clinton), many voters still engage in gender stereotyping and assume that men are stronger and more decisive than women on issues surrounding national security and the War on Terror. Research shows that Americans associate traits such as "self-confident," "assertive," and "tough" with men, while women are associated with traits such as "compassionate," "emotional," and "sensitive" (Lawless 2004: 482). Moreover, Americans are more likely to say that men have the traits necessary to handle a military crisis. Consequently, voters who prioritize national security—even Democrats who would presumably support Hillary Clinton—are "significantly less" willing to vote for a woman presidential candidate (Lawless 2004: 486). And second, while it does seem that a very high percentage of the electorate is willing to vote for a female presidential candidate, there is some evidence that many respondents are giving the socially desirable answer. Indeed, when Americans are asked how they would feel about a female president, "26 percent of the public is 'angry or upset'" (Streb et al. 2008: 77). In other words, instead of Gallup's 5% of voters who would not vote for a well-qualified female presidential candidate, perhaps up to 26% of Americans remain unwilling to vote for a female presidential candidate.

These two barriers remind us that even a well-qualified presidential candidate such as Hillary Clinton will face significant barriers simply because of her gender. However, given her record and the issues she is highlighting as she positions herself for a presidential run, Clinton can potentially minimize the impact of these two barriers. First, regarding national security, Clinton served as secretary of state and, as we discuss below, has recently staked out positions expressing a willingness to flex U.S. muscle in the Middle East, Russia, and Iran. In other words, she is positioning herself as decisive, strong, and willing to use diplomatic and military means to promote American interests. And given the ongoing importance of the War on Terror (from Afghanistan and Iraq to the rise of the so-called Islamic State or ISIS in Iraq and Syria), this will likely be a key factor in the 2016 presidential election. And second, regarding the social desirability phenomenon, Gallup found significant "anti-Hillary" sentiment in the electorate in 2007. Indeed, 44% of Americans stated they "definitely would not vote for Clinton" for president in 2008; and, when asked why they would not vote for her, the top reason (25%) was that they "didn't like her" (Jones 2007). However, by 2011 Gallup found that 66% of Americans had a favorable view of Hillary Clinton (one point off her all-time high of 67%) while 31% had an unfavorable view of her (Saad 2011). With this level of favorability, and with a significant number of liberal Democrats who are more likely to vote for a female presidential candidate, perhaps Hillary Clinton can overcome any residual unwillingness by some voters to support a female president.

American Exceptionalism

There are deeper elements of American political culture, entwined with the notion of "American Exceptionalism," that a female presidential candidate—even Hillary Clinton—will have to embody as well as overcome. In its most basic form, American Exceptionalism views the U.S. as *at least* a qualitatively unique—and *at most* a superior—nation when compared to its liberal democratic counterparts in Europe. And if the U.S. is assumed to be a superior nation, American Exceptionalism imbues the U.S. with a moral and political responsibility to exercise its power as a global leader. As summarized by Stephen Walt, "Most statements of 'American Exceptionalism' presume that America's values, political system, and history are unique and worthy of universal admiration. They also imply that the United States is both destined and entitled to play a distinct and positive role on the world stage" (Walt 2011).

Upon closer inspection, American Exceptionalism is a multidimensional concept: first, it blends descriptive observations and normative judgments; second, it comes in "moderate" and "strong" forms; and third, it is connected to a recent debate between those who see American Exceptionalism as declining and those who think the U.S. remains the world's indispensable nation. In this section we briefly unpack these dimensions to provide a more nuanced understanding of American Exceptionalism and to highlight the paradox that American Exceptionalism is one of the reasons why the U.S. has not yet had a woman serve as president.

Descriptive and Normative

Most scholars who study American Exceptionalism engage in a descriptive analysis of what makes the U.S. *unique*—that is, different—when compared to other industrialized liberal democracies (Lipset 1997). This approach typically does not generate claims that the U.S. is superior, only that it is qualitatively different when compared to other nations. However, when some journalists, political candidates, and elected leaders invoke American Exceptionalism in their speeches and books (Hirsch 2003; Gingrich 2011a; Romney 2011; Obama 2009, 2012), they often claim that the U.S. is uniquely exceptional and has an obligation to serve as a global leader.

When describing what makes the U.S. unique and different, scholars typically highlight the unique history of the U.S. and pay close attention to its founding documents, core ideals, and political culture. For example, Seymour Lipset identifies two basic reasons why the U.S. is exceptional: first, the American Revolution established the U.S. as the first "new nation" in modern times; and second, American political culture is based on a unique set of unifying ideals embodied in the "American Creed" that includes the principles of liberty, individualism, egalitarianism, populism, and laissez-faire economics (1997: 17–19). Additionally, Peter Bienart suggests that contemporary proponents of American Exceptionalism emphasize religiosity, patriotism, and mobility to describe what makes the U.S. exceptional (Bienart 2014a). And Charles Murray writes that American Exceptionalism refers to the historical fact that from its founding through the 19th century, the U.S. was exceptional because of the ideology and constitutional structure of limited government as well as a culture rooted in a strong work ethic, religiosity, and civic engagement (Murray 2013). However, to say that the U.S. is unique is *not* the same as saying it is superior. Instead, the unique history and political culture make the U.S. "qualitatively different" when compared to other liberal democratic countries (Lipset 1997: 18). Even Charles Murray, a prominent conservative intellectual, concludes that American Exceptionalism does not refer to American superiority but only to what made the U.S. *unique* when compared to its counterparts in the 1700s–1800s (Murray 2013).

The uniqueness of American political culture is evident when we compare Americans to their counterparts in other nations. First, there is ample evidence that Americans have unique cultural attitudes toward work and individualism. For example, a 2014 Pew Global Attitudes Survey found that 73% of Americans believe in the importance of working hard to "get ahead in life" compared to a global mean of 50%; and 57% of Americans *disagree* that "success in life is pretty much determined by forces outside our control" compared to a global mean of 38% (Pew 2014c: 5). Another Pew survey compared American attitudes to their counterparts in Great Britain, Germany, France, and Spain, and on the question of which is more important, 58% of Americans opted for "Freedom to pursue life's goals without state interference" compared to a European average of 35%, while 35% of Americans opted for "State guarantees nobody is in need" compared to a European average of 62% (Pew 2011b: 7). The gap between Americans and Europeans on the theme of individualism is a strong indicator that there is something "unique" about American political culture. This attitude, according to conservative commentator George Will, sheds light on American Exceptionalism: "Americans are exceptionally committed to limited government because they are exceptionally confident of social mobility through personal striving" (Will 2011).

Second, on matters of religion Americans also are qualitatively different than their European counterparts. According to Pew Research, while "half of Americans deem religion very important in their lives; fewer than a quarter in Spain (22%), Germany (21%), Britain (17%) and France (13%) share this view" (Pew 2011b: 8). When asked if a belief in God is necessary to be a moral person, 53% of Americans agree compared to 33% in Germany, 20% in Britain, 19% in Spain, and 15% in France (Pew 2011b: 8–9). And when asked which identity was more important—religious or national—American Christians split, with 46% seeing themselves primarily as Christians and another 46% seeing themselves primarily as Americans. However, "majorities of Christians in France (90%), Germany (70%), Britain (63%) and Spain (53%) identify primarily with their nationality rather than their religion" (Pew 2011b: 10). On many issues, but especially individualism and religiosity, there is indeed something qualitatively unique about American culture.

At the same time, the scholarly approach to American Exceptionalism also highlights some inner tensions and contradictions. According to Lipset, American Exceptionalism is a "double-edged sword" whereby key principles of the American Creed conflict with—and undermine—each other. For example, individualism and laissez-faire economics allow Americans to pursue happiness in their own way, but these cultural beliefs often gloss over structural inequalities that limit opportunities for women, people of color, and low-income Americans and constrain their ability to participate as equals in American society. Moreover, unfettered individualism and laissez-faire economics often generate extreme inequality that undermines egalitarianism. And the egalitarian notion that all Americans are equal under law has been undermined by a history of slavery, discrimination, and glass ceilings. Indeed, if men and women were treated equally in the U.S., the pay gap in which women earn 78 cents to every 1 dollar men earn would not be so intractable. And when the core values of religiosity, patriotism, and mobility diverge from reality or justify unpopular policies, it can generate a backlash that ultimately undermines American Exceptionalism (Bienart 2014a). Moreover, religiosity and religious traditionalism in the U.S. serve as cultural barriers that make it more difficult for women candidates to win national elections in the U.S. (Layman and Carmines 1997; Streb et al. 2008).

In contrast to the scholarly descriptions of what makes American political culture qualitatively different, American politicians and their speechwriters are more likely to invoke American Exceptionalism as proof that the U.S. is a unique and superior nation. Ever since President Reagan invoked the metaphor of the U.S. as a "shining city on a hill" (Reagan 1989), presidential hopefuls must assert their faith that America is a unique and superior nation with a special duty to be a global leader. At the 2004 Republican national convention President George W. Bush hinted at a divinely inspired justification of American global leadership:

> I believe that America is called to lead the cause of freedom in a new century . . . because freedom is not America's gift to the world; it is the Almighty God's gift to every man and woman in this world . . . Now we go forward, grateful for our freedom, faithful to our cause, and confident in the future of the greatest nation on Earth (2004).

Newt Gingrich echoed this sentiment at a Republican presidential candidate forum in 2011 when he said, "the fact is that what makes American exceptionalism different is that we are the only people I know of in history to say power comes directly from God to each one of you" (Gingrich 2011b). In 2012, Republican presidential candidate Mitt Romney frequently invoked themes of American Exceptionalism in his campaign speeches and his book, *No Apology: The Case for American Greatness* (2011). And President Obama has asserted his belief in American Exceptionalism on several occasions—indeed, he has used the phrase "American Exceptionalism" more often than his predecessors—despite critics' attempts to paint him as less than fully committed to the idea (Obama 2009, 2011; Streich and Marrar 2014). In short, the political claims of American Exceptionalism rest on the same underlying observations made by scholars. However, because politicians seek to reassure voters and secure their political support, their claims do not simply describe the U.S. as qualitatively different but assert that it is indeed a uniquely superior nation.

Moderate and Strong

Is the U.S. one of many great countries, or is it the greatest country? The answer to this question distinguishes the "moderate" and "strong" versions of American Exceptionalism. In short, when Americans think the U.S. is "the best country" they uphold the strong version, and when they think the U.S. is "one of many great countries" they uphold the moderate version.

Looking more closely at the strong version, many of those who believe in American Exceptionalism also believe that the U.S. is not just a unique nation but a superior one. According to a 2010 Gallup survey, 80% of all Americans, including 91% of Republicans and 73% of Democrats, "agree that the United States has a unique character because of its history and Constitution that sets it apart from other nations as *the greatest in the world*" (Jones 2010, emphasis added). Moreover, because of this unique character, 66% of Americans say the United States has "a special responsibility to be the leading nation in world affairs" (Jones 2010).

By using phrases such as "the greatest country in the world" and "special responsibility" to lead, Gallup measured the degree to which Americans believe in the *strong form* of American exceptionalism.

However, surveys conducted by the Pew Research Center help us distinguish the strong and moderate forms of American exceptionalism. In 2011, Pew found that 53% of Americans agree that the U.S. "is one of the greatest countries in the world, along with some others" (Pew 2011a), a number that rose to 58% in 2014 (Pew 2014b: 34). This phrasing measures the *moderate form* of American exceptionalism in which the U.S. is a unique nation but not necessarily superior when compared to others. By contrast, in 2011, 38% of Americans agreed that the U.S. "stands above all other countries in the world" (Pew 2011a), a number that decreased to 28% in 2014 (Pew 2014b: 34). This phrasing measures the strong form of American Exceptionalism in which the U.S. is unique *and* superior. Additionally, the strong version of American Exceptionalism contains a corresponding belief in American cultural superiority. In 2011, Pew Research found that 49% of Americans agreed that "Our people are not perfect, but our culture is superior to others," but support for this view has declined from 60% in 2002 and 55% in 2007 (Pew 2011b: 5–6).

Partisanship, ideology, and age shape how Americans view American exceptionalism. For example, 52% of Republicans but only 33% of Democrats agree that the U.S. "stands above all others" while 43% of Republicans and 59% of Democrats agree that the U.S. is "one of the greatest countries, along with some others" (Pew 2011a). Among "Steadfast Conservatives" 46% believe that the U.S. "stands alone above all other countries" while 46% believe it is "one of the greatest, along with some others" (Pew 2014b: 34). By contrast, only 11% of "Solid Liberals" believe that the U.S. "stands alone above all other countries" while 71% believe it is "one of the greatest, along with some others" and 16% believe "there are other countries that are better than the U.S." (Pew 2014b: 34).[1] And among Americans age 65 and older, 50% believe the U.S. "stands above all others" while 46% believe the U.S. is "among the greatest" nations. By contrast, 59% of Americans ages 18–29 agree with that the U.S. "among the greatest" nations, 27% agree that the U.S. "stands above all others," and 12% say that there are "other countries" that are better than the U.S. (Pew 2011a). Similar differences appear on the question of the cultural superiority of the U.S. By ideology, 63% of conservatives agree with American cultural superiority compared to 45% of moderates and 34% of liberals (Pew 2011b: 6).[2] And, when broken down by age, 60% of Americans age 50 and over agree that the U.S. is culturally superior compared to 37% of Americans age 30 and under (Pew 2011b: 6).

It is clear from survey research that American Exceptionalism is a strongly held belief. However, upon closer inspection, it is also clear that there are two versions. On one hand, Republicans, conservatives, and older Americans are more likely to believe in the strong form in which the U.S. is unique, exceptional, and culturally superior when compared to other nations. And on the other hand, Democrats, liberals, and younger Americans are more likely to support the modest form in which the U.S. is unique, not superior, and one of many great countries in the world. As Clinton prepares for a presidential campaign, her stance on American Exceptionalism will either attract or repel different groups of voters.

Decline or Indispensable

A third dimension of American Exceptionalism revolves around a recent debate between those who believe that American power and status on the world stage are declining and those who believe the U.S. remains the indispensable nation. On one hand, many of President Obama's critics have argued he has chosen a course of "decline" (Krauthammer 2009) and is allowing Americans to commit "pre-emptive superpower suicide" (Kagan 2012b). In particular, critics argue that

President Obama does not embrace or embody American Exceptionalism and is therefore steering the U.S. into an era of decline by shying away from global leadership, avoiding unilateral military force in favor of multilateral diplomacy, and failing to increase military spending. As former Vice President Dick Cheney stated, "I don't think that Barack Obama believes in the U.S. as an exceptional nation . . . Our adversaries no longer fear us. Our friends no longer trust us" (Shabad 2013). Instead, Obama's critics argue that the U.S. must protect its unique global position by maintaining a dominant military role throughout the world and a willingness to project unilateral force when necessary (Romney 2011; Kagan 2012a).

Others, not necessarily critics of President Obama, have suggested that the U.S. is not the premier global power it once was because of the emergence of countries such as China, India, and Brazil as economic powers (Zakaria 2008; Friedman 2005). As Fareed Zakaria famously observed, we are not witnessing American decline so much as "rise of the rest," as countries such as Brazil, India, and China "catch up" to the U.S. economically and other countries such as Finland, South Korea, and Canada "pass" the U.S. educationally (Zakaria 2008). Given that the strength of the U.S. economy rests on an educated and innovate workforce, this trend worries many observers. However, those who take this view do not blame President Obama, but instead argue that bipartisan commitment and political willpower is needed to renew the strength and competitive edge of the U.S. both domestically and internationally (Friedman and Mandelbaum 2011).

In contrast, there remains strong support for the idea that the U.S. remains the indispensable nation on the world stage. While Secretary of State Madeline Albright famously described the U.S. as "the indispensable nation" (1998), this view has been re-asserted by President George W. Bush and President Barack Obama. Indeed, speaking to Air Force Academy graduates, Obama responded to his critics when he stated, "Let's start by putting aside the tired notion that says our influence has waned or that America is in decline" (Obama 2012). He then reminded his critics to "never bet against the United States of America. And one of the reasons is that the United States *has been, and will always be, the one indispensable nation in world affairs*" (Obama 2012, emphasis added).

What Does Hillary Clinton Say about American Exceptionalism?

Like any potential presidential candidate, Hillary Clinton embraces the idea of American Exceptionalism. However, she blends elements of both moderate and strong versions of American Exceptionalism in a way that will help her overcome some of the gender stereotyping she will inevitably face as a female presidential candidate. But in doing so, she risks alienating some liberal Democrats who are more than ready to support a female presidential candidate but who might find Hillary Clinton too centrist and too ready to adopt an interventionist foreign policy agenda as commander in chief.

First, recall that embedded in American Exceptionalism are core principles such as individualism, mobility, and opportunity. Hillary Clinton has strongly defended the idea that the U.S. is exceptional because it is a society in which a person's talents and hard work, not structures beyond their control, can determine their fate. At a political event to promote Democratic women candidates in 2014, Clinton stated, "This country will maintain a level playing field so whether you're the grandchild of a president, or the grandchild of a janitor, whether you were born in a city or a small rural village, no matter who you are you have the right to inherit the American dream" (Newton-Small 2014). While Clinton's declaration that the U.S. will *maintain* a level playing field is an assertion that everyone should have a fair chance at social, economic, and political opportunities, there is a risk that such a position is out of synch with Americans who increasingly think the playing field is unfair. Indeed, Pew Research finds that 62% of all Americans and 88% of solid liberals believe the U.S. "economic system unfairly favors the powerful" (Pew 2014b: 41). Similarly, 78% of all Americans and 95% of solid liberals agree that too much power is concentrated in the hands of a few large corporations (Pew 2014b: 41–42). Thus, Clinton must embrace the idea of mobility and opportunity that are part of American Exceptionalism—indeed, she must *embody* the principles of mobility and opportunity—but she must also be aware that many Americans are increasingly skeptical that hard work and fair play are enough to get ahead. If she does not respond to the growing sense that the economic system is stacked against ordinary Americans in favor of Wall Street and large campaign contributors, she might be vulnerable to a more populist campaign from another rising star in the Democratic Party, Senator Elizabeth Warren of Massachusetts.[3]

While it is common to invoke the idea that everyone in America is equal and has a fair chance at success, it is all too simple a statement when confronted with the history of exclusion, discrimination, and inequality that undermine the principles of fairness and equality. For example, while Americans embrace the ideals of equality and opportunity, women still are under-represented in the political and corporate worlds. For this reason, it is arguable that American Exceptionalism has always been more of a self-deluding myth than a reality (Hodgson 2009). On this issue, Hillary Clinton has offered a more nuanced answer that both embraces American Exceptionalism while acknowledging the country's imperfections. In a June 2014 interview, Jane Pauley (herself a groundbreaking female journalist) asked Clinton if she still believes in American Exceptionalism. Clinton's answer was yes, and that she believes it even more today than before she became secretary of state. When asked why, she stated that the U.S. is one of the longest surviving democracies in the world. Furthermore, Clinton suggested that American Exceptionalism is evident in the many changes (Amendments, laws, norms, etc.) that have been made to create a more perfect union. Indeed, while the U.S. may not be perfect and does not claim perfection, Clinton notes that it is exceptional because of its self-awareness and willingness to make changes to live up to its founding principles (CBS News 2014).

Thus, American Exceptionalism not only lies in the founding principles of the U.S. but in the constant struggle to eliminate the gap between those principles and historical practices that have excluded women.

Indeed, Clinton's views are very similar to the view expressed by President Obama in a speech to the United Nations in September 2014. While most of the speech focused on problems of global warming and terrorism, President Obama closed his speech with reference to the civil unrest that occurred in Ferguson, Missouri, after an unarmed black teenage male was shot and killed by a white police officer in August 2014. Obama used Ferguson not to indict the U.S. for falling short of its professed principles but as an example of how even though the U.S. is far from perfect it is unique in the way that it allows for debate and change to address its shortcomings:

> I realize that America's critics will be quick to point out that at times we too have failed to live up to our ideals. That America has plenty of problems within its own borders. This is true. In a summer marked by instability in the Middle East and Eastern Europe, I know the world also took notice of the small American city of Ferguson, Missouri, where a young man was killed and a community was divided. So, yes, we have our own racial and ethnic tensions, and like every country, we continue to wrestle with how to reconcile the vast changes by greater diversity with the traditions that we hold dear. But we welcome the scrutiny of the world. Because what you see in America is a country that has steadily worked to address our problems, to make our union more perfect, to bridge the divides that existed at the founding of this nation. America is not the same as it was 100 years ago or 50 years ago or even a decade ago. Because we fight for our ideals, and we are willing to criticize ourselves when we fall short. Because we hold our leaders accountable and insist on a free press and independent judiciary. Because we address our differences in the open space of democracy with respect for the rule of law, with a place for people of every race and every religion and with an unyielding belief in the ability of men and women to change their communities and their circumstances and their countries for the better (Obama 2014).

In short, both Obama and Clinton share the idea that what makes America an exceptional nation is its willingness to use the democratic process to self-critique, self-correct, and make progress toward making the American democracy a "more perfect union."

Indeed, this view also straddles a tension in American politics. When Pew Research investigated what Americans thought was the key to the country's success, "51% say the country has been successful more because of its ability to change, while 44% say it is more because of its reliance on long-standing principles" (Pew 2014a: 35). Thus, a slim majority share the Clinton-Obama view that what makes America great is its ability to change and improve. But underneath there is a stark ideological and partisan split: 78% of "steadfast conservatives" but only 17% of "solid liberals" agree that success is due to America's reliance on its founding principles; and only 17% of "steadfast conservatives" but 79% of "solid liberals" agree that the country has been successful because of its ability to change (Pew 2014a: 35). By embracing the core principles of the American Creed as well as the ability to change in order to live according to those principles, Clinton embraces American Exceptionalism at the same time she reconciles one of its inner tensions. But she does so in a way that appeals more to liberals who embrace the willingness to change, which may alienate conservatives who hold tight to long-standing principles.

Where Hillary Clinton *differs* from President Obama is on matters of foreign policy, where she is staking out a more aggressive stance on the use of American power as a way to address global problems. Indeed, since leaving the State Department, Clinton has made it known that she would be an advocate of a tougher stance against Iran's nuclear program, defending Crimea and Ukraine from Russian aggression, and arming Syrian rebels attempting to topple Bashar al Assad. Her 2002 vote in the U.S. Senate to authorize the use of force against Iraq is a reminder that on foreign policy matters she has always taken a more conservative line than some of her fellow Democrats. And, ironically, it was this vote to authorize the use of force that came back to haunt her in 2008 as then Senator Obama positioned himself as a critic of an unpopular war that then Senator Clinton helped start.

To distinguish herself from President Obama as she prepares for a White House run, Clinton is aware that Obama's foreign policy is increasingly seen as ineffective and weak. In August 2014 Pew Research found that 54% of Americans say, "Obama is not tough enough in his approach on foreign policy and national security issues," up from 41% in September 2012 prior to his re-election (Pew 2014d: 4). And as crises intensify in Iraq and Syria, 31% of Americans say, "the U.S. does too little to address global problems" (up from 17% in November 2013) while 39% of Americans say the U.S. is doing "too much" (down from 51% in November 2013) (Pew 2014d: 1). Numbers such as these allow Obama's critics to portray him as weak, indecisive, and choosing a path of American "decline."

At the same time, these numbers give Hillary Clinton an opportunity to establish her own foreign policy strategy while distancing herself from an unpopular president. Over the summer of 2014 she did just that. In an appearance on *The Daily Show with Jon Stewart*, Hillary Clinton offered insight into her foreign policy approach. Since *The Daily Show* caters to a young audience, she remarked that when she became secretary of state she was surprised at how many people had no memory of the U.S. liberating Europe in World War II and defeating the Soviet Union in the Cold War. Her takeaway point was that because people around the world, and young people in the U.S., are not aware of the sacrifices the U.S. has made to keep the world safe and it is values that guide it, the U.S. has to do a better job of telling its story. She reminded the audience that while the U.S. is not perfect, it has a great story to tell about human rights, freedom, and opportunity. Not only should the world hear this story, Clinton said, but Americans must tell it to themselves to renew their faith in American Exceptionalism (*The Daily Show* 2014).

Here Clinton once again acknowledges the U.S. is not perfect, but she implicitly invokes the idea that the 20th century was "the American Century" with the U.S. as the indispensable nation that sacrificed itself in order to promote freedom, opportunity, and human rights. While President Obama has made similar claims (Obama 2009, 2012), Clinton suggests that the problem with American Exceptionalism is that Americans no longer believe in their own greatness. And ultimately, for Clinton, the problem is not one of policy but packaging: U.S. influence on the world stage is waning because it is doing a poor job of "telling" the story of American indispensability. On this point, we must note, Clinton did not engage in self-critique to admit that the U.S. has often blocked progress on issues such as climate change and all too often backs autocratic allies (Walt 2011; Bienart 2014a), perhaps because when President Obama made such admissions he was accused of apologizing for American greatness (Romney 2011).

Hillary Clinton offered more insight into her foreign policy approach in a 2014 interview with the *Atlantic*. Elaborating on her position that the U.S. should have intervened in Syria to assist anti-Assad rebels, Clinton stated, "The failure to help build up a credible fighting force of the people who were the originators of the protests against Assad—there were Islamists, there were secularists, there was everything in the middle—the failure to do that left a big vacuum, which the jihadists have now filled" (Goldberg 2014). And while Clinton is quick to commend President Obama as intelligent and thoughtful, she accuses him of responding too cautiously to global crises, a position not unlike those expressed by Republicans John McCain and Dick Cheney (Bienart 2014b). For his part, President Obama has summarized his foreign-policy doctrine as "Don't do stupid stuff," which highlights his pragmatic response to various crises; after all, he is aware that efforts to arm insurgents often backfire, and he wants to vet those rebels and know who the U.S. is backing. But Clinton's response to this doctrine reveals a much different approach: "Great nations need organizing principles, and 'Don't do stupid stuff' is not an organizing principle" (Goldberg 2014). Obama's pragmatism is, for Clinton, too cautious and is an insufficient principle to guide U.S. foreign policy. And when Clinton reinforces this narrative it allows her to occupy a middle ground between the bellicose posturing of George W. Bush and the cautiousness of Barack Obama.

Hillary Clinton's views on American foreign policy, and the U.S. as an indispensable nation, are clear evidence that she believes in American Exceptionalism. But there is also a paradox: on one hand, by carving out a more assertive foreign policy, Clinton may be able to tap into American concerns that the U.S. is not doing enough to address global crises at the same time that she overcomes the gender stereotype that women are not as strong and decisive on military and security questions; but on the other hand, her more assertive foreign policy approach is ironically closer to the views of Republican voters and can potentially alienate the very Democratic voters whose enthusiastic support she will need if she wants to win the White House in 2016 (Bienart 2014b). The voters Clinton is trying to woo are actually closer to the policies pursued by President Obama in Syria and Iran, even if they think President Obama is too cautious in pursuing them.[4] If Clinton pursues stronger goals in a more assertive manner, she can certainly overcome the stereotype that women are not tough and decisive even as she risks being seen as too bellicose. For her part, however, Clinton is sure that the U.S. remains an exceptional and indispensable nation. And if the U.S. does a better job of "telling its story," then Americans as well as our allies around the world can once again believe in America's greatness.

The Exception to the Rule: U.S. History, Political Institutions, and Women in Politics

To fully understand the barriers that Hillary Clinton has both overcome and will continue to face as a female politician, we now look at some of the historical and institutional factors that shape a political environment that has historically been hostile to women candidates. The fact that Hillary Clinton is potentially a frontrunner in 2016's presidential campaign may not seem unique in our modern times; however, given the historical and institutional barriers that have hindered women and minorities in gaining elective office, this is nothing we should take for granted. While Hillary Clinton's popularity, political experience, and articulation of American Exceptionalism make her a viable candidate for the 2016 presidential election, many women who have previously run for the presidency did not enjoy her popularity nor did they have a legitimate chance of winning. The historical, social, and legal changes the U.S. underwent in the 20th century have indeed put Hillary Clinton in a unique position as she runs for the presidency. But like many women before her, she still has some barriers to overcome.

The 1872 election was the first election with a female presidential candidate, Victoria Woodhull, who made waves simply by attempting to vie for the White House. Her attempt was hard-fought and historically symbolic, especially since women were not supposed to be involved in the rough and tumble of the political arena. As an equal rights activist, Woodhull focused on a platform of universal suffrage (Underhill 1995; Gabriel 1998).[5] Since Woodhull's first campaign for the American presidency, only thirteen other women with significant national presence, including Hillary Clinton, have vied for the president's office, but they too have failed to win the position.[6] However, the failure to win the presidency should not overshadow the number of women who have run for or even successfully won political seats in the U.S. In 1975, women comprised 8.1% of all elected representatives in U.S. state legislatures and 3.6% of Congress. But by 2014, women held over 40% of the seats in state legislatures in states such as Arizona, Colorado, and Vermont while averaging 24.2% of legislative seats for all 50 states (National Conference of State Legislatures [NCSL] 2014; also, see Center for Women and American Politics [CAWP] 2014). As such, women hold a higher percentage of the seats than at the national level, where women comprise just 18.3% of the House of Representatives and Senate (NCSL 2014). Currently the U.S. ranks 85th out of 189 countries in the percentage of women in national office (Inter-Parliamentary Union [IPU] 2014).[7] By comparison, Pakistan, which ranks 72nd out of 189 countries, has a higher percentage of women in political office than the U.S. (IPU 2014).

Considering the strides that women have made in U.S. politics since Woodhull's 1872 campaign, especially since the ratification of the 19th Amendment in 1920 that secured the franchise for women, one would think that by now women would have climbed to higher rungs on the political ladder. While there are various cultural reasons why this has not come to fruition (as we discussed above), there are also historical and institutional factors that help us understand why the U.S. ranks so low on the number of women who hold a national political office. It is indeed ironic that while the U.S. champions the core principles of equality, mobility, and opportunity, countries with undemocratic systems actually have more women in political office than does the U.S. (McDonagh 2002; 2009; 2010).

Wither the Women? A Historical Paradox

Taking a global perspective, there have not been many women who have served as the leaders of their nation (Jackson 1990). Many women were starting to be elected to national legislatures during the 1970s, but most of the increase in women's representation occurred three decades ago when "the number of new female national leaders nearly quadrupled in the 1980s and 1990s and again the 2000s" (Jalazai and Krook 2010: 6). However, scholars find that countries that have had a history of stringent and highly exclusive political rights have had more women in political office and more instances of women as head of state (McDonagh 2002, 2009, 2010). Using the Freedom House rankings, an extensive review of countries' global political liberties and rights, the U.S. has consistently ranked 1 out of 7 (1 being the "most free" and 7 being the "least free") while other countries with more instances of female office holders rank as "less free" (Freedom House 2014).[8] While some countries fully expanded political rights to citizens, others have remained fairly exclusive in granting them. For example, Pakistan ranked as a 4 in political rights and a 5 in civil liberties according to the 2014 Freedom House rankings, yet in 2014 the Pakistani parliament consisted of higher proportions of women than the U.S., with women comprising 20.7% of national representatives in the lower chamber. Further, in 1988, Pakistanis elected their first female prime minister, Benazir Bhutto, even when Freedom House listed the country as only "partly free" and Pakistan was criticized for putting women's rights on the back burner (Weiss 2003, 2012). Within the same region, both India and Bangladesh rank lower on the Freedom House ratings for political rights than the U.S., yet Indira Gandhi became prime minister of India in 1966 and Khaleda Zia became the first female prime minister of Bangladesh in 1991, a country that also has a parliament with a higher percentage of women than the U.S. Congress. This is not a regional idiosyncrasy: Latin American countries have also topped the U.S. in the percentage of female lawmakers and leaders. For example, Argentina has had two female presidents: Isabel Peron. who was installed in 1974. and Christina Kirchner. who was elected in 2007.[9] Additionally, in 2014, in Argentina women hold 37.8% of the seats in the national legislature, yet until 2003 it was only a "partly free" country according to Freedom House rankings.

One reason why some countries have a higher percentage of women in their national legislatures when compared to the U.S. (even when they rank as "partly free") can be explained by the historical context in which they developed their political systems. Looking at the U.S., some scholars explain why so few women have been elected to national political office by looking at how the U.S. was founded and how it developed as a nation. The U.S. is unique, recall, because it was the first modern nation to reject rule by an inherited monarchy and create a republic, which ironically "increased the political citizenship of some men" and "decreased the political citizenship of all women" (McDonagh 2002: 535). At that time, women had virtually no role in politics except to raise children to be good citizens, a form of "Republican Motherhood" (Kerber 1979; see also McDonagh 2002, 2010). At the American founding, gender differences were pointed out as primary reason to exclude women from politics (Wilson 1976; Pateman 1988), blocking any pathway for women to participate in politics, much less hold political office. Still, the fact that women were legally set apart from men does not in itself explain why the U.S. has not had a female head of state when other countries, with similar or even more entrenched gender inequalities, have had a woman appointed or elected as their head of state.

Indeed, one factor that is not necessarily intuitive but is indeed important is that countries with an inherited monarch provide an automatic pathway for women to rule due to kinship (McDonagh 2002, 2009, 2010). Monarchical systems not only provide an avenue for women to be the head of state, but create a history of political rule by women. In fact, McDonagh points out that monarchies open to female rule often have currency with women leaders on them, and this serves to "remind people on an everyday basis that being a woman and being a political leader can and do go together" (2009: 66). While Margaret Thatcher, for example, may have been the first female Prime Minister of the United Kingdom elected in 1979, the United Kingdom already had a history of six reigning queens (Waller 2006). In short, citizens in monarchical countries often have a history of female rulers, and in those countries the "glass ceiling" is easier to break; indeed, these countries have more females in their national legislatures (McDonagh 2002, 2010). If Hillary Clinton wins the presidency in 2016, the final "glass ceiling" of American politics will finally be shattered.

There are, of course, additional psychological factors involved. Women's participation in politics is reduced when there is a dearth of female candidates or sitting female representatives (Plutzer and Zipp 1996; Verba, Burns, and Schlozman 1997; Dolan 1998; Atkenson 2003; Campbell and Wolbrecht 2006; Lawless and Fox 2013). Not only are females less likely to run for political office when women are absent in the political arena, but they are also less likely to engage in political discussion. This creates a mutually reinforcing dynamic that makes the political environment even less inviting for women. Overall, the absence of women from politics reinforces the perception that politics a "man's game" not one that is "gender-integrated" (McDonagh 2002: 538). The relatively low percentage of women in the U.S. Congress might still reinforce this perception in the mind of American voters who remain fixed on the assumption that only men can be the commander in chief. Thus, as far as Hillary Clinton has come in her political career, she still must overcome institutional and cultural barriers that reinforce the political "glass ceiling" blocking access to the presidency.

Constitutionalizing Gender Equality: Diminishing Barriers via Codifying Women's Rights

Breaking away from a monarchical system in the 18th century is exceptional in itself as the United States became a beacon of self-government and individual freedom. However, the U.S. also broke away from an important historical factor that has historically enhanced the presence of women in the political arena: a monarchy that was open to rule by women. Adding to this phenomenon is another component unique to the United States. The U.S. was founded at a time when gender roles were deeply embedded, and consequently the idea of including women as citizens in the political arena was absent when the Constitution was drafted and ratified (Wilson 1976; Pateman 1988). This has had a lasting effect on the election of women into political office. A majority of democracies in the world today developed after World War II and skyrocketed in the 1970s into the 1990s (Geddes 1999). These "newer democracies" developed alongside global feminist movements, and in turn gender equality was often embedded into the language of their constitutions. While famous for its culture of individualism and liberty, the U.S. has been comparatively slow to institutionalize gender equality in its political system.

While a global discussion was taking place about implementing such mechanisms into the political structure of new democracies, the U.S. Supreme Court, for example, had just ruled that women had a constitutional right to serve on a jury.[10]

Scholars find that countries that have constitutional provisions and policies that mandate gender equality are much more likely to have higher percentages of women in legislatures and parliaments (Norris 2006; Lambert and Scribner 2009; Jalaizai and Krook 2010; McDonagh 2010). This is still the case even when accounting for cultural norms that promote gender inequality (Lambert and Scribner 2009). These constitutional provisions include economic equality in employment, maternity leave, free day care for children, and quota requirements for parliaments.[11] Why do constitutions matter even in places where cultural norms subordinate women? Constitutions are important in defining relationships by "codifying gender rights" (Waylen 2006: 1210). A country's constitution is the "core of the institutional structure and legal system of a state and defines the relationships between the state and its citizens as well as among the citizens themselves" (Waylen 2006: 1210). Moreover, countries with such constitutional provisions *combined with* a history of a hereditary monarchy have *more* women in political office than countries with mandated gender equality policies (McDonagh 2010).

Some of these constitutional provisions have their roots in the efforts of the Commission on the Status of Women (CSW) and a variety of global and local feminist movements (Bystydziensky and Sekhon 1999; Htun and Weldon 2010). In 1949, in the shadow of World War II and during the formation of the United Nations (UN), the UN developed CSW, which became a hallmark for the advancement of women's global rights. Addressing issues such as the right for a woman to consent to marriage in the 1960s to a spectrum of rights in the 1970s, CSW, along with numerous organizations, developed a Convention on the Elimination of All Forms of Discrimination Against Women (CEDAW). In 1979, 64 countries signed CEDAW, which is a commitment to implement policies for gender equality. Although U.S. President Jimmy Carter signed CEDAW, the U.S. Congress failed to ratify it. This movement has helped to develop provisions of gender equality in countries with strict gender roles, even in the development of the Afghan constitution (Farhoumand-Sims 2009).

Thus, in the 1970s and 1980s many countries were poised to implement policies meant to alleviate discrimination based on gender. And by the late 1980s many women's groups were emerging as active participants in the development of national constitutions, especially in Latin America (Bystydziensky and Sekhon 1999; Htun and Weldon 2010). Meanwhile, the United States was struggling to pass the Equal Rights Amendment (ERA), which would have given a constitutional guarantee to the equal status of women. The ERA failed to be ratified in 1979 and again in 1982, a failure that can be attributed to organizations aligned with conservative Christians (Mansbridge 1986) which were becoming politically influential within the Republican Party. This is an important reminder that one of the ways in which the U.S. is exceptional is that, when compared to other liberal democracies, it contains a strong component of religiosity and religious traditionalism which mitigate steps toward codifying gender equality. Even though the ERA did not guarantee political office for women, its ultimate defeat put the U.S. out of step with the global trends in an era when other countries started to write guarantees of gender equality into their constitutions as well as implement a system of quotas for women in legislatures and in parliament.

Guaranteeing Political Representation: Quotas and Electoral Systems

Gender quotas have also had a significant influence on women's access to national political office. There are currently 24 countries that reserve seats for women in their national legislature. Over 75 countries either have quota requirements for potential candidates in the general election or have reserved seats for women in the national legislature. These quota systems are aimed at creating a "critical mass" of women in political office while balancing gender inequity in governance (Dahlerup 2006). The adoption of quota systems began in Argentina in 1991 and swiftly gained steam during that decade, with 17 other countries following in Argentina's footsteps (Dahlerup and Freidenvall 2005). Some quota requirements range from granting women five seats or up to 50% of legislative seats. For example, Rwanda has a 30% gender quota in elected offices, Tanzania has a 20% requirement, and France has a 50% requirement. Quota systems not only open the door for women to serve in elective office, but they help create a "history of rule by women" which, in turn, creates a cultural norm that is inclusive of women in politics. Indeed, some countries are consistently electing women to parliament above and beyond their country's gender quota requirements. In 2014, for example, Rwanda had 64% of women making up the lower chamber of their national legislature and 38% of the upper chamber. Additionally, countries such as Bangladesh and Zimbabwe have about 8% more women beyond their quotas in their lower legislative chambers, while Afghanistan, Burundi, and Niger have between 1% and 3% more women than the required quota in their national legislature.

Getting Jane There: Party Leaders, Candidate Recruitment, Electoral Systems, and Incumbency Advantage

Not all countries that have adopted quota systems have reserved seats in their national legislatures. Many countries that have adopted quota systems require political parties to ensure that women are a certain percentage of their candidates. This allows women to enter into the political career ladder, especially when there are preconceived notions by party leaders that some districts are not friendly to female candidates. In a comparative U.S. state-level study, it has been found that when party leaders do not perceive females as viable candidates in the upcoming election, they will be less likely to recruit them (Sabonmatsu 2009). Interestingly, in countries that have quota systems for party candidate lists, there is a "contagion effect" where party leaders may urge the party to nominate female candidates to run in the general election if other political parties have female candidates poised to be on the upcoming ballot (Caul 2001; Sanbonmatsu 2009). Indeed, parties may place women on the ballot to illustrate their commitment to women's rights (Sabonmatsu 2009: 109).

Contrary to conventional wisdom, in the U.S. women are *not* more likely than men to lose an election in both state-level and national-level elections (Darcy, Welch, and Clark 1994; Burrell 1994; Seltzer, Newman, and Leighton 1997). This is despite the fact that some citizens, especially those concerned about national security, are less willing to vote for a female candidate (Lawless 2004). Further, female candidates in the U.S. actually have the same financial advantage in raising funds for their campaigns (Seltzer, Newman, and Leighton 1997; Werner 1997). If this is the case, then why does the U.S. continue to have such a low number of women in state legislatures and the U.S. Congress? Some of this has to do with incumbency advantage (Welch, Ambrosius, Clark, and Darcy 1985; Darcy, Welch, and Clark 1994) and the *perception* by the public as well as some party leaders that women will have a harder time getting elected (Sanbonmatsu 2009). In American politics it is hard enough to be a viable candidate and get your name on the ballot, let alone climb the political ladder to the presidency. In order to do so, one must be a skilled and polished politician, which takes time to cultivate. However, if party leaders do not recruit women candidates at the state level, this prevents women from getting into the political pipeline, where they can acquire the necessary experience to be successful candidates at the national level.

Additionally, incumbency advantages in American politics block access to Congress for challengers of both genders, but especially women. Once elected to Congress, representatives have a very high reelection rate of about 90% or higher over the past 40 years (Dodd and Oppenheimer 2005; Center for Responsive Politics 2014). Additionally, incumbents have similar reelection rates in state legislatures (Breaux 1990; Hogan 2004).[12] The advantage incumbents have are multiple: they typically have more money to run their campaigns; they can claim credit for what they done in office (Fenno 1974); they are quality politicians, and their challengers are not often strategic (Jacobson and Kernell 1983; Jacobson 1989)[13]; and the districts they represent are often drawn to their advantage by their political party, insulating them from opposition (Dodd and Oppenheimer 2005). But why would incumbency advantage have an effect on female representation more so than males'? As with any career, women have historically had a hard time pursuing political ones. This can, in part, be attributed to gender differences and perceptions about women's role in society (Sabonmatsu 2009: 16). The U.S. political environment did not have many women entering national politics until the 1970s, and even then there was a very slow increase in the number of women running for political office (Palmer and Simon 2008). This inertia has been attributed to societal views about gender roles which have contributed to a dearth of female candidates in the first place (Burrell 1994). And since "most incumbents win reelection, and most incumbents happen to be men," then opportunities for women to enter into politics due to a combination of residual gender roles along with incumbency advantage constitute major barriers for women candidates even at the state level (Sabonmatsu 2009: 17).

Some state legislatures, however, do have features that allow women to overcome incumbency advantage. States that have imposed term limits on their state legislators have more women representatives than states without term limits (Carroll and Jenkins 2001),[14] in part because term limits force incumbents out and increase the overall number of open seats in state legislative elections (Kousser 2005; Carey, Niemi, Powell, and Moncrief 1998). And where the state legislature is not as professionalized, that is, they have lower salaries, staff, and days in session, a state's term-limit policy can have a synergistic effect on women's representation in the legislature. In short, when state legislatures are less professionalized and are not full-time jobs, women seem to be more likely to run for election. Further, un-professionalized and term-limited seats are not attractive to men who would like to make politics their career (Lawless and Fox 2013). Additionally, term-limited state legislatures open seats up in state senates, which allows women to overcome incumbency advantage and move up the political ladder (Carroll and Jenkins 2001). At the national level, term limits do not exist, thus incumbency advantage is a hard and fast obstacle, so both men and women have to wait until an incumbent retires, dies, or there is some sort of significant political scandal.

Another barrier for women that begins at the candidacy stage is that party leaders serve as both recruiters and gatekeepers for potential candidates. Recruitment means that party leaders field potential candidates and ask them to run under their party name. This also means that they act as "gatekeepers" by allowing only certain individuals to have their endorsement (Sabonmatsu 2009). Although it has not been found that there is systematic bias by party leaders in asking a man to run for their party over a woman (Sabonmatsu 2009), there are serious projections that party leaders do make in considering their electability. First, the recruitment pool is severely limited by their eligibility, meaning that women do not often take on jobs that help make them attractive potential candidates, such as being a lawyer or a business owner. Further, they tend to have the "double burden" when family obligations such as child rearing take up time and resources even if they have complementary careers for candidacy. Second, party leaders field candidates based on electability within a particular district. Based on their projections as to how the district may react to a female candidate, party leaders may only ask male candidates to run, even though research illustrates that male and female candidates fare the same in electoral wins and losses (Darcy, Welch, and Clark 1994; Burrell 1994; Seltzer, Newman, and Leighton 1997). Without party nomination quotas, the U.S. seems to be the exception to the rule among democracies, since over 50 other countries have a quota system at the level of the party nomination process while the U.S. does not. So, the U.S. has fewer women in elected office in part because fewer women are asked to run for those offices.

Once on the ballot, another institutional barrier for women seeking political office is the election system. The U.S. Congress and 87% of the U.S. state legislatures have single-member districts (SMDs) and a plurality threshold, an election system in which the candidate with the most votes wins that district's seat in the legislature. This is a different election structure than multi-member districts (MMDs) and proportional representation (PR) systems. In MMDs, there can be multiple seats to represent one district; for example, one district might have three seats, and the top three candidates win those seats. PR systems have multi-member districts and political parties win seats for their candidates based on the proportion of votes they receive. If a party receives 30% of the votes, then candidates of that political party will hold about 30% of the seats in the legislature. Research on electoral systems consistently demonstrates that women are more likely to be elected into office in MMD and PR systems than in the single-member districts used in the U.S. (Norris 1985, 2006; Matland 1998; Reynolds 1999; King 2002).

Multi-member districts not only allow for more seats for women to potentially compete for, but these systems also give party leaders more leeway in putting women on their party's list of nominees, especially when having women on the ticket can increase votes for their political party (Caul 1999; Jalalzai and Krook 2010). This allows political parties to balance their tickets and strategically illustrate that their party is "gender-inclusive." Also, if there are a higher number of seats to be filled, party leaders may be more likely to support females even if they have doubts about the district being "female friendly." In U.S. national elections, however, these strategies cannot occur because of single member districts.

***

The United States is an exceptional nation. Its political culture, history, and electoral system create a unique mixture of principles, attitudes, practices, and institutions that are qualitatively different from those found in other democratic countries. From this perspective, the U.S. is a leading and even an exceptional nation. It is, as Americans like to believe, a land of opportunity, mobility, equality, and freedom that remains a beacon of democracy for many at home and around the world. However, this same mixture of principles, attitudes, practices, and institutions also make the U.S. exceptional not because it leads but because it lags. When it comes to electing women to the national legislature and as head of state, the U.S. is exceptional because it is the exception to the rule. Many other countries around the world, from advanced democracies in Europe to developing nations in Asia and Africa, have higher percentages of women in their national legislative bodies, and have elected one or more women as prime minister or president. Paradoxically, upward political mobility for women has been blocked due to the very same cultural attitudes that set it apart as unique. In short, for women candidates in the U.S., upward political mobility and opportunity are blocked by cultural phenomena such as gender stereotyping and religious traditionalism as well as institutional practices that fail to recruit, nominate, and elect women to state and national legislative bodies. And because women are not recruited or nominated by party leaders, this reinforces the cultural assumption that women do not have what it takes to hold the highest elected office of the land.

Hillary Clinton has a chance to once again prove that America is an exceptional nation. If she emerges victorious in the 2016 presidential election, she will shatter the last remaining political glass ceiling. While Clinton has extensive political experience (both elected and appointed) and other advantages such as name recognition, popularity, and fund-raising capabilities, she will still have to contend with the deeply entrenched attitudes and practices that place women candidates at a disadvantage. For example, even though she has served as secretary of state and has staked out a strong stance on the use of American influence in global politics, she still must overcome the gender stereotype that she is not "tough" and "decisive" because of her gender. And even though many Americans say they are willing to vote for a qualified woman for president, the idea of a "Madam President" still makes many Americans upset.

Rather than complaining about these barriers, Clinton is poised to attack them head on. Indeed, by highlighting the core principles of opportunity and equality that are at the heart of American Exceptionalism and simultaneously arguing that what makes the U.S. exceptional is not only these principles but the ability to improve itself over time by dismantling discriminatory barriers, she has deftly positioned herself as the embodiment of American Exceptionalism. On matters of domestic policy, she must embody upward mobility and opportunity at the same time she overcomes the barriers that too often hinder women candidates. And, on matters of foreign policy, she has positioned herself as a strong leader who is willing to make "hard choices"[15] in contrast to the bellicose posturing of George W. Bush and overly cautious approach of President Obama.

In short, as we have shown, if Hillary Clinton hopes to become the first female president of the United States, she will have to both *embody* American Exceptionalism by highlighting what makes the U.S. unique and exceptional at the same time she *overcomes* its inner contradictions that make the U.S. the exception to the rule when it comes to women serving as head of state.

References

1 PEW describes "Steadfast Conservatives" as Americans who consistently take the conservative position on a range of social and economic issues, while "Solid Liberals" consistently take the liberal position on those same issues.
2 By contrast, in Britain and France, "only about a third or fewer (32% and 27%, respectively) think their culture is better than others" (Pew 2011b: 6).
3 In fact, Senator Bernie Sanders of Vermont took up this challenge and is campaigning for the Democratic nomination by focusing on themes of income inequality and the political power of the "billionaire class."

4 For instance, while Clinton favors arming rebels in Syria as part of an effort to oust Bashar al Assad from Syria, only 20% of Americans support this policy while 70% oppose it; and while Clinton favors stronger sanctions against Iran for its nuclear enrichment program, only 35% of Americans support tougher sanctions while 61% support a deal that would limit (but not prohibit) Iran's ability to enrich uranium (Bienart 2014b).

5 Woodhull also ran with ex-slave Fredrick Douglass as her vice presidential candidate on the 1872 presidential ticket. Although Douglass was nominated by the Equal Rights Party, he did not actively campaign with Woodhull (Underhill 1995; Gabriel 1988).

6 Based on Rutgers University's Center for American Women in Politics (2012) selection of female candidates that have "achieved major historic firsts; were named in national polls; achieved prominence by holding significant elected or appointed office; appeared on the general election ballot in a majority of states; and/or became eligible for federal matching funds." Overall, 48 women have run for the president's seat. Available at: www.cawp.rutgers.edu/fast_facts/levels_of_office/documents/prescand .pdf. [Accessed: December 1, 2014.]

7 Statistics from IPU (2014) were collected via the PARLINE database on national parliaments and are available at: www.ipu.org/parline-e/parlinesearch.asp.

8 See the Freedom in the World data-set available at https://freedomhouse.org/report-types/freedom-world#.VIB4ZFJAQuM. [Accessed: December 1, 2014.]

9 Isabel Peron was not elected but succeeded her husband, Juan Peron, in 1974.

10 It was not until the Supreme Court ruling in the 1975 case of *Taylor v. Louisiana* that women gained the right to serve as jurors. Prior to this court ruling, women were omitted from jury lists.

11 Currently twenty-four countries have constitutional quota requirements for women in parliament. See the Comparative Constitutional Database compiled by UN Women. Available at: http://constitutions.unwomen.org. [Accessed: December 1, 2014.]

12 Also see the National Institute on Money in State Politics. Available at: http://classic .followthemoney.org/press/ReportView.phtml?r=361&ext=5. [Accessed: December 1, 2014.]

13 Strategic candidates run in open seat elections because they understand incumbency advantage and their chances of winning the election.

14 Arkansas, Arizona, California, Colorado, Florida, Louisiana, Maine, Michigan, Missouri, Montana, Nebraska, Nevada, Ohio, Oklahoma, and South Dakota have term-limited state legislative seats (National Conference of State Legislatures 2014).

15 Consider the title of her book which is widely seen as her first step towards a presidential campaign, *Hard Choices* (2014).

Bibliography

Albright, Madeline. 1998. "Transcript: Albright Interview on NBC-TV February 19," February 19, available at: www.fas.org/news/iraq/1998/02/19/98021907_tpo.html. [Accessed: December 6, 2014.]

Atkeson, Lonna Rae. 2003. "Not All Cues are Created Equal: The Conditional Impact of Female Candidates on Political Engagement," *Journal of Politics* 65 (November): 1040–1061.

Bienart, Peter. 2014a. "The End of American Exceptionalism," *Atlantic*, February 3, available at: www.theatlantic.com/politics/archive/2014/02/the-end-of-american-exceptionalism/283540/. [Accessed: August 14, 2014.]

Bienart, Peter. 2014b. "How Money Warps U.S. Foreign Policy," *Atlantic*, August 13, available at: www.theatlantic.com/international/archive/2014/08/how-money-warps-us-foreign-policy/376035/?single_page=true. [Accessed: December 7, 2014.]

Breaux, David. 1990. "Specifying the Impact of Incumbency on State Legislative Elections: A District-Level Analysis," *American Politics Quarterly* 18(3): 270–286.

Burrell, Barabara C. 1994. *A Woman's Place Is in the House: Campaigning for Congress in the Feminist Era.* Ann Arbor: University of Michigan Press.

Bush, George W. 2004. "Remarks Accepting the Presidential Nomination at the Republican National Convention in New York City," September 2, available at: www.presidency.ucsb.edu/ws/index.php?pid=72727#axzz1Xs4CwFYP. [Accessed: August 14, 2014.]

Bystydzienski, Jill M. and Joti Sekhon, eds. 1999. *Democratization and Women's Grassroots Movements.* Bloomington, IN: Indiana University Press.

Campbell, David E., and Christina Wolbrecht. 2006. "See Jane Run: Women Politicians as Role Models for Adolescents," *Journal of Politics* 68 (March): 233–247.

Carey, John M., Richard G. Niemi, and Lynda W. Powell. 1998. "The Effects of Term Limits on State Legislatures," *Legislative Studies Quarterly* 23 (May): 271–300.

Carroll, Susan J., and Krista Jenkins. 2001. "Do Term limits Help Women Get Elected?" *Social Science Quarterly* 82(1): 197–201.

Caul, Miki. 2001. "Political Parties and the Adoption of Candidate Gender Quotas: A Cross-National Analysis," *Journal of Politics*, 63(4): 1214–1229.

Caul, Miki. 1999. "Women's Representation in Parliament: The Role of Political Parties," *Party Politics* 5(1): 79–98.

CBS News. 2014. "Hillary Clinton: I Still Believe in American Exceptionalism," June 15, available at: www.cbsnews.com/videos/hillary-clinton-i-still-believe-in-american-exceptionalism/. [Accessed: December 1, 2014.]

Center for Responsive Politics. 2014. "Reelection Rates Over the Years," available at: www.opensecrets.org/bigpicture/reelect.php. [Accessed: August 14, 2014.]

Center for Women and Politics. 2014. "Fact Sheet: Women in State Legislatures," Eagleton Institute for Politics, Rutgers University, available at: www.cawp.rutgers.edu/fast_facts/levels_of_office/documents/stleg.pdf. [Accessed: August 14, 2014.]

Center for Women and Politics. 2014. "Fact Sheet: Women in U.S. Congress," Eagleton Institute for Politics, Rutgers University, available at: www.cawp.rutgers.edu/fast_facts/levels_of_office/documents/cong.pdf. [Accessed: August 14, 2014.]

Clinton, Hillary. 2014. *Hard Choices.* New York: Simon & Schuster.

Dahlerup, Drude, and Lenita Freidenvall, Lenita. 2005. "Quotas as a 'Fast Track' to Equal Representation for Women," *International Feminist Journal of Politics*, 7(1): 26–48.

Dahlerup, Drude, ed. 2006. *Women, Quotas and Politics.* Routledge: London and New York.

Darcey, R., Susan Welch, and Janet Clark. 1994. *Women, Elections, and Representation*, 2nd ed. Lincoln: University of Nebraska Press.

Dodd, Lawerence C., and Bruce I. Oppenhiemer. 2005. *Congress Reconsidered.* Washington DC: CQ Press.

Dolan, Kathleen. 1998. "Voting for Women in the 'Year of the Woman,'" *American Journal of Political Science* 42 (March): 272–293.

Farhoumand-Simms, Cheshmak. 2009. "CEDAW and Afghanistan," *Journal of International Women's Studies* 11(1): 136–156.

Fenno Jr., Richard F. 1978. *Home Style: House Members in Their Districts.* Boston: Little Brown.

Freedom House. 2014. "Freedom in the World 2014," available at: www.freedomhouse.org/report/freedom-world/freedom-world-2014. [Accessed: December 1, 2014.]

Friedman, Thomas. 2005. *The World Is Flat: A Brief History of the Twenty-First Century*. New York: Farrar, Strauss and Giroux.

Friedman, Thomas, and Michael Mandelbaum. 2011. *That Used to Be Us: How America Fell Behind in the World It Invented and How We Can Come Back*. New York: Farrar, Strauss and Giroux.

Gabriel, Mary. 1998. *Notorious Victoria: The Life of Victoria Woodhull Uncensored*. Algoquin Books of Chapel Hill: North Carolina.

Geddes, Barbara. 1999. "What Do We Know about Democratization after Twenty Years?" *Annual Review of Political Science* 2: 115–144.

Gingrich, Newt. 2011a. *A Nation Like No Other: Why American Exceptionalism Matters*. Washington, DC: Regnery Publishing.

Gingrich, Newt. 2011b. "Newt Gingrich Explains American Exceptionalism," *Real Clear Politics*, September 5, available at: www.realclearpolitics.com/video/2011/09/05/newt_gingrich_explains_american_exceptionalism.html. [Accessed: September 22, 2014.]

Goldberg, Jeffrey. 2014. "Hillary Clinton: 'Failure' to Help Syrian Rebels Led to the Rise of ISIS," *Atlantic*, August 10, available at: www.theatlantic.com/international/archive/2014/08/hillary-clinton-failure-to-help-syrian-rebels-led-to-the-rise-of-isis/375832/. [Accessed: December 7, 2014.]

Hirsh, Michael. 2003. *At War with Ourselves: Why America Is Squandering Its Chance to Build a Better World*. New York: Oxford University Press.

Hodgson, Godfrey. 2009. *The Myth of American Exceptionalism*. New Haven, CT: Yale University Press.

Hogan, Robert E. 2004. "Challenger Emergence, Incumbent Success, and Electoral Accountability in State Legislative Elections," *Journal of Politics* 66(4): 1283–1303.

Htun, Mala, and S. Laurel Weldon. 2010. "When Do Governments Promote Women's Rights? A Framework for the Comparative Analysis of Sex Equality Policy," *Perspectives on Politics* 8: 207–216.

Jackson, Guida M. 1990. *Women Who Ruled*. Santa Barbara, CA: ABC-CLIO.

Jacobson, Gary C. 1989. "Strategic Politicians and the Dynamics of U.S. House Elections, 1946–1986," *American Political Science Review* 83: 773–793.

Jacobson, Gary C., and Samuel Kernell. 1983. *Strategy and Choice in Congressional Elections*, 2nd ed. New Haven: Yale University Press.

Jalazai, Farida, and Mona Lena Krook. 2010. "Beyond Hillary and Benazir: Women's Political Leadership Wordwide," *International Political Science Review* 31(1): 5–21.

Jones, Jeffrey M. 2007. "What Is Behind Anti-Hillary Sentiment?" available at: www.gallup.com/poll/102907/What-Behind-AntiHillary-Sentiment.aspx. [Accessed: November 24, 2014.]

Jones, Jeffrey M. 2010. "Americans See U.S. as Exceptional; 37% Doubt Obama Does," available at: www.gallup.com/poll/145358/Americans-Exceptional-Doubt-Obama.aspx. [Accessed: August 14, 2014.]

Jones, Jeffrey M. 2012. "Atheists, Muslims See Most Bias as Presidential Candidates," available at: www.gallup.com/poll/155285/Atheists-Muslims-Bias-Presidential-Candidates.aspx. [Accessed: November 24, 2014.]

Kagan, Robert. 2012a. *The World America Made*. New York: Knopf.

Kagan, Robert, 2012b. "Not fade Away: Against the Myth of American Decline," January 11, *New Republic*, available at: www.newrepublic.com/article/politics/magazine/99521/america-world-power-declinism. [Accessed: December 6, 2014.]

Kerber, Linda. 1976. "The Republican Mother: Women and the Enlightenment—An American Perspective," *American Quarterly* 28(2): 187–205.

King, James D. 2002. "Single-Member Districts and the Representation of Women in American State Legislatures: The Effects of Electoral System Change," *State Politics and Policy Quarterly* 2: 161–175.

Kousser, Thad. 2005. *Term Limits and the Dismantling of State Legislative Professionalism.* Cambridge: Cambridge University Press.

Krauthammer, Charles. 2009. "Decline Is a Choice: The New Liberalism and the End of American Ascendancy," *Weekly Standard*, available at: www.weeklystandard .com/Content/Public/Articles/000/000/017/056lfnpr.asp. [Accessed: December 5, 2014].

Lambert, Priscilla A., and Druscilla L. Scribner. 2009. "A Politics of Difference versus a Politics of Equality: Do Constitutions Matter?" *Comparative Politics* 41(3): 337–357.

Lawless, Jennifer. 2004. "Women, War, and Winning Elections: Gender Stereotyping in the Post-September 11th Era," *Political Research Quarterly* 57(3): 479–490.

Lawless, Jennifer L., and Richard L. Fox. 2013. "Girls Just Wanna Not Run: The Gender Gap in Young American's Political Ambition," Women & Politics Institute: Washington, DC, available at: www.american.edu/spa/wpi/upload/girls-just-wanna-not-run_policy-report.pdf. [Accessed: December 1, 2014.]

Layman, Geoffrey, and Edward Carmines. 1997. "Cultural Conflict in American Politics: Religious Traditionalism, Postmaterialism, and U.S. Political Behavior," *Journal of Politics* 59(3): 751–777.

Lipset, Seymour. 1997. *American Exceptionalism: A Double-Edged Sword.* New York: W.W. Norton.

Mansbridge, Jane J. 1986. Why We Lost the ERA. Chicago: University of Chicago Press.

Matland, Richard E. 1998. "Women's Representation in National Legislatures: Developed and Developing Nations," *Legislative Studies Quarterly* 23(1): 109–125.

McDonagh, Eileen. 2002. "Political Citizens and Democratization: The Gender Paradox," *American Political Science Review* 96(3): 535–552.

McDonagh, Eileen. 2009. *A Motherless State: Women's Political Leadership and American Democracy.* Chicago: University of Chicago Press.

McDonagh, Eileen. 2010. "It Takes a State: A Policy Feedback Model of Women's Political Representation," *Perspectives on Politics* 8(1): 69–91.

Murray, Charles. 2013. *American Exceptionalism: An Experiment in History.* Washington, DC: AEI Press.

National Conference of State Legislatures. 2014. "Women in State Legislatures for 2014," available at: www.ncsl.org/legislators-staff/legislators/womens-legislative-network/women-in-state-legislatures-for-2014.aspx. [Accessed: December 1, 2014.]

Newton-Small, Jay. 2014. "Hillary Clinton Pledges to Campaign for Female Democratic Candidates," September 19, available at: http://time.com/3404189/hillary-clinton-2014-midterm-elections/ [Accessed: September 22, 2014.]

Norris, Pippa. 1985. "Women in European Legislative Elites," *West European Politics* 8(4): 90–101.

Norris, Pippa. 2006. "The Impact of Electoral Reform on Women's Representation," *Acta Politica* 41: 197–213.

Obama, Barack. 2009. "News Conference by President Obama," April 4, available at: www.whitehouse.gov/the-press-office/news-conference-president-obama-4042009. [Accessed: December 6, 2014.]

Obama, Barack. 2012. "Remarks Made by the President at the Air Force Academy Commencement," May 23, available at: www.whitehouse.gov/the-press-office/2012/05/23/remarks-president-air-force-academy-commencement. [Accessed: December 6, 2014].

Obama, Barack. 2014. "Remarks by President Obama in Address to the United Nations General Assembly Available," September 24, available at: www.whitehouse .gov/the-press-office/2014/09/24/remarks-president-obama-address-united-nations-general-assembly. [Accessed: November 30, 2014.]

Palmer, Barbara, and Dennis Simon. 2008. *Breaking the Political Glass Ceiling: Women and Congressional Elections*, 2nd ed. New York: Routledge.

Pateman, Carole. 1988. *The Sexual Contract*. Cambridge: Polity Press.

Pew Research Center. 2011a. "U.S. Seen as Among the Greatest Nations, But Not Superior to All Others," available at: www.people-press.org/2011/06/30/u-s-seen-as-among-the-greatest-nations-but-not-superior-to-all-others/. [Accessed: August 15, 2014.]

Pew Research Center. 2011b. "The American-Western European Values Gap: American Exceptionalism Subsides," available at: www.pewglobal.org/2011/11/17/the-american-western-european-values-gap/. [Accessed: August 15, 2014.]

Pew Research, 2014a. "For 2016 Hopefuls, Washington Experience Could Do More Harm than Good," available at: www.people-press.org/2014/05/19/for-2016-hopefuls-washington-experience-could-do-more-harm-than-good/ [Accessed: October 1, 2014.]

Pew Research, 2014b. "Beyond Red vs. Blue: The Political Typology," available at: www.people-press.org/files/2014/06/6-26-14-Political-Typology-release1.pdf [Accessed: October 15, 2014.]

Pew Research, 2014c. "Emerging and Developing Economies Much More Optimistic Than Rich Countries about the Future," available at: www.pewglobal.org/files/2014/10/Pew-Research-Center-Inequality-Report-FINAL-October-17-2014.pdf [Accessed: November 1, 2014.]

Pew Research, 2014d. "As New Dangers Loom, More Think the U.S. Does 'Too Little' to Solve World Problems," available at: www.people-press.org/files/2014/08/8-28-14-Obama-and-Foreign-Affairs-release.pdf. [Accessed: December 7, 2014.]

Plutzer, Eric and John F. Zipp. 1996. "Identity Politics, Partisanship, and Voting for Women Candidates," *Public Opinion Quarterly* 60: 30–57.

Reagan, Ronald. 1989. "Farewell Address," available at: http://millercenter.org/president/speeches/speech-3418. [Accessed: July 27, 2014.]

Reynolds, Andrew. 1999. "Women in the Legislatures and Executives of the World: Knocking at the Highest Glass Ceiling," *World Politics* 51(4): 547–572.

Romney, Mitt. 2011. *No Apology: The Case for American Greatness*. New York: St. Martin's Press.

Saad, Lydia. 2011. "Hillary Clinton Favorable Near Her All-Time High," available at: www.gallup.com/poll/146891/Hillary-Clinton-Favorable-Near-Time-High.aspx. [Accessed: November 24, 2014.]

Sanbonmatsu, Kira. 2009. *Where Women Run: Gender and Party in the American States* Ann Arbor, MI: The University of Michigan Press.

Seltzer, Richard A., Jody Newman, and Mellissa Vorhees Leighton. 1997. *Sex as a Political Variable: Women as Candidates and Voters in U.S. Elections*. Boulder, CO: Rienner.

Shabad, Rebecca. 2013. "Cheney: Obama Doesn't Believe in American Exceptionalism," *The Hill*, available at: http://thehill.com/blogs/blog-briefing-room/news/192466-cheney-obama-doesnt-believe-in-american-exceptionalism#ixzz37fZ73AiE. [Accessed: December 7, 2014.]

Streb, Matthew J., Barbara Burrell, Brian Frederick, and Michael A. Genovese. 2008. "Social Desirability Effects and Support for a Female American President," *Public Opinion Quarterly* 72(1): 76–89.

Streich, Gregory, and Khalil Marrar. 2014. "President Obama and American Exceptionalism: Is the United States an Indispensable Nation in a Multipolar World?" in *The Global Obama: Crossroads of Leadership in the 21st Century*, Dinesh Sharma and Uwe P. Gielen, eds. (New York: Routledge), 31–44.

The Daily Show with Jon Stewart. 2014. "Hillary Clinton Extended Interview," available at: http://thedailyshow.cc.com/extended-interviews/aw9j6p/hillary-clinton-extended-interview. [Accessed: December 7, 2014.]

UnderHill, Lois Beachy. 1995. *The Woman Who Ran for President: The Many Lives of Victoria Woodhull*. Penguin: New York.

Verba, Sidney, Burns, Nancy, and Schlozman, Kay L. 1997. "Knowing and Caring about Politics: Gender and Political Engagement," *Journal of Politics* 59 (04): 1051–1072.

Waller, Maureen. 2006. *Sovereign Ladies: Sex, Sacrifice and Power: The Six Reigning Queens of England*. St. Martin's Press: New York.

Walt, Stephen. 2011. "The Myth of American Exceptionalism," *Foreign Policy*, available at: www.foreignpolicy.com/articles/2011/10/11/the_myth_of_american_exceptionalism?page=full. [Accessed: November 21, 2014.]

Waylen, Georgina. 2006. "Constitutional Engineering: What Opportunities for the Enhancement of Gender Rights?" *Third World Quarterly* 27(7): 1209–1221.

Weiss, Anita M. 2003. "Interpreting Islam and Women's Rights: Implementing CEDAW in Pakistan," *International Sociology* 18(581): 581–601.

Weiss, Anita M. 2012. "Moving Forward with the Legal Empowerment of Women in Pakistan," United States Institute of Peace, Special Report 305, available at: www.usip.org/sites/default/files/SR305.pdf. [Accessed: December 1, 2014.]

Welch, Susan, Margery M. Ambrosius, Janet Clark, and Robert Darcy. 1985. "The Effects of Candidate Gender on Election Outcomes in State Legislative Races," *Western Political Quarterly* 38: 464–465.

Werner, Brian. 1997. "Financing the Campaigns of Women Candidates and Their Opponents: Evidence from Three States: 1981–1990," *Women & Politics* 18(1): 81–97.

Will, George. 2011. "A Congress That Reasserts Its Power." *Washington Post*, January 16.

Wilson, Joan Hof. 1976. "The Illusion of Change: Women and the American Revolution," in Alfred F. Young, ed., *The American Revolution*. Dekalb, IL: Northern Illinois University Press.

Zakaria, Fareed. 2008. *The Post-American World*. New York: W. W. Norton.

3

HILLARY CLINTON

Feminist and Activist

Florence L. Denmark, Hillary I. Goldstein, Kristin Thies and Adrian Tworecke

This chapter covers the highlights of Hillary Rodham Clinton's life from her years at Wellesley College and her activities as First Lady of the United States and after, up to the present day. She had a keen intellect and was very outspoken. Hillary fought within the system for the things she believed in including women's rights and correcting social injustice.

> *"My mother and my grandmothers could never have lived my life; my father and my grandfathers could never have imagined it. But they bestowed on me the promise of America, which made my life and my choices possible."*
>
> —Hillary Clinton, *Living History*, 2003

Wellesley College Years

Upon graduation from Maine Township High School South in 1965, Hillary Rodham was in the top 5 percent of her class and was voted Most Likely to Succeed by her peers (*Encyclopedia of Arkansas History & Culture*, 2014). That fall, she arrived at Wellesley College near Boston, where she majored in political science and minored in psychology (*Encylopedia of World Biographies*, 2014.). Coming from a Republican household in the Chicago suburb of Park Ridge, Illinois, she had circulated pamphlets for Barry Goldwater's, aka "Mr. Conservative," 1964 presidential campaign the previous fall. Rodham was resolved to ascend quickly through the ranks of Wellesley's Young Republican's chapter. As such, during her freshman year, she was elected president of the organization. With this Rockefeller Republican-oriented group, she supported the elections of U.S. Congressman John Lindsay in New York and U.S. Senator Edward Brooke from Massachusetts (Clinton, 2003).

The tumultuous years of the 1960s as well as the influence of a liberal arts education opened Hillary's mind to new political perspectives. This environment encouraged her evolving worldview. After hearing Dr. Martin Luther King Jr. speak in 1962, Hillary began to develop strong opinions about the American civil rights movement, social justice, and the Vietnam War (Clinton, 2003). As such, Clinton stepped down from her position as president of the Wellesley Young Republicans. At this time she wrote a letter to her youth minister, describing herself as "a mind conservative and a heart liberal" (Bernstein, 2007, p. 50).

In the upheaval of the 1960s Rodham found herself exploring the political landscape and working for politicians of both parties. During her junior year, Rodham supported the antiwar presidential nomination campaign of Democrat Eugene McCarthy (D-Minn) as well as hawkish Republican congressman Melvin Laird's campaign for the seventh district in Wisconsin. To help her better realize her shifting political ideals, Professor Alan Schechter assigned Rodham to intern at the House Republican Conference, and she attended the "Wellesley in Washington" summer program (Leibovich, 2007). Rodham was asked by moderate New York Republican Representative Charles Goodell to assist in Governor Nelson Rockefeller's campaign for the Republican nomination. As such, Rodham attended the 1968 Republican National Convention in Miami. However, she was put off by the way Richard Nixon's campaign represented Rockefeller and by what she perceived as the convention's obscure prejudices. "All of a sudden you get all these veiled messages, frankly, that were racist," Mrs. Clinton said of the convention. "I may not have been able to explain it, but I could feel it" (Leibovch, 2007, pg. 2). Further, she observed the protests at the Democratic National Convention in Chicago that year. Before the end of that year, Rodham chose to leave the Republican Party for good—or as she later put it, "it left her" (Clinton, 2003).

Though the zeitgeist of the 1960s tended toward extreme and revolutionary actions against the political system, Clinton aimed to pursue change within it (Kenney, 1993). A natural speaker, she motivated many of the movements for social change that occurred on the Wellesley college campus. Following the assassination of Martin Luther King Jr., Rodham joined a rally in Post Office Square in Boston, coming back to campus wearing a black armband. Worried that the assassination would provoke riots and unrest as it had on other campuses, Rodham organized a two-day student strike and worked with Wellesley's Black students to recruit more Black students and hire Black professors (Leibovich, 2007). Avoiding the bullhorns and protests that were common on campuses, she instead arranged meetings, lectures, and seminars, designed to be informative rather than disruptive. Rodham worked as a liaison to direct productive discourse and significant action. In 1968, she was elected president of the Wellesley College Government Association and served through early 1969; she was influential in keeping Wellesley from being caught up in the student disturbances widespread at many colleges (Kenney, 1993).

During her senior year, Rodham worked on her 92-page honors dissertation, a critique of Saul Alinsky, an antipoverty champion and community advocate. In her paper, Rodham endorsed Mr. Alinsky's principal criticism of government anti-poverty agendas—that is, that they tended to be detached from the needs of individuals and were too top-down (Dedman, 2007). However, Rodham differed with Mr. Alinsky over a fundamental idea. He pledged to "rub raw the sores of discontent" and coerce action through agitation. This, Rodham believed, contradicted her belief in effecting transformation within the system (Leibovich, 2007, p. 3). When Rodham became First Lady, access to her thesis was limited at the request of the White House, which became the focus of some conjecture.

In 1969, Rodham graduated with a Bachelor of Arts, with departmental honors in political science. She became the first student in Wellesley College history to deliver its commencement address. In her address she lay out the "rules" for women striving to weigh family and work, saying:

> As women today, you do face tough choices. You know the rules are basically as follows: If you don't get married, you're abnormal. If you get married, but don't have children, you're a selfish yuppie. If you get married and have children, but then go outside the home to work, you're a bad mother. If you get married and have children, but stay home, you've wasted your education. And if you don't get married, but have children and work outside the home as a fictional newscaster, you get in trouble with the vice president. (Rodham, 1969)

Rodham's speech received a standing ovation lasting seven minutes and marked Rodham as a prominent leader for the young women of her generation. Further, the speech received national notice and introduced her not just as an esteemed young mind but also an outspoken voice (*Huffington Post*). In her speech, she critiqued the previous speaker, Massachusetts Senator Edward Brooke, and suggested that he was out of touch with the action that her generation desired. Weeks later, she was featured in *Life* magazine as an exceptional paradigm of the Class of 1969.

Yale Law School

The summer before law school, Rodham worked at what later became the Children's Defense Fund. That fall, 1969, she enrolled in Yale Law School in New Haven, Connecticut, where she continued to pursue her interests in politics, social justice, and children and families. She served on the editorial board of the *Yale Review of Law and Social Action* (*Encyclopedia of Arkansas History & Culture*, n.d.). In law school, Yale alumna Marian Wright Edelman, a lawyer and children's rights advocate, inspired Rodham. Through her work with Edelman, she further developed her strong interest in family law and a concern for protecting the welfare of children and families. In the summer of 1970, Rodham was awarded a grant to work at Edelman's Washington Research Project. She was appointed to the Subcommittee on Migratory Labor, chaired by Senator Walter Mondale, where she researched significant issues affecting migrant workers such as health, housing, sanitation, and education. Edelman became an important mentor for Rodham (Morris, 1996).

Law school allowed Rodham to combine her keen aspirations for social activism with her budding legal career. In her second year in law school, she worked at the Yale Child Study Center. Here, she learned about innovative research on brain development in early childhood. Further, she worked as a research assistant, contributing to the influential piece *Beyond the Best Interests of the Child* (1973). In addition, Rodham provided free legal advice to low socioeconomic families at New Haven Legal Services and assumed various cases of child abuse at the Yale–New Haven Hospital (Gerth & Van Natta, 2007).

Rodham continued to be active politically in law school and was recruited by Anne Wexler, a political advisor, to work on the 1970 campaign of Joseph Duffey, a U.S. Senate candidate from Connecticut. In the summer of 1971, Rodham interned at the law firm of Treuhaft, Walker, and Burnstein in Oakland, California. The firm was well known for its support of activist causes, constitutional law, and civil rights. Here Rodham was also able to advocate for children and families, working on child custody and other cases (Bernstein, 2007). The following summer, Rodham campaigned in Texas for candidate George McGovern, a democrat who ran unsuccessfully in the 1972 presidential election (Gerth & Van Natta, 2007).

Rodham graduated with honors in 1973. She then went on to enroll at the Yale Child Study Center, where she studied child development and medicine, completing one year of post-graduate study (PBS, 2015). Rodham's first academic article, "Children Under the Law," was published in the *Harvard Educational Review* in 1973. In it, she discussed the children's rights movement, and advocated for "child citizens." Rodham argued that children should not be considered consistently incompetent from birth to reaching legal age and that one should acknowledge the unique needs of children as lawfully enforceable rights (Rodham, 1973).

During her postgraduate study, Rodham simultaneously served as staff attorney for the Children's Defense Fund and as a consultant to the Carnegie Council on Children (Bernstein, 2007). She continued advocating tirelessly for children and their families.

In 1974, Rodham moved to Washington, D.C., to work as a member of the impeachment inquest staff counseling the House Committee on the Judiciary during the Watergate investigation. Under the guidance of Chief Counsel John Doar and senior member Bernard Nussbaum, Rodham researched impeachment processes and the historical bases and criteria for impeachment. The committee's efforts concluded in the resignation of President Richard Nixon in August of 1974 (Gerth & Van Natta, 2007).

The Move to Arkansas

In August 1974, Rodham moved to Fayetteville, Arkansas, to be with her future husband, Bill Clinton, whom she had met in law school; he was teaching law and running for a seat in the U.S. House of Representatives in his home state. Rodham became one of only two female faculty members in the School of Law at the University of Arkansas, Fayetteville. There, she taught classes in criminal law and became the first director of the law school's legal aid clinic where she continued her advocacy work (Clinton, 2003).

Though Bill Clinton lost the congressional race in 1974, in November 1976 he was elected Arkansas Attorney General. Thus, the newly married couple moved to the state capital of Little Rock. When Bill and Hillary married in October 1975, Rodham chose to keep her maiden name in order to keep their professional and personal lives separate.

In February 1977, Rodham joined the well-established and esteemed Rose Law Firm, a paradigm of Arkansan governmental and financial power and influence. Rodham specialized in patent infringement and intellectual property law. Within a few years, she became the first woman to be named a full partner (Bernstein, 2007).

Rodham's sustained interest in children and family law, manifested in the publishing of the scholarly articles "Children's Policies: Abandonment and Neglect" in 1977 and "Children's Rights: A Legal Perspective" in 1979. The latter article continued her argument set forth in her first scholarly article that children's legal competencies depended upon their age and other conditions. Further, Rodham continued her longstanding practice of activism by also working pro bono in child advocacy, co-founding Arkansas Advocates for Children & Families in 1977. Rodham also stayed true to her political roots, serving as Jimmy Carter's Indiana campaign director of field operations in 1976 (Gerth & Van Natta, 2007). In 1977, President Jimmy Carter appointed her to the board of directors of the Legal Services Corporation, where she served from 1978 until the end of 1981. During her tenure at Legal Services Corporation, she served as the chair of the board and was the first woman to do so.

First Lady of Arkansas

In November 1978, Bill Clinton was elected Governor of Arkansas, and Rodham became First Lady of Arkansas in January 1979. Clinton appointed her as the chair of the Rural Health Advisory Committee. In this role, she procured federal funds to develop medical services in Arkansas's most needy districts while keeping doctors' fees unchanged (Bernstein, 2007).

In November 1980, Bill Clinton was defeated for reelection as governor. During this time, many voters saw Hillary Rodham as a scholarly feminist with a thriving career and were perhaps put off by her independence. Bill Clinton's advisers believed Rodham's use of her maiden name was one of the reasons that he, in fact, lost the 1980 gubernatorial election (Kelly, 1993). Rodham Clinton states, "I learned the hard way that some voters in Arkansas were seriously offended by the fact that I kept my maiden name" (Rodham Clinton, 2003, pp. 91–93). Therefore, during the 1982 campaign, Rodham went by Hillary Rodham Clinton and was instrumental in coordinating his comeback campaign.

Bill Clinton returned to the governor's office, winning the election in 1982. Rodham Clinton was appointed chair of the Arkansas Educational Standards Committee in 1983. In this position she continued advocating on behalf of the youth in Arkansas. She pursued the reform of the court-sanctioned public education system in the state. One of the her most significant initiatives was a protracted but eventually efficacious fight against the Arkansas Education Association, to institute compulsory teacher testing and improve standards for classroom size in the state of Arkansas (Old State House Museum, 1993). This political battle for education reform was perhaps her most noteworthy achievement in her life as the First Lady of Arkansas (Bernstein, 2007). Also as First Lady of Arkansas, Rodham Clinton introduced Arkansas's Home Instruction Program for Preschool Youth in 1985 (HIPPY-USA). This international program aims to enhance the home learning environment by providing parents with educational activities for preschool preparedness and literacy. Currently, there are 135 HIPPY program sites in 21 states and the District of Columbia, serving 15,000 children and their families (Hippyusa.org).

Rodham Clinton was the first chair of the American Bar Association's Commission on Women in the Profession and served from 1987 to 1991. This organization was formed to bring attention to gender prejudice in the legal profession and encourage the association to implement methods to fight such bias. In 1988 and in 1991 Rodham Clinton was named by the *National Law Journal* as one of the 100 most influential lawyers in America. Rodham Clinton also continued her involvement in critical causes by serving on the boards of the Children's Defense Fund (as chair, 1986–1992) and the Arkansas Children's Hospital Legal Services (1988–1992) (The White House, n.d.).

Rodham Clinton was the first female member on Wal-Mart's board, where she advocated effectively for Wal-Mart to implement more environmentally responsible practices. However, she was generally ineffective in her movement to have more women be added to the corporation's administration (Barbaro, 2007).

Clinton Presidential Campaign

In 1992, Hillary Clinton received continued national notice when her husband became a candidate for the Democratic presidential nomination. Reports of Bill's extramarital affair with Gennifer Flowers, an actress and model, surfaced during the campaign for the New Hampshire primary. In response, Bill and Hillary appeared together on *60 Minutes*, where Bill Clinton denied the affair but acknowledged, "causing pain in my marriage" (*Washington Post*, 1992).

In addition, questions of conflict of interest regarding state business and the law firm at which Hillary Rodham Clinton was a partner arose during the campaign. Clinton argued the questions were unfounded because all state fiscal transactions had been deducted before Hillary's firm pay was agreed upon.

During the election, Bill Clinton joked that in electing him, the nation would "get two for the price of one," referring to the prominent role his wife would assume. And in fact, when Bill took office as president in January 1993, Hillary was the first First Lady to hold a postgraduate degree and to have her own professional career up to the time of entering the White House (Kelly, 1993).

The Clinton Presidency

On November 3, 1992, Bill Clinton was elected the 42nd president of the United States (PBS, 2001). As first lady, Hillary was now a prominent public figure and had a new forum to spread her work as an activist. She was a role model to many middle-class American women, showing them that they could be strong, smart, and raise kids all while being successful in the workplace (Boyer, 2006). Hillary Rodham Clinton entered the White House with a successful career and salaried job. She was the first First Lady in history to do so (Barringer, 1992).

Hillary Clinton forced the American public to reevaluate the role of women in politics, the role of the First Lady, and the roles of women, spouses, and partners in general. Although never calling herself a feminist, Hillary Rodham Clinton's success in the public is due to her adoption of asertive male-coded behavior (Burrell, 2001). If society were designed for women to flourish, there would be more consideration of female embodiment and women's concerns, such as reproduction. The Clintons always presented themselves as equal partners both in marriage and in politics (Burrell, 2001). Hillary did not appear subservient to her husband. As a woman succeeding on men's terms in society, adopting male-coded behaviors, and bringing women's needs to the agenda of the patriarchal public sphere as it is, Hillary Rodham Clinton fits into the paradigm of liberal feminism (Burrell, 2001).

Hillary Rodham Clinton was one of the most active First Ladies in modern memory (Hastedt & Eksterowicz, 2006). Her early life experiences were instrumental in forging the optimism and vision that she applied to the foreign policy area. She combined her knowledge of and commitment to the issues most important to her with her relationship with the president to strengthen her influence in the political world (Hastedt & Eksterowicz, 2006). Her office was integrated with the White House Office. Hillary practiced foreign policy in synch with the Clinton administration, although establishing some independence in her trips abroad. Hillary Clinton also optimized her influence in foreign policy through her alliances of power (Hastedt & Eksterowicz, 2006).

As First Lady, Hillary Clinton demonstrated her commitment to civil rights and women's and children's issues. She was involved in health care, adoption, women's right to choose, mitigation of domestic violence, and electoral rights (Hastedt & Eksterowicz, 2006). During her term as First Lady, she engaged in extensive contacts with legislators, testified before the Congress, and formed alliances both inside and outside of Washington with activist groups such as Vital Voices and the Children's Defense Fund (Hastedt & Eksterowicz, 2006). She fought for universal health care for the United States; however, this endeavor failed.

Prior to her husband's presidency, Hillary was cognizant of the contributions of prior First Ladies who had increased the influence, size, and prominence of the First Lady's office (Hastedt & Eksterowicz, 2006). Hillary Rodham Clinton too sought to increase her office's influence as First Lady. She was the first First Lady to have her office in the West Wing, and an additional office in the Old Executive Office Building, just down the hall from other offices in President Clinton's West Wing office (Pear, 1993). Dee Dee Myers, President Clinton's press secretary, announced that the First Lady would have an office in the West Wing. When asked why by reporters, Ms. Myers said, "Because the President wanted her to be there to work. She'll be working on a variety of domestic policy issues. She'll be there with other domestic policy advisers" (Pear, 1993). In regard to this situation, Hillary stated, "Some of my staff would be part of the West Wing team. I thought they should be integrated physically as well . . . These physical and staff changes were important if I was going to be involved in working on Bill's agenda, particularly as it related to issues affecting women, children, and families" (Hastedt & Eksterowicz, 2006). These were Hillary's primary areas of interest and advocacy while she served her tenure as First Lady.

Hillary Clinton's personal relationship with her husband and his own activism heightened her position as a global activist (Hastedt & Eksterowicz, 2006). Many of her areas of interest, such as health care and human rights, were also a focus of President Clinton. The strength of the Clinton Administration, policy synchronization, and the professional and personal partnership of the Clintons contributed to Hillary's overall influence as an activist during her tenure as First Lady (Hastedt & Eksterowicz, 2006). By the end of the Clinton presidency, the public came to expect a certain amount of advocacy from Hillary Clinton due to the evolution of her office (Burrell, 2001). Hillary Clinton was one of the most active modern First Ladies in both domestic and foreign policy issues (Hastedt & Eksterowicz, 2006).

In July 1993, Hillary Rodham Clinton first traveled abroad as First Lady to the G-7 economic summit in Japan with her husband (Hastedt & Eksterowicz, 2006). Then, in early 1994, she made her first official trip abroad without the president, leading the American delegation to the Winter Olympics in Norway. Later that year, Hillary acted as a last-minute replacement for the president as a member of the US delegation to the presidential inauguration of Nelson Mandela in South Africa (Hastedt & Eksterowicz, 2006). In March 1995, the First Lady took her first lengthy trip abroad without the president when she traveled to South Asia. In September she traveled to China, where in Beijing, she served as honorary chair of the American delegation and delivered a key address at the United Nations Fourth World Conference on Women (Hastedt & Eksterowicz, 2006). This conference was aimed at empowering women economically, socially, and politically, ensuring the improvement of all women, a cause dear to Clinton's heart (United Nations, 2015). She stated:

> We are here to find common ground so that we may help bring dignity and respect to women and girls all over the world- and in so doing, bring new strength and stability to families as well. By gathering in Beijing, we are focusing world attention on issues that matter most in the lives of women and their families: access to education, health care, jobs, and credit, the chance to enjoy basic legal and human rights and participate fully in the political life of their countries." (Clinton, 1995)

Hillary Clinton continued to discuss her experiences in meeting women across the world who are suffering and those who are succeeding, highlighting the progress that had been made and what still needed to be done, and noting the gender inequalities across the globe. She emphasized the goal of this conference "to strengthen families and societies by empowering women to take greater control over their own destinies" but this "cannot be fully achieved unless all governments—here and around the world—accept their responsibility to protect and promoted internationally recognized human rights" (Clinton, 1995).

With her role as First Lady came increased political resources and activism, allowing for the pursuit of her own foreign policy agenda (Hastedt & Eksterowicz, 2006). This first became evident at her speech in Beijing at the Fourth World Conference on Women:

> Prior to Beijing when we traveled on official visits abroad I accompanied Bill where appropriate and attended spouses' programs. In mid-November when we made state visits to Australia, the Philippines and Thailand, I followed my own agenda as well as Bill's. . . . I usually branched off from Bill's official delegations . . . and reinforced the message that a nation's prosperity is linked to the education and well-being of girls and women." (Clinton, 2003)

In November of 1995, she joined the president on an official trip to England, Ireland, Germany, and Spain (Hastedt & Eksterowicz, 2006). The next summer, she partnered with the United Nations Ambassador, Madeleine Albright, on a tour of Eastern and Central Europe. Together, they created the Vital Voices Democracy Initiative in 1997 after the United Nations Fourth World Conference on Women (Vital Voices, 2015). The goal of this initiative was to promote the advancement of women as a United States foreign policy goal. Hillary Rodham Clinton acted as the keynote speaker at the Vital Voices: Women in Democracy meeting at a NATO Summit in Madrid. Under the leadership of the *Vital Voices Democracy Initiative*, the U.S. government, in partnership with the Inter-American Development Bank, the United Nations, the World Bank, the Nordic Council of Ministers, the European Union, and other governments has coordinated Vital Voices conferences throughout the world, promoting women in leadership and giving them a venue to unite (Vital Voices, 2015). These conferences launched regional Vital Voices initiatives that continue to give women the skills and resources they need to empower themselves, their communities, and their countries. The overwhelmingly positive response to the *Vital Voices Democracy Initiative* led to the creation of Vital Voices Global Partnership as a nonprofit nongovernmental organization (NGO) in June 2000, something Clinton has noted to be very proud of (Vital Voices, 2015). Vital Voices continues the work of advancing women's economic, political and social status around the world, by providing skills, networking and other support to women around the world (Vital Voices, 2015).

Traditionally, foreign travel by First Ladies has been categorized under the heading of symbolic representation of the United States, showing our support to other countries (Hastedt & Eksterowicz, 2006). Hillary Rodham Clinton's diplomacy was much more than symbolism. In March of 1999, Hillary gave a speech on Women's Rights at the United Nations International Women's Day, a day used to celebrate women's achievements throughout history and across nations (United Nations, 2015). Her speech highlighted the progress of women's rights, and her outreach to women throughout the world. She advocated for and brought awareness to women's rights:

> My hope is that into the next century we will not only continue to see progress, but advancements in every part of the world. We will see a world in which all citizens—men and women—enjoy the freedoms of liberty; in which all children are valued and given equal opportunities whether they are boys or girls; and in which every citizen can live in dignity, free from fear, and filled with hope. Only then will we be able to say—with honesty—that yes, women not only can but do hold up half the sky. And that sky over all of us is filled with a bright future for our boys and, especially, our girls. (Clinton, 1999)

In *Living History*, Hillary Clinton stated, "One of the most important lessons I learned during my years as First Lady was how dependent the affairs of the state are on the personal relationships among leaders . . . But this sort of diplomacy requires constant nurturing and informal dialogue among the principals" (Clinton, 2003). Through her contacts with foreign leaders and their spouses, Hillary Rodham Clinton was able to advocate for her belief in women's and children's rights.

First Lady Hillary Clinton utilized public diplomacy throughout her tenure in office (Hastedt & Eksterowicz, 2006). Public diplomacy consists of statements and actions of representatives of states that are intended to influence the public rather than the official leadership in another country (Hastedt & Eksterowicz, 2006). It is a major shift from classic diplomacy, which emphasizes secrecy and confidential bargaining among like-minded elites. Public diplomacy is conducted through public statements, press briefings, and state visits (Hastedt & Eksterowicz, 2006). In practicing public diplomacy, Hillary Clinton's principal audiences were individuals attending conferences or citizens to whom she sought to bring a message of hope, inspiration, and empowerment.

On her trip to Japan for the G-7 summit, she visited with a group of prominent Japanese women, the first of many meetings of this kind she would hold in her travels as a First Lady (Hastedt & Eksterowicz, 2006). In India, she spoke at the Rajiv Gandhi Foundation. In Nepal, she visited a women's health clinic. This was her most politically charged venture to date, both for its content and its timing, coming shortly after the arrest, imprisonment, and then release of Chinese dissident Harry Wu (Hastedt & Eksterowicz, 2006). Later, she delivered the keynote address at a Vital Voices forum in Vienna (Vital Voices, 2015). Hillary Clinton's frequent trips to Africa during her tenure as First Lady were intended to highlight the self-help efforts of African women as supported by U.S. foreign aid (Hastedt & Eksterowicz, 2006).

The issues Hillary Rodham Clinton chose to stress were those which have long been a staple of American domestic politics: health care, children, education, and the position of women in society. She once stated, "In the new global economy, individual countries and regions would find it difficult to make economic or social progress if a disproportionate percentage of their female population remains poor, uneducated, unhealthy, and disenfranchised" (Clinton, 2003).

A trip to Nicaragua brought her attention to Mothers United, a microcredit organization supported by USAID, and inspired her advocacy in 1994 for a Community Development Financial Institutions Fund, which would provide financial assistance to distressed areas that were not being serviced by the established banking system. A visit to an AIDS information center in Uganda revealed how HIV testing at this USAID-funded facility had already been used in the United States (Hastedt & Eksterowicz, 2006).

Bill Clinton's presidency came to an end in 2001, and with that Hillary Rodham Clinton was no longer First Lady (PBS, 2001). Her influence and activism throughout her tenure in the office is still evident today through the advancements in women's rights, health care, and children's issues. It is of no surprise to the public that Hillary Rodham Clinton sought to continue her activism and remain in the political arena after the Clinton presidency. Even during Bill Clinton's impeachment trial due to inappropriate conduct with a female staff member, the Clintons remained a cohesive and united front, not weakening their influence in foreign or domestic diplomacy (Hastedt & Eksterowicz, 2006).

Post-Presidency

Senate Election of 2000

In November of 1998, in the midst of Bill Clinton's final term as president, longstanding New York State senator Daniel Patrick Moynihan announced his retirement, leaving his seat open in the upcoming 2000 election. Almost immediately, multiple leaders within the Democratic party urged Hillary Clinton to run for the vacant seat, including Charles Rangel, the 14-term congressman from Harlem (Ratnesar, 1999). Though speculation and rumors swirled for months, Clinton ultimately decided to run. While she faced challenges along the way, including allegations of carpetbagging, Clinton won the election against Republican Rick Lazio that November and was sworn in as the United States senator for the state of New York in January of 2001 (*Encylopedia of World Biographies*, 2014). This election was a victory on multiple levels, and Clinton made history that day: not only was she the first woman elected to the United States Senate from the state of New York, but also she became the first and only wife of a president to run for and be elected to national office (Center for American Women and Politics, 2014).

During her first term as senator, Clinton served on five committees, including the Committee on the Budget; the Committee on Armed Services; the Committee on Environment and Public Works; the Committee on Environment, Education, Labor, and Pensions; and the Special Committee on Aging. In addition, Clinton served as commissioner of the Commission on Security and Cooperation in Europe, as well as chairwoman of the Steering and Outreach Committee and vice chairwoman of committee outreach in the Senate Democratic caucus (Gerth & Van Natta, 2007).

In addition to actively working as a member of a number of committees, Clinton made many notable accomplishments during her first term. For example, Clinton was serving as one of the major political figures in New York at the time of the September 11, 2001, attacks. Following this, Clinton worked with Charles Schumer, the senior senator for New York at the time, to secure funding related to improving security and recovery measures (Gerth & Van Natta, 2007; Bernstein, 2008). Clinton also worked actively to facilitate investigations into the resulting health difficulties experienced by first responders. She also took a strong stance toward resultant issues in the Middle East. In particular, she advocated for military action in Afghanistan, which was seen as the country from which Al Queda organized the attacks on 9/11 in the United States. Her advocacy for military action in Afghanistan and Iraq was viewed as an opportunity to impede terrorism and address issues related to women's lives and well-being under the current regime in the country (Clinton, 2001). Though Clinton's viewpoint proved to be controversial within the Democratic party, she remained strong in her position, even taking frequent trips to both Afghanistan and Iraq following the beginning of the Iraq war.

Clinton also demonstrated her consciousness of and commitment to issues relating to social justice during her first term. For example, she voted against the Federal Marriage Amendment in both 2004 and 2006 (VoteSmart.org, n.d.). This amendment sought to deny lesbian, gay, and bisexual (LGB) individuals the right to same-sex marriage. Clinton's attention to social issues was not only evident in the legislation that she supported or opposed, but was also apparent in the organizations that she helped form and worked alongside. For example, Clinton was key in the founding of the Center for American Progress (CAP) and Media Matters for America (MMfA) (Gerth & Van Natta, 2007). CAP is a progressive organization that conducts public policy research and advocacy work. MMfA is a nonprofit progressive media watchdog group that identifies and corrects misinformation put forth by the conservative media in the United States.

In terms of economic issues, Clinton worked to reduce the national debt and voted against tax cuts that President Bush put forth (VoteSmart.org, n.d.). She also introduced an amendment that would support and fund the creation of jobs to modernize public schools (Nagourney, 2000). Moreover, Clinton worked across the aisle with Newt Gingrich, a Republican and the former Speaker of the House, on a proposal for universal health care (Hernandez, 2005).

Senate Re-Election and Second Term

Clinton announced her decision to run for re-election and a second term in the Senate in November of 2004. Though she was initially confronted with some opposition from the Democratic party due to her demonstrated support for the Iraq War, she eventually received the support of the party and won the Democratic nomination with ease. The nomination for the Republican party was John Spencer. Clinton won the election with 67% of the vote (NYS Board of Elections, 2006). It is important to note Clinton's growing popularity in New York state: the margin of her win during the 2006 election was significantly greater than the victory margin from the 2000 election. In addition, she won 58 of the 62 counties in the state (Dance & Ericson, 2006).

During Clinton's second term, social issues related to immigration were a focus in the Senate. In particular, in 2007 a comprehensive immigration reform bill, titled the Secure Borders, Economic Opportunity and Immigration Reform Act of 2007, was introduced. The bill was intended to be a compromise between increasing border security and creating avenues to citizenship and providing legal status to the millions of illegal immigrants in the United States. Though it was presented as a compromise, the bill was hugely controversial and criticized by both sides of the debate. Clinton voted against two separate amendments that attempted to offset the bill's passage and also worked on her own amendment that would foster the efforts of legal immigrants to bring their family members into the United States (U.S. Senate Roll Call Votes, 2007a, 2007b; Santora, 2007).

Clinton also supported the DREAM Act, which proposed to provide conditional permanent residency to immigrants who meet particular criteria.

Clinton also continued to address pertinent issues in the Middle East throughout her second term in the Senate. Though she had initially shown strong support for military action in Afghanistan, Clinton voted for a resolution in the Senate against the troop surge in Iraq in 2007. Around the same time, she also voted to support a bill that required the withdrawal of troops. Similarly, in 2008 she stated her belief that the time had come to withdraw the troops (Bosman, 2008).

With regard to economic issues, during her second term Clinton voted in support of a bill that would expand an economic stimulus package proposed by President Bush, which would include additional benefits for unemployed individuals as well as senior citizens and disabled veterans. This expanded version of the stimulus package had strong support; however, following a filibuster in the Senate, the bill failed to pass (Levey, 2008). As a result of scheduling conflicts and presidential campaign commitments, Clinton was unable to participate in the final vote. Ultimately, the version put forth by President Bush and the House of Representatives received great support and became the Economic Stimulus Act of 2008.

Presidential Campaign of 2008

In January of 2007, in the midst of her second term in the United States Senate, Clinton formed an exploratory committee for the 2008 presidential election. This pursuit did not come as a surprise, as she had been considering running for president and reportedly preparing since as early as 2003 (Bernstein, 2007). However, that is not to say that her announcement did not have a polarizing effect on the nation. Numerous anti–Hillary Clinton organizations had already formed, including Stop Her Now and the Stop Hillary PAC. Both organizations aimed to raise funds and impede her progress toward the presidency. In spite of these efforts, in early 2007, leading up to the primaries, Clinton was one of the top choices for the Democratic party. Other prime contenders included Barack Obama, then senator for Illinois, and John Edwards, a former North Carolina senator. Clinton's campaign sought to address many important social and economic issues. One of her main platforms was a proposed universal health care plan, which included individual mandates requiring coverage for all. Though Clinton continued to receive some criticism with regard to her previous demonstration of support for the Iraq War, she remained in the lead for the nomination throughout the remainder of 2007 (Balz & Johnson, 2009).

By the fall of 2007, however, Clinton's grip on the lead gradually loosened, beginning with a particularly difficult debate against the other Democratic candidates in Philadelphia that resulted in a much closer race. By January of 2008, polls placed her behind both Obama and Edwards (Kornblut, 2009). Though she remained a strong candidate and presence within the race and won the

New Hampshire primary, her campaign was marked by criticism related to voter perceptions of remarks made by both Hillary and Bill concerning Obama's race. John Edwards left the campaign by late January, leaving Clinton and Obama in a tense competition, with Clinton losing much key support from the African American population (Balz & Johnson, 2009). As the primaries wore on, Clinton's campaign struggled to maintain funds and faced financing and staff adjustments (Balz & Johnson, 2009). In the spring of 2008, following a string of losses or very close wins, it became clear that the possibility of Clinton taking the nomination was no longer a reality. Despite this, Clinton did not quit or drop out of the campaign; rather, she remained a candidate in the final primaries, winning some though never overtaking the lead established by Obama (Kornblut & Balz, 2008).

On June 7, 2008, Clinton gracefully accepted the loss, officially endorsed Obama as the nominee, and concluded her campaign. Though she had not succeeded in becoming the Democratic nominee for the 2008 presidential election, she was a fierce competitor in the primaries and achieved many other notable accomplishments during her campaign, including being the first woman to run in the primary of every state. She was also arguably the first female candidate to come so close to receiving the nomination for presidential candidacy for a major party (Cafferty, 2012). As such, though Clinton was by no means the first female to run for President of the United States, issues of gender were prominent throughout the 2008 campaign.

As a powerful woman in the political spotlight, much attention was placed on Clinton's presentation and appearance. For example, some speculated that she had undergone plastic surgery during the previous decades and now looked more attractive, while others discussed perceptions regarding the modesty and decency of her attire within the Senate (Givhan, 2007; Preson, 2006). Beyond discussing Clinton's physical beauty and dress, her personality was also attacked, her "likeability" questioned, and she was frequently referred to by multiple publications within the media with the term "bitch" or as strident, frightening, or overbearing (Jamieson & Dunn, 2008; Black, 2007; Daum, 2008).

Issues of gender and femininity were explicitly brought to the forefront at particular moments during the campaign. For example, at an appearance in Portsmouth, New Hampshire, while discussing the pressure and difficulty of campaigning, Clinton briefly choked up. Her small display of emotion garnered huge media attention and was viewed as controversial, with many pundits speculating that it would lead to her downfall in the campaign. However, others argued that her mildly emotional episode, as well as the way she managed it afterward, opened up a public conversation regarding issues of gender and the bias inherent in the media's coverage of the campaign (Shepard, 2008). Ultimately, Clinton succeeded in New Hampshire. Shortly following this event, media judgments regarding Clinton's femininity also led to her backing out of a commitment to appear on the cover of *Vogue* magazine. It was reported that campaign staff members feared this cover shoot would cause Clinton to come across as "too feminine" (Smith, 2008).

In response, *Vogue* editor Anna Wintour shared her dismay that in the year 2008 a female nominee for United States president would have to shy away from looking feminine in order to be perceived as a serious politician (Mesure, 2008).

In addition, once Sarah Palin, then governor of Alaska, was nominated for vice president following the Republican National Convention in 2008, numerous comparisons were drawn between the two women. Unfortunately, rather than celebrating the presence of two women within the 2008 election, the media often pitted the two against each other. For example, Clinton was often presented as more experienced, with Palin lacking depth, knowledge, and expertise (Healy, 2008a; Healy, 2008b). However, Clinton refused to give in to the media's need to create unnecessary and unrelated competition between the women. Rather, Clinton brought the focus back to the political issues at hand by stating her disagreement with John McCain and Palin's policies while also demonstrating her support: she deemed Palin's nomination "historic," congratulated her, and expressed her pride in Palin's accomplishment (Nichols, 2008).

Secretary of State

In November of 2008, following her presidential campaign and Obama's election victory, Clinton directly expressed her request to assume a leadership position within the Senate; alternatively, she requested to serve as the head of a task force to address the issue of health care reform. Though there were discussions with leaders regarding these potentialities, neither of these requests came to fruition. Around the same time, Obama and Clinton began discussing the possibility of Clinton receiving the nomination to serve as the United States secretary of state. Though Clinton was hesitant initially, she eventually accepted the position, and Obama made a formal announcement indicating that Clinton was his nominee. Clinton was approved by the Senate Foreign Relations Committee and confirmed by the Senate in January of 2009. Clinton was the third female to hold the position of secretary of state and the only former First Lady to serve as a member of the Cabinet of the United States.

Clinton's time as secretary of state may not be remembered for a single, monumental breakthrough in foreign relationships or diplomatic policy. Rather, Clinton herself cited her strategy as "smart power" or a combination of military hard power with the soft power of creating alliances, establishing relationships, developing the global economy and technology, and advocating for human rights (Calabresi, 2011). Her goal then was not to reform the department but achieve lasting effects through small, incremental changes (Ghattas, 2013). A comprehensive review of her tenure is well beyond the scope of this chapter, but Clinton worked tirelessly from 2009 to 2013. Visiting more than 110 countries within this period of time, Clinton traveled more than any previous secretary of state (Davidson, 2013). In addition to extensive traveling, she helped her daughter, Chelsea, prepare for her wedding in 2010 and was also the center of much ongoing media scrutiny during her tenure. However, this chapter will highlight a number of Clinton's specific accomplishments while in office.

Through Clinton's foreign policy work, she continued to actively address numerous social issues around the world. For example, one of Clinton's greatest and most ambitious reforms for the State Department was the Quadrennial Diplomacy and Development Review (Allen & Parnes, 2014). The purpose of this review, to be completed every four years, is to analyze the United States' diplomacy work overseas and to identify areas of reform and changes that needed to be made. The first review was conducted in 2010. Clinton also specifically cited her aim of incorporating and institutionalizing goals that would work toward empowering women and girls internationally. The purpose of institutionalizing such goals was to ensure that this type of work with the female population around the globe would continue after Clinton's tenure was complete (Lemmon, 2011). One particular global cause that Clinton actively worked toward was the adoption of cookstoves in developing countries, to reduce energy consumption and the significant health problems many women experience that are associated with cooking over an open fire.

Clinton also relegated $1.2 billion of the State Department budget to programs addressing women and girls internationally, particularly global health programs (Lemmon, 2011). In addition, Clinton formed the Women in Public Service Project, in conjunction with the Seven Sisters colleges, an association of liberal arts schools in the Northeast that were historically women's colleges. The hope of this initiative was to attract more women to the public service sector in order to create a more equitable balance between men and women working in that arena (U.S. Department of State, 2011). Moreover, Clinton cited her ongoing commitment to issues related to women's well-being and quality of life at a keynote speech for the International Crisis Group, a nongovernmental organization focused on conflict prevention. In this speech she described women around the world as an underutilized source of talent and expertise and expressed her belief that the global empowerment of women would continue to grow (Combe, 2012).

Clinton also worked to combat issues of worldwide hunger through the Global Hunger and Food Security Initiative (U.S. Department of State, 2011). By incorporating these issues as an essential part of the United States foreign policy work, Clinton hoped that hunger would be addressed strategically and on an ongoing basis, rather that only during acute crises. Clinton placed women at the forefront of this endeavor to develop agriculture due to their role as farmers around the globe. Clinton was also an active advocate for national and international gay rights during her time as secretary of state. For example, in a 2011 speech for the United Nations Human Rights Council, Clinton stated, "Gay rights are human rights" and pledged her commitment to advocate for legal protection and rights for lesbian, gay, and bisexual individuals around the world (Allen & Parnes, 2014).

Clinton stated as early as 2011 that she would not continue on in her position as Secretary of State should Obama win re-election. When Obama did win in November of 2012, Clinton indicated that she would continue to serve until Obama nominated her successor. Ultimately, John Kerry became the next secretary of state, and Clinton resigned officially in February of 2013. Though Clinton's service was not free of criticism, she remained largely popular with high approval ratings. During her time in office, between the years of 2009 to 2012, Clinton was consistently named the most admired woman in the world in the annual Gallup poll (Jones, 2013).

Recent Endeavors

Though Clinton is no longer engaged in the high-profile international work that characterized her most recent position in government, she has remained a dynamic figure in the public eye, continuing her work as an activist and feminist. Soon after her resignation as secretary of state, Clinton joined the Clinton Foundation, a nonprofit organization created by her husband to address issues related to global health, economic growth, leadership, and empowerment around the world. When Clinton joined in 2013, she added the focus of improving opportunities for and empowering women and young girls internationally. Part of her efforts through the Clinton Foundation included starting Too Small to Fail, which emphasizes promoting the health and well-being of young children through research and work with parents, businesses, and communities in the United States (Clinton Foundation, n.d.). With her daughter, Chelsea Clinton, she also created and led an initiative called No Ceilings: The Full Participation Project, the purpose of which is to gather and analyze data regarding the status of women around the world in order to foster their full participation and advance the status of women and young girls across countries (Clinton Foundation, n.d.). Clinton also began working on a program to promote the enrollment of girls in secondary schools around the world in order to increase girls' access to quality education (Thomas, 2014).

In addition to these pursuits, Clinton also published her second memoir, *Hard Choices*, in June 2014. This book primarily serves as her account of her time as secretary of state. Clinton went on a month-long promotional book tour throughout the United States, Canada, and Europe following publication (Frumin, 2014). Clinton also became a grandmother in 2014, when Chelsea gave birth to a baby girl, Charlotte, in September.

When Clinton has not been busy with advocacy work, writing, and being a grandmother, she has also made paid speaking appearances at events for various organizations. These appearances have continued to add fuel to the speculation regarding a potential run for president in 2016, particularly because they have provided her with an opportunity to build her image in front of large crowds and discuss policy issues such as health care, immigration, national security, and international conflicts (Chozick, 2013). Though Clinton herself continues to remain relatively quiet on the issue of the 2016 presidential campaign, speculation runs rampant. Clinton already has a large group of supporters, as evidenced by the

Ready for Hillary super PAC. Created in 2013, the PAC raised over $4 million in its first year (Caldwell, 2014). Clinton recently returned to Iowa to make a keynote address in September 2014; this marked her first appearance in Iowa since 2008, following her loss to Obama. With the timing and location of the event, many have come to view her speech as an unofficial kickoff to her campaign for 2016 (Newton-Small, 2014). Though Clinton would admit only that she has been "thinking" about the presidency in 2016, she came onto the stage by declaring, "I'm back!" At this time, it is anybody's guess what these two words might mean for Hillary Clinton's future. A glance back at her pursuits thus far illustrates a life that is far from predictable and characterized by progress, commitment, empowerment, and action, and one can surmise that she will continue down this same path. Whether this path will lead to her being the first female president of the United States or in a slightly different direction, one thing is clear: she's back.

References

Allen, P., & Parnes, A. (2014). *HRC: State Secrets and the Rebirth of Hillary Clinton*. New York, NY: Crown Publishers.

Balz, J., & Johnson, H. (2009). *The Battle for America 2008: The Story of an Extraordinary Election*. New York, NY: Penguin Group.

Barbaro, Michael (May 20, 2007). "As a Director, Clinton Moved Wal-Mart Board, but Only So Far." *New York Times*. Retrieved August 26, 2014, from www.nytimes.com/2007/05/20/us/politics/20walmart.html?_r=1&.

Barringer, F. (1992). "The Transition: The President-Elect's Wife; Hillary Clinton's New Role: The Job Description Is Open." *New York Times*, p. 1A.

Bernstein, C. (2008). *A Woman in Charge: The Life of Hillary Rodham Clinton*. New York, NY: Vintage Books.

Bernstein, C. (2007). *A Woman in Charge: The Life of Hillary Rodham Clinton*. New York, NY: Knopf.

Biography.com. (2014). "Hillary Diane Rodham Clinton." Retrieved from www.biography.com/people/hillary-clinton-9251306#related-video-gallery.

Black, E. (2007, March 28). "There's Just Something about Her That Feels Castrating, Overbearing, and Scary." *Star Tribune*. Retrieved from http://politicalblogs.startribune.com/bigquestionblog/?p=624.

Bosman, J. (2008, April 10). "President Is Boss, Clinton Says." *New York Times*. Retrieved from http://thecaucus.blogs.nytimes.com/2008/04/10/president-is-boss-clinton-says/?gwh=CFB4961E530567384BBDA455A8C64037&gwt=pay.

Boyer, H. J. (2006). *Hillary Rodham Clinton: Feminism, Success, and the First Ladyship* (Unpublished honors theses). Florida Atlantic University, Boca Raton, FL.

Burell, B. (2001). *Public Opinion, the First Ladyship and Hillary Rodham Clinton*. New York, NY: Routledge.

Cafferty, J. (2012, January 4). "What Will It Take for This Country to Elect a Woman President?" *CNN.com*. Retrieved from http://caffertyfile.blogs.cnn.com/2012/01/04/what-will-it-take-for-this-country-to-elect-a-woman-president/.

Calabresi, M. (2011, November 7). "Hillary Clinton and the Rise of Smart Power." *Time*. Retrieved from http://content.time.com/time/magazine/article/0,9171,2097973,00.html.

Caldwell, P. (2014, February 18). "How Two Hillary Clinton Superfans Became Super-PAC Power Players." *Mother Jones*. Retrieved from www.motherjones.com/politics/2014/02/ready-for-hillary-clinton-super-pac.

Center for American Women and Politics (2014). *Firsts for Women in U.S. Politics*. Retrieved from www.cawp.rutgers.edu/fast_facts/resources/Firsts.php.

Chozick, A. (2013, July 11). "Hillary Clinton Tapes Speechmaking Gold Mine. *New York Times*." Retrieved from www.nytimes.com/2013/07/12/us/politics/hillary-clinton-hits-the-lucrative-speechmaking-trail.html?pagewanted=all&_r=0&gwh=F254C05D8FBAFE0AC27A361AA6D907E6&gwt=pay.

Clinton Foundation (n.d.). *No Ceilings: The Full Participation Project*. Retrieved from www.clintonfoundation.org/our-work/no-ceilings-full-participation-project.

Clinton Foundation (n.d.). *Too Small to Fail*. Retrieved from www.clintonfoundation.org/our-work/too-small-fail.

Clinton, H. R. (2003). *Living History*. New York, NY: Simon & Schuster.

Clinton, H. (2001, November 24). "New Hope for Afghanistan's Women." *Time*. Retrieved from http://content.time.com/time/nation/article/0,8599,185643,00.html.

Clinton, H. R. (1999, March). *United Nations International Women's Day Speech on Women's Rights*. Speech presented at the United Nations International Women's Day, New York, NY. Retrieved from http://clinton2.nara.gov/WH/EOP/First_Lady/html/generalspeeches/1999/19990304.html.

Clinton, H. R. (1995, September). *Remarks for the United Nations Fourth World Conference on Women*. Speech presented at the United Nations Fourth World Conference on Women, Beijing, China. Retrieved from http://clinton3.nara.gov/WH/EOP/First_Lady/html/China/plenary.html.

Combe, R. (2012, April 5). "At the Pinnacle of Hillary Clinton's Career." *Elle*. Retrieved from www.elle.com/life-love/society-career/at-the-pinnacle-of-hillary-clintons-career-654140.

Dance, G. & Ericson, M. (2006). "Election 2006." *New York Times*. Retrieved from www.nytimes.com/ref/elections/2006/Senate.html.

Daum, M. (2008, January 12). "Hillary's Gotta Have It." *Los Angeles Times*. Retrieved from www.latimes.com/news/la-oe-daum12jan12-column.html.

Davidson, K. A. (2013, February 2). "Hillary Clinton: Countries Visited by the Most-Traveled Secretary of State in History." *Huffington Post*. Retrieved from www.huffingtonpost.com/2013/02/02/hillary-clinton-countries-travels_n_2602541.html

Dedman, Bill (May 9, 2007). "Reading Hillary Rodham's Hidden Thesis." *MSNBC.com*. www.nbcnews.com/id/17388372/#.U_z1Kigx8lJ

Encyclopedia of Arkansas History & Culture. Hillary Diane Rodham Clinton (1947–). Retrieved August 26, 2014, from www.encyclopediaofarkansas.net/encyclopedia/entry-detail.aspx?entryID=2744.

Encylopedia of World Biographies. (2014). "Hillary Rodham Clinton Biography." Retrieved from www.notablebiographies.com/Ch-Co/Clinton-Hillary-Rodham.html.

Frumin, A. (2014, May 22). "Hillary Clinton's *Hard Choices* Book Tour Comes Together." *MSNBC.com*. Retrieved from www.msnbc.com/msnbc/hillary-clinton-hard-choices-book-tour.

Gerth, J. & Van Natta, D. (2007). *Her Way: The Hopes and Ambitions of Hillary Rodham Clinton*. New York, NY: Little, Brown and Company.

Ghattas, K. (2013). *The Secretary: A Journey with Hillary Clinton from Beirut to the Heart of American Power*. New York, NY: Times Books.

Givhan, R. (2007, July 20). "Hillary Clinton's Tentative Dip into New Neckline territory. *Washington Post*. Retrieved from www.washingtonpost.com/wp-dyn/content/article/2007/07/19/AR2007071902668_pf.html.

Hastedt, G. P., & Eksterowicz, A. J. (2006). "First Lady Diplomacy: The Foreign Policy Activism of First Lady Clinton." *The Whitehead Journal of Diplomacy and International Relations*, (7) 57–66.

Healy, P. (2008a, August 31). "McCain's Pick May Foster Bigger Campaign Role for Clinton." *New York Times*. Retrieved from www.nytimes.com/2008/09/01/us/politics/01clinton.html?_r=1&ref=todayspaper&oref=slogin.

Healy, P. (2008b, September 5.). "The Real '08 Fight: Clinton v. Palin? *New York Times*. Retrieved from www.nytimes.com/2008/09/06/us/politics/06web-healy.html?_r=0.

Hernandez, R. (2005, May 14). "New Odd Couple: Hillary Clinton and Newt Gingrich." *New York Times*. Retrieved from www.nytimes.com/2005/05/13/world/americas/13iht-clinton.html.

Jamieson, K. H., & Dunn, J. (2008). "The 'B' Word in Traditional News and on the Web." *Nieman Reports*. Retrieved from niemanreports.org/articles/the-b-word-in-traditional-news-and-on-the-web/.

Jones, J. M. (2013, December 30). "Obama, Clinton Continue Reign as Most Admired." *Gallup*. Retrieved from www.gallup.com/poll/166646/obama-clinton-continue-reign-admired-man-woman.aspx.

Kelly, Michael (1993, February 14). "Again: It's Hillary Rodham Clinton. Got That?" *New York Times*.

Kenney, Charles (1993, January 12). "Hillary: The Wellesley Years: The Woman Who Will Live in the White House Was a Sharp-Witted Activist in the Class of '69." *Boston Globe*. Retrieved from www.highbeam.com/doc/1P2-8210491.html.

Kornblut, A. E. (2009). *Notes from the Cracked Ceiling: Hillary Clinton, Sarah Palin, and What It Will Take for a Woman to Win*. New York, NY: Crown Books.

Kornblut, A. E., & Balz, D. (2008, June 5). "She Could Accept Losing. She Could Not Accept Quitting." *Washington Post*. Retrieved from www.washingtonpost.com/wp-dyn/content/article/2008/06/04/AR2008060404312_pf.html.

Leibovich, Mark (2007, September 7). "In Turmoil of '68, Clinton Found a New Voice." *New York Times*. Retrieved from www.nytimes.com/2007/09/05/us/politics/05clinton.html?_r=0.

Lemmon, G. T. (2011, March 6). "The Hillary Doctrine." *Newsweek*. Retrieved from www.newsweek.com/hillary-doctrine-66105.

Levey, N. (2008, February 7). "Senate Democrats Fail to Expand Stimulus Bill." *Los Angeles Times*. Retrieved from http://web.archive.org/web/20080211183755/www.latimes.com/news/printedition/asection/la-na-stimulus7feb07,1,2385014.story.

Mesure, S. (2008, January 20). "Wintour Goes Nuclear over Hillary's Snub to *Vogue*." *The Independent*. Retrieved from www.independent.co.uk/news/world/americas/wintour-goes-nuclear-over-hillarys-snub-to-vogue-771263.html.

Morris, Roger. (1996). *Partners in Power: The Clintons and Their America*. New York, NY: Henry Holt.

Nagourney, A. (2000, March 12). "Mrs. Clinton Assails Mayor on Schools." *New York Times*. Retrieved from www.nytimes.com/2000/03/12/nyregion/mrs-clinton-assails-mayor-on-schools.html.

New York State Board of Elections (2006). *United States Senate Election Returns Nov. 7, 2006.* Retrieved from www.elections.ny.gov/NYSBOE/elections/2006/general/2006_ussen.pdf.

Newton-Small, J. (2014, September 14). "Hillary Clinton Flips a Steak in Iowa." *Time.* Retrieved from http://time.com/3373772/hillary-clinton-iowa-steak-fry/.

Nichols, J. (2008, August 30). "Clinton Praises Palin Pick." *The Nation.* Retrieved from www.thenation.com/blog/clinton-praises-palin-pick.

Old State House Museum. (Spring 1993). Hillary Clinton Guides Movement to Change Public Education in Arkansas. Retrieved August 26, 2014, from www.oldstatehouse.com/collections/classroom/arkansas_news.aspx?issue=29&page=1&detail=528.

PBS (2015). *The Clinton Years.* Retrieved from www.pbs.org/wgbh/pages/frontline/shows/clinton/.

Pear, R. (1993). "Settling In: First Lady; Hillary Clinton Gets Policy Job and New Office." *The New York Times.* Retrieved from www.nytimes.com/1993/01/22/us/settling-in-first-lady-hillary-clinton-gets-policy-job-and-new-office.html.

Preson, M. (2006, October 23). "Opponent Denies Knocking Senator Clinton's Looks." *CNN.com.* Retrieved from https://web.archive.org/web/20070321133945/www.cnn.com/2006/POLITICS/10/23/spencer.remarks/index.html.

Ratnesar, R. (1999, March 1). "Hillary Clinton: A Race of Her Own." *Time.* Retrieved from http://content.time.com/time/magazine/article/0,9171,990324,00.html.

Rodham, Hillary (1979). "Children's Rights: A Legal Perspective." in Patricia A. Vardin and Ilene N. Brody (eds.), *Children's Rights: Contemporary Perspectives.* New York, NY: Teacher's College Press, pp. 21–36.

Rodham, Hillary (June 1977). "Children's Policies: Abandonment and Neglect." *Yale Law Journal 86* (7): 1522–1531.

Rodham, Hillary (1973). "Children Under the Law." *Harvard Educational Review, 43*(4), 487–514.

Rodham, Hillary (May 31, 1969). "Hillary D. Rodham's 1969 Student Commencement Speech." Wellesley College. Retrieved August 26, 2014, from www.wellesley.edu/events/commencement/archives/1969commencement/studentspeech.

Santora, M. (2007, November 1). "Immigration is Fodder for Clinton Rivals." *New York Times.* Retrieved from www.nytimes.com/2007/11/01/us/politics/01immig.html.

Shepard, R. (2008). "Confronting Gender Bias, Finding a Voice: Hillary Clinton and the New Hampshire Crying Incident." *Argumentation and Advocacy, 46,* 64–77.

Smith, S. (2008, January 18). "Memo pad: Sharp Words . . . Shutter Fly . . . Close, but No Cigar . . . " *Women's Wear Daily.* Retrieved from https://web.archive.org/web/20080120151630/www.wwd.com/issue/article/121588?page=0.

Solnit, A., Goldstein, J., & Freud, Anna. (1973). *Beyond the Best Interests of the Child.* New York, NY: The Free Press.

Thomas, K. (2014, September, 24). "Hillary Clinton Pushes School Program for Girls." *The Big Story.* Retrieved from http://bigstory.ap.org/article/17cfd06eb2ca4558abb5c8bee0ffc1c1/hillary-clinton-pushes-school-program-girls.

United Nations (2015). *Beijing and Its Follow-Up.* Retrieved from www.un.org/womenwatch/daw/beijing/.

United Nations (2015). *History of International Women's Day.* Retrieved from www.un.org/en/events/womensday/history.shtml.

United States Department of State (2011, December 6). *U.S. Department of State Announces "The Women in Public Service Project."* Retrieved from www.state.gov/r/pa/prs/ps/2011/12/178394.htm.

United States Department of State (2011, September 19). *Women and Agriculture: Improving Global Food Security.* Retrieved from https://blogs.state.gov/stories/2011/09/19/women-and-agriculture-improving-global-food-security.

United States Senate. (2007a). *United States Senate Roll Call Votes 110th Congress—1st Session: On the Amendment Coleman Amdt. No. 1158.* Retrieved from www.senate.gov/legislative/LIS/roll_call_lists/roll_call_vote_cfm.cfm?congress=110&session=1&vote=00177.

United States Senate. (2007b). *United States Senate Roll Call Votes 110th Congress—1st Session: On the Amendment Vitter Amdt. No. 1157.* Retrieved from www.senate.gov/legislative/LIS/roll_call_lists/roll_call_vote_cfm.cfm?congress=110&session=1&vote=00180.

Vital Voices (2015). *History.* Retrieved from www.vitalvoices.org/about-us/history.

VoteSmart.org. (n.d.). "Senator Hillary Rodham Clinton: Voting record." Retrieved from http://votesmart.org/candidate/key-votes/55463/hillary-clinton#.VI73SGTF8td.

Washington Post. (January 26, 1992). In 1992, Clinton Conceded Marital "Wrongdoing." Retrived December 4, 2014, from www.washingtonpost.com/wp-srv/politics/special/clinton/stories/flowers012792.htm.

White House, The. (n.d.) "Hillary Rodham Clinton." Retrieved August 22, 2014, from www.whitehouse.gov/about/first-ladies/hillaryclinton.

www.hippyusa.org/.

www.huffingtonpost.com/2013/08/03/hillary-clinton-wellesley-speech_n_3692257.html.

www.pbs.org/wgbh/americanexperience/features/biography/clinton-hillary/.

4

HILLARY AND ELEANOR

The Rise of Smart Power and National Security Feminism

Dinesh Sharma

The political science and psychological evidence that women are treated differently than men in the US elections is incontrovertible. The finding that women face a significant deficit of "trust" and "likeability" when they run for public office is so well established that it is not even worth debating it. How else can you explain the wide gender lag in female representation for political office at the local, state, and national levels? This is what anthropologist and sociologists call a systemic variable that permeates all aspects of social and political life. While women are making strides in all aspects of life, they really have a long way to go in holding a publicly elected office in the US. The old slogan from the 1970s billboards, "You've come a long way, baby," is at best only partly true or overblown! The US ranks far behind other developed and developing nations in female representation for political office, approximately 20% in both houses.[1]

As Stephen Hill points out in a recent article, while "the United States may join the UK, Germany, Brazil, and Argentina as democracies that have had a woman as their top leader," women still hold less than 20 percent of congressional seats and rank low internationally.[2]

This is precisely why many international experts and most foreign travelers find the American outcry for women's rights movement worldwide through its agencies of development so poignant yet ironic at the same time. Shouldn't the change begin at home, as many women's rights advocates have argued for more than half a century? When we look at the life narrative of one of the most prominent woman politicians, namely Hillary Clinton, we find the contradictions and complexities at the heart of American body politic still remain perplexingly knotted at the nexus of gender, race, history, and the founding of the American democracy. The cultural forces that were pervasive during Eleanor Roosevelt's time at the turn of the previous century with the struggle for the passage of the Nineteenth Amendment, Hillary Clinton continues to run against in this century as women are still not fully represented in the government.

Daughters of Liberty

While the American history books discuss both the sons and daughters of liberty, history itself has been more kind to the sons than to the daughters of the American Revolution. As the Royal Massachusetts Governor Thomas Hutchinson observed in 1760, the daughters of liberty had an equal hand in fomenting protest in the colonies: "The Daughters of Liberty performed equally important functions. Once non-importation became the decided course of action, there was a natural textile shortage. Mass spinning bees were organized in various colonial cities to make homespun substitutes."[3] The daughters may have been the real unsung heroes of the American Revolution.

As Kathryn Halpin describes in her research on women's history of the workplace—from the daughters of liberty to women reporters at *Newsweek* in the 1970s to the women COOs at tech giants like Facebook and Yahoo—the gender roles of what Simone de Beauvoir called "the second sex" are still evolving.[4] Hillary Clinton said recently, "Women can't push to be paid equally if they don't know they're not paid equally."[5] While the gender wage gap still persists in 2015 (79 cents on the dollar)[6] even as a majority of women prefer to work outside the home,[7] we can only hold out hope that with greater reform, our daughters will be able to earn just as well as our sons in the coming decades.

First Wives Club

On the Fourth of July we celebrate the founders and the independence from Britain, but hardly mention the "mothers who raised a nation," suggests Cokie Roberts. From Martha Washington, Abigail Adams, and Deborah Sampson to Molly Pitcher, women have played a significant role in the founding of this nation, but are often the unsung heroes of the struggle for independence.[8]

At a recent fundraiser in Silicon Valley, Hillary was asked by an audience member if she was similar to Eleanor Roosevelt, to which she replied with a self-deprecating humor, brushing aside any strong linkages between the two women's careers. This was a change in strategy from the earlier times when Hillary ran for office in 2008. Hillary has welcomed the comparison with her historical role model—inspirational and imaginary mentor—with whom she once said to have "communicated" regularly through ESP and the clairvoyant medium.

However, the fact remains that as a member of the first wives club, she has many remarkable similarities with the longest-serving former First Lady. Professionally, both shared a passion for civil rights, human rights, and women's rights. Much has been written, rewritten, and revised about their similar interests and outspoken views on feminism.

Blanche Wiesen Cook, a recent Eleanor Roosevelt biographer, has claimed there are significant parallels between Eleanor, who entered the White House in 1933, and Hillary, who moved in 60 years later. "Each was attacked and mocked in the press, but refused to be silent," claimed Cook.[9] The difference was that Clinton was a nationally recognized lawyer steeped in politics before she became First Lady. As a result she may have become a polarizing figure. Her husband, President Clinton, boldly predicted that the nation was "getting two leaders for the price of one."

Franklin Roosevelt never publicly credited Eleanor's role in his decision-making, even though she was a vocal feminist in the 1920s. Cook notes, "So she was filled with dread before the inauguration in 1933, because Washington was such a small, ungenerous town. She feared she would have to give up her roles as educator and journalist, as her predecessor, Lou Henry Hoover, had done."

Roosevelt became an activist, touring the slums of Washington and launching a public housing campaign. Once, she went onstage during an opera intermission to collect donations for people suffering from the Great Depression. She crusaded vigorously for a series of domestic reforms, worked to protect Jewish refugees during World War II, embarked on a quest for human rights and drafted the UN charter.

Hillary Clinton, arguably the most activist First Lady in recent history, has been seen by many historians as constructing the first co-presidency. However, FDR's grandson Curtis Roosevelt, who knew his grandparents in the White House and lived with them, has revealed that the comparison is really misguided. While Eleanor remained an "amateur politician," eschewing policy-making or an elected office, Hillary has broken her teeth in politics. Eleanor was a distinctive First Lady, wrote Curtis Roosevelt about his memories of some 80 years ago, in *Too Close to the Sun*, but Eleanor "didn't wish to be a professional. Hillary Clinton is a professional . . . and that is a basic difference."[10] Perhaps it might be more accurate to speculate Hillary Clinton has appropriated and professionalized the concerns and projects championed by Eleanor Roosevelt for the next generation of women, especially as they relate to civil rights, human rights, and women's rights.

Gender Matters in Politics

Today, gender preferences are one of the significant drivers of voting behaviors in US elections, otherwise known as the gender gap, accounting for differences in men and women at the ballot box. Despite decades of women's rights activism, there is rampant discrimination when it comes to women political candidates. People say they are ready to elect a woman president, but will they actually vote for the first woman president in a crowded field of male candidates? This remains to be seen in the 2016 elections.

We can identify seven factors that contribute to the gender gap, according to the Women and Politics Institute at American University, which can directly impede women's ambition, making the decision to run more complicated for women than men. "Given the persistent gender gap in political ambition, we are a long way from a political reality in which women and men are equally likely to aspire to attain high level elective office.... But many barriers to women's interest in running for office can be overcome only with major cultural and political changes," according to the report.[11]

1. Women perceive the electoral environment as highly biased against female candidates.
2. Hillary Clinton and Sarah Palin's candidacies have deteriorated women's perceptions of the gender bias.
3. Women are more likely than men to think they are less qualified to run for elected office.
4. Female candidates feel less confident and more risk-averse than male counterparts to run for office.
5. Women have more negative reactions than men to the politics of the modern campaign.
6. Women receive fewer suggestions to run for office than their male counterparts.
7. Instead, women continue to feel higher responsibility and pressures for childcare and household tasks.

We also know that women and men vote differently for political candidates. As Kelly Ditmar points out in her research at Rutgers University, "Women and men are political actors with distinct political preferences. These differences—or gender gaps—emerged in the 1980s and have been persistent since then in vote choice, party identification, and presidential performance ratings."[12]

Starting in the 1980s women have a shown strong preference for the Democratic platform and candidates, ranging from a 4% to 11% gender gap. In 2012, women preferred Obama by an almost 10% margin compared to Romney (55% vs. 44%), significantly contributing to the Democratic victory. For a viable woman candidate in the general election, such as Hillary Clinton, the gender gap may be even larger.

A larger percentage of women self-identify as Democrats. This trend has been in place since the Equal Rights Amendment translated to the ballot box. Women also view Democratic presidents more favorably than men do and are more likely to give them better approval ratings overall. In a recent poll, women gave Obama an 8% higher rating than men did.

In terms of turnout, women also come out to vote in larger numbers than men do. Voter turnout among women has been at higher rates than among men beginning in 1980, and significantly higher in numbers since 1964. In 2012, almost

10 million more women voted than men (71.4 vs. 61.6 million). Eligible women voters went to the polls in higher proportions in 2012 than eligible men voters (63.7% vs. 59.8%). Finally, almost 10 million more women registered to vote than men in 2012 (81.7 vs. 71.4 million). All these trends might put a Democratic woman candidate at an advantage in the general election, but again we must wait for the 2016 elections.

Clearly, women's vote can sway a close election, especially if the historical trends remain steady. In presidential elections, women come out to vote in larger numbers than men; especially, black women are the most reliable voting bloc, followed by Latinos, young people, and unmarried women, based on the 2012 and 2014 turnout data. Women invariably feel concerned about the economic well-being of their families, which has over time drawn them to the polls in higher numbers. While the "war on women" will draw both sides to their electoral base, Democrats might gain a bigger surge at the ballot box from a woman presidential candidate in 2016.

Nexus of Gender and Race

While in 2008 and 2012, race trumped gender in the US primaries and the general election, will 2016 be the year of the female candidate? The evolving complexities of race, gender and ethnicities in the US election continue to pose challenges for politicians, especially as the country changes demographically in some interesting and dramatic ways.

According to the US Census, beginning in 1996 the number of eligible voters has increased in all presidential elections. "Overall, 133 million people reported voting in 2012, a turnout increase of about 2 million people since the election of 2008," according to a report by US Census.[13] Over two decades, turnout increases have fluctuated but are always larger than in 2012, "reaching a high of about 15 million additional voters in 2004," when George Bush ran for office. Almost 1.7 million additional Black voters went to the polls in 2012 compared to 2008, as did 1.4 million additional Hispanics, and approximately 550,000 additional Asians. On the other hand, "the number of non-Hispanic White voters decreased by about 2 million between 2008 and 2012." Predictably, since 1996 the race group that has decreased in net votes from one election to the next is the White majority, while the increase in the 2012 voting population arose from minority voters.

Just as the older voters (ages 35–65 years) are most politically active, the Black voters are more active now when compared with the majority White voters, stretching back to the Voting Rights Act of 1965. African American voters are more active in the political process than other minority groups, showing the highest level of voter registration and participation in elections compared to other groups: 64.7% in 2008 and 66.2% in 2012 turned out to vote. Although Latino groups form a substantial political bloc, only 49.9% and 48% of eligible Latino voters voted in the 2008 and 2012 presidential elections, respectively; similarly, only 48% and 47% of Asian Americans turned out to vote, respectively.[14]

The gender gap by ethnicity demonstrates that the Black women voters have been the most reliable set of voters. Since 1996, the gender voting gap has shown that Black women come out to vote at higher rates than Black men by a range of 7 to 8 percentage points through 2008, a large number of them voting for Democrats. Similarly, Black women voted at higher rates by 9 percentage points compared to Black men, approximately 6 percentage points greater than other ethnic groups. For non-Hispanic Whites, the gap has been smaller than for Blacks but consistently present across elections. For Hispanics, the gender voting gap has been present in every election except for 2000. This clearly bodes well for a Democratic woman candidate in 2016, given that ethnic women bring out greater votes for issues that are central to the Democratic platform and have a deep concern for women's rights.

Feminism and the Rise of Smart Power

There is a congruence between the history of feminism and the rise of soft power in Western societies. Hard power consists of military and economic capital that influences the behavior or interests of other nations. Often aggressive, hard power is most effective when there is an asymmetrical relationship between countries, where the stronger country has the advantage. Unlike hard power, soft power comes from diplomacy, culture, and history. According to Joseph Nye at Harvard, who coined the term, soft power is "the ability to use the carrots and sticks of economic and military might to make others follow your will" or to co-opt "another to act in ways in which that entity would not have acted otherwise."[15] While in the history of Western civilization, the use of hard power has a long trajectory, the use of soft power, according to Nye, is the new form of power in the arsenal.[16]

Soft power is the ability to shape the preferences of others through appeal and attraction. A defining feature of soft power is that it is noncoercive; the currency of soft power is culture, political values, and foreign policies. Recently, the term has also been used in changing and influencing social and public opinion through relatively less transparent channels and lobbying through powerful political and nonpolitical organizations. In 2012, Nye explained that with soft power, "the best propaganda is not propaganda," further explaining that during the Information Age, "credibility is the scarcest resource."[17]

When used in conjunction with hard power, soft power can be transformed into "smart power." Smart power is devising a platform of hard and soft power strategies into a successful plan. During the Cold War, the US managed such a combination of different strategies, but more recently US foreign policy has relied more heavily on hard power as the evidence of American strength. "The Pentagon is the best trained and best resourced arm of the government, but there are limits to what hard power can achieve on its own," according to Nye.[18] Nation building—democracy, human rights, and development of civil society—is not achieved with more boots on the ground. American military has an impressive operational capacity, but the practice of turning to the Pentagon for every foreign excursion offers an over-militarized foreign policy.

The notion of smart power has reemerged in the past decade, but the concept has much earlier roots in American history and is a well-known idea in international relations. In 1901, it was Theodore Roosevelt who proclaimed that leadership meant to "speak softly and carry a big stick!" During the late 1940s, the United States initiated soft power programs with the passage of the Smith-Mundt Act, which consisted of broadcasting, exchange, and information to combat the Soviet Union worldwide. Interestingly, this closely followed on heels of the ratification of the UN charter in 1945, drafted and approved with the leadership and support of many American philanthropists and foreign policy experts. The longest-serving former First Lady formally approved the UN charter: "We the people of the United Nations have determined . . . to save the succeeding generations from the scourge of war."[19] The synchrony between UN and US policy-making is today seen as one of the hallmarks of smart power, which is deeply rooted in the feminist movement in the US, as women were seen on the frontlines of progressive change, trying to create a more egalitarian and harmonious world through peacemaking rather than conflict.

Experts have recently suggested that the UN is the most critical tool in the US foreign policy tool-kit. Investing in a "New Multilateralism," a report issued by the Center for Strategic and International Studies in January 2009 discussed the role of the UN as an instrument of US smart power strategy.[20] In an increasingly multipolar world, the UN cannot be discarded as an outdated institution of the great powers and is an essential player in the multilateralism that the US faces. An effective smart power strategy will align the interests of the US and the UN, thereby effectively addressing threats to peace and security, climate change, global health, and humanitarian operations.

Eleanor Roosevelt as the Matriarch of Soft Power

Eleanor Roosevelt was the original champion of human rights and fully grasped the spirit behind the UN charter after the horrors of two world wars. Issues of women's rights were first prominently highlighted by Eleanor Roosevelt from her perch at the White House, more than sixty years later these ideas were fully integrated as part of the US foreign policy by Hillary Clinton. It is the cornerstone of what Hillary Clinton thinks is smart power, the compliment to America's hard military power, often deployed in concert with military power. Whereas Eleanor was the original champion of America's soft power after WWII and help found the UN charter, Hillary Clinton has fully integrated that institutional strength as part and parcel of America's smart power by establishing it as a fixture of the State Department.

Mary Ann Glendon, former ambassador to the Vatican and professor of comparative human rights law at Harvard University, agrees that Eleanor understood the force of UN charter was primarily cultural. "Mrs. Roosevelt understood that where human rights are concerned culture is prior to law. That understanding was shared by most of her colleagues on the U.N.'s first Human Rights Commission, but she was the one who expressed it best: 'Where, after all, do human rights begin? In small places, close to home.'"[21]

Nathan Gardels, editor of *New Perspective Quarterly*, traces the rise of American soft power to its post–Cold War heydays and its demise since the invasion of Iraq. He focuses on the clash between Muslim populations and the West, including the play of cultural contradictions in which the American majority, swayed by postmodern mass culture, is at loggerheads with an Islam that is culturally very conservative. Gardels argues that the chief consequence of going to war in Iraq against the tide of global public opinion has been the downgrading of America from a global superpower to a preponderant military bully. "By willfully ignoring the interests of others as expressed in their public opinion," Gardels writes, "the US unilateralist approach to Iraq and other issues has pushed the multi-polar world order out of its post–Cold War womb."[22] Likewise, William Schulz, former director of Amnesty International, has suggested that the Bush administration compromised the leadership on human rights in the aftermath of the 9/11 attacks built on decades of soft power cultivated by Eleanor Roosevelt and many others, philanthropists and founders of the UN. The US must try to reform soft power into smart power and regain the higher moral ground.

The dominant myth, according to the editor of *The Eleanor Roosevelt Papers, Volume I: The Human Rights Years, 1945–1948*, Allida Black, is that Eleanor was "a meek, mushy-headed liberal." Black has argued, "We did the book because everybody thinks of Eleanor as this great, bleeding liberal conscience who had no experience in crafting hard-nosed realistic policy."[23] That is factually inaccurate; Eleanor Roosevelt shaped policy from her role as the First Lady and afterwards, protected by her traditional image in the cloak of a humanitarian activist. Eleanor was one of the original champions of America's soft power in the twentieth century.

Smart Power after 9/11

In the wake of September 11, 2001, the spread of non-state actors who migrate across civilian populations, borderless communities, and terrorist groups pose daunting new challenges to the security of the United States. Conventional methods of security are no longer adequate. "Novel, unconventional threats and enemies can only be anticipated and overcome through the multidimensional and flexible application of smart power, the balanced synthesis of hard and soft power," according to a report by CACI International.[24] There seems to be a consensus among national security experts that American smart power is perhaps the best way to tackle these global problems. Smart power, consisting of government institutions, the private sector, and America's cultural reach, is the multipronged strategy that can win over threats to security. An integrated approach can blunt the asymmetric threats posed by violent Islamic extremism, drug trafficking, nuclear proliferation, global poverty, impending natural disasters, and other asymmetric threats, according to CACI International.

CSIS launched a smart power initiative to counter the threats to American image abroad.[25] Fostering America's leading role in global affairs, CSIS recommended we must elicit optimism and hope, not fear, among the global populations. The United States must deploy smart power strategy by continuing to invest in global goods and offer peoples and governments things that they cannot afford. In the absence of American leadership, peoples and governments will turn to other powers to fill the vacuum. Specifically, the United States should focus on five critical areas:

1. Global alliances to meet twenty-first century challenges
2. Global development aligning self-interest with the aspirations of people around the world
3. Global diplomacy to bring foreign populations to our side
4. Economic integration to benefit the global economy, growth, and prosperity
5. Technology and innovation for energy security and climate change

According to CSIS, the next president should consider a number of creative solutions to maximize smart power.

Hillary Clinton as the National Security Grandmother

As the former Secretary of State, Senator, and an advocate for America's soft power, Hillary is best equipped to deal with the challenges of the implementation of smart power. She has actually dealt with the day-to-day challenges of balancing American foreign policy—with democracy, development, and diplomacy—at the cutting edge of the globalized world order. She in many ways represents the rise of the national security moms across the US agencies—CIA, Department of Defense, and the military—to blunt the challenges of homeland security in the world shaped by the 9/11 security concerns, on the one hand, and the domestic challenges posed by the globalization of the economy, on the other[26].

On December 8, 2010, at the TEDWomen Conference in Washington, DC, Clinton explicitly stated,

> So the United States has made empowering women and girls a cornerstone of our foreign policy, because women's equality is not just a moral issue, it's not just a humanitarian issue, it is not just a fairness issue; it is a security issue. It is a prosperity issue and it is a peace issue. . . . Give women equal rights, and entire nations are more stable and secure. Deny women equal

rights, and the instability of nations is almost certain. The subjugation of women is, therefore, a threat to the common security of our world and to the national security of our country.[27]

In *Hard Choices* she further stated that this doctrine was crucial to development and diplomacy:

> It was no coincidence that the places where women's lives were most undervalued largely lined up with the parts of the world most plagued by instability, conflict, extremism, and poverty. This was a point lost on many of the men working across Washington's foreign policy establishment, but over the years I came to view it as one of the most compelling arguments for why standing up for women and girls was not just the right thing to do but also smart and strategic....The correlation was undeniable, and a growing body of research showed that improving conditions for women helped resolve conflicts and stabilize societies. "Women's issues" had long been relegated to the margins of U.S. foreign policy and international diplomacy, considered at best a nice thing to work on but hardly a necessity. I became convinced that, in fact, this was a cause that cut to the heart of our national security.[28]

On the domestic front, Clinton promises to bring back the prosperity of the 1990s when her husband Bill Clinton was president, on the one hand, and continue the policies of the Obama administration, on the other, to make America the land of prosperity; she espouses centrist, progressive economic policies.[29] The decline of the middle class has eroded incomes and created inequalities that Americans have not seen since the Great Depression. It has forced the Democratic presidential race to deal with job creation for the majority of the population. Clinton's policies try to alleviate the middle class economic pains—try to secure better futures and expand opportunities through greater access to education—by evenly distributing wealth and prosperity.

Hillary wants to restore the American dream by growing productivity—GDP, jobs, and innovation or entrepreneurship. She has said the "defining economic challenge of our time is raising incomes for hardworking Americans." Clinton wants to invest in education and infrastructure, rebuild small businesses, and increase labor participation that has fallen recently, especially for women.

Clinton has been arguing for fair growth, given corporate earnings have been at a record high, while wages for middle- and working-class Americans have not grown and have been declining. She has proposed to achieve greater prosperity by profit sharing, increasing wages, ensuring that the well-off pay their fair share in taxes, and expanding educational opportunities for young adults and children.

Clinton has claimed she wants to achieve long-term growth and encourage companies to plan for long-run gains instead of short-term capital returns or quarterly capitalism. She plans to further increase regulation on the banks, deter risky speculations, and build for long-term stability of the economy. Her proposals are progressive and in no small measure continue to build on the legacy of the previous two Democratic presidents that have preceded her: Barack Obama, her former boss and 44th president and Bill Clinton, her husband, the 42nd president.

Pushing the national security record of the Obama administration toward a more "hawkish" and proactive direction, Hillary Clinton would try to put down ISIS using a multilevel strategy. Her strategy for combating terrorism intensifies in many significant ways the efforts of the Obama administration. She recently outlined her plan at CFR: "Our strategy should have three main elements: one, defeat ISIS in Syria, Iraq, and across the Middle East; two, disrupt and dismantle the growing terrorist infrastructure that facilities the flow of fighters, financing arms, and propaganda around the world; three, harden our defenses and those of our allies against external and homegrown threats."[30] Many bipartisan supporters agreed that her speech was much tougher and clearly headed in the right direction. In many ways, her national security speech and credentials represented the strong stance some feminists have taken in stamping out terrorism as seen across the media landscape (in TV shows like *Supergirl, Quantico,* and movies like *Zero Dark Thirty*).

Her smart power approach has delivered the results in terms of changing America's image abroad: "In that way, the objectives of using a smart-power approach and rebuilding America's standing meshed perfectly. America would increase its influence in the world by taking advantage of opportunities to engage other countries in trade, investment, philanthropic partnerships, and military coalitions."[31] Similarly, in the use of smart power to defeat terrorism, Clinton has called for coalition building, bringing together powerful groups, "traditional allies, emerging powers, and Muslim-majority countries" to establish a global counterterrorism offensive.[32] Clinton has also called for a smart power approach in Afghanistan and Pakistan, combining "daring military action, careful intelligence gathering, dogged law enforcement, and delicate diplomacy."[33] Her smart power approach on foreign policy in Asia strengthened alliances, expanded relations with China, and worked with ASEAN and APEC in order to pivot toward Asia.[34]

The evolution of race and gender in the American electorate has moved haltingly, in fits and starts. In the 2016 election, the 240th year of its founding, America seems much closer to achieving some semblance of gender representation in the executive branch. The candidacy of the former First Lady, former US senator, and former Secretary of State Hillary Clinton seems to be the best opportunity Americans have for placing a woman in the White House. This will lead to a more inclusive government at home, and especially abroad, where the US development and diplomatic agencies constantly sound the clarion call for liberation of women worldwide. At least having a woman president would finally give real meaning to America's global political rhetoric on the part of half of the world's population caught in the struggle for equality and democracy.

References

1 Women in national parliaments, last updated Dec. 1, 2015; last accessed on April 30, 2016; www.ipu.org/wmn-e/classif.htm.
2 Hill, S. (2014). "Why does the US still have so few women in office?," *The Nation*, Mar 7; last accessed Feb. 24, 2016; www.thenation.com/article/why-does-us-still-have-so-few-women-office/.
3 E-Pluribus Unum, US History, Sons and daughters of liberty; last accessed on Feb. 24, 2016; www.ushistory.org/us/10b.asp.
4 Halprin, K. (2014). "The evolution of women in the workforce," in Michele A. Paludi, (ed.). *Women, Work, and Famil : How Companies Thrive with a 21st-Century Multicultural Workforce*. Santa Barbara, California: Praeger.
5 Foley, E. (2015). "Hillary Clinton: Women can't push to be paid equally if they don't know they're not paid equally," *Huffington Post*, Oct. 20; last accessed on Feb. 24, 2016; www.huffingtonpost.com/entry/hillary-clinton-equal-pay-women_us_561fe6a3e4b0c5a1ce627372.
6 O'Brien, S. A. (2015). "Seventy-eight cents on the dollar: The facts about the gender wage gap," April 14; last accessed on Feb. 24, 2016, http://money.cnn.com/2015/04/13/news/economy/equal-pay-day-2015/.
7 Saad, L. (2012). "In U.S., half of women prefer a job outside the home," Gallup, Sep 7; last accessed on Feb. 24, 2016; www.gallup.com/poll/157313/half-women-prefer-job-outside-home.aspx.
8 Roberts, C. (2015). *Founding Mothers: The Women Who Raised Our Nation*. New York: Harper.
9 Gilbert, D. (1993). "Biographer of Eleanor Roosevelt compares her with Hillary Clinton," *The University Record*, April 12; last accessed on April 30, 2016, http://ur.umich.edu/9293/Apr12_93/14.htm.
10 Bedard, P. (2010). "Eleanor Roosevelt Was No Hillary Clinton," *US News and World Report*, Feb 4; last accessed on April 30, 2016; www.usnews.com/news/blogs/washington-whispers/2010/02/04/eleanor-roosevelt-was-no-hillary-clinton.
11 Lawless, J. L. and Fox, R. L. (2012). *Men Rule: The Continued Under-Representation of Women in U.S. Politics*, Washington, DC: Women and Politics Institute; last accessed on Feb. 24, 2016; www.american.edu/spa/wpi/upload/2012-Men-Rule-Report-web.pdf.
12 Ditmar, K. (2014). "The Gender Gap," Center for American Women and Politics, July 15; last accessed on April 30, 2016; www.cawp.rutgers.edu/sites/default/files/resources/closerlook_gender-gap-07-15-14.pdf.
13 File, T. (2013). *The Diversifying Electorate—Voting Rates by Race and Hispanic Origin in 2012 (and Other Recent Elections)*, May; last accessed on Feb. 24, 2015; www.census.gov/prod/2013pubs/p20-568.pdf.
14 Frey, W. (2013). *Minority Turnout Determined the 2012 Election*, Brookings Institute, Washington, DC; last accessed on Feb. 24, 2015; www.brookings.edu/research/papers/2013/05/10-election-2012-minority-voter-turnout-frey.
15 Joseph Nye (January 10, 2003). "Propaganda isn't the way: Soft power." *International Herald Tribune*. Retrieved October 1, 2012; last accessed on Feb. 24, 2016; www.nytimes.com/2003/01/10/opinion/10iht-ednye_ed3_.html.
16 Barzegar, K. (2008). *Joseph Nye on Smart Power in Iran-U.S. Relations*, Q&A, July 11, 2008; last accessed on Feb. 24, 2016; http://belfercenter.ksg.harvard.edu/publication/18420/joseph_nye_on_smart_power_in_iranus_relations.html.
17 Nye, Joseph (2012). "China's soft power deficit: To catch up, its politics must unleash the many talents of its civil society." *Wall Street Journal*, May 8; last accessed

on Feb. 24, 2016; www.wsj.com/articles/SB10001424052702304451104577389923098678842.

18 Nye, J. (2007). "Recovering America's 'smart power'," *Korea Times*, Dec. 18, 2007; last accessed on Feb. 24, 2016; http://belfercenter.hks.harvard.edu/publication/17787/recovering_americas_smart_power.html.

19 From the *Charter of the United Nations* © 1945 United Nations. Reprinted with the permission of the United Nations.

20 Forman, J. (2009). "Investing in new multilateralism." *CSIS Report*, Jan 2009; last accessed on Feb. 24, 2016; http://csis.org/files/media/csis/pubs/090128_mendelsonforman_un_smartpower_web.pdf.

21 Donnelly, D. (2008). "Soft power and hope," *America: The Catholic Review*, November 24, Issue; last accessed on Feb. 24, 2016; http://americamagazine.org/issue/677/article/soft-power-and-hope.

22 Gardels, N. (2008). "The rise and fall of America's soft power," *New Perspectives Quarterly*, Winter 2008; last accessed on Feb. 24, 2016; www.digitalnpq.org/archive/2005_winter/02_gardels.html.

23 Baird, J. (2007). "The Real Eleanor: Smart disciplined strong," *Newsweek*, Dec 15; last accessed on Feb. 24, 2016; www.newsweek.com/real-eleanor-roosevelt-smart-disciplined-strong-94321.

24 CACI International. (2009). *Dealing with Today's Asymmetric Threat to U.S. and Global Security Symposium Three: Employing Smart Power*; last accessed on Feb. 24, 2016; http://asymmetricthreat.net/docs/asymmetric_threat_3_exec_sum.pdf.

25 Armitage, R. and Nye, J. (2007). "CSIS Commission of smart power: A smarter, more secure America," Washington, DC: *CSIS Reports*; last accessed on Feb. 24, 2016; http://csis.org/files/media/csis/pubs/071106_csissmartpowerreport.pdf.

26 Drum, K. (2015). "Hillary Clinton Is Strongly Trusted on National Security," *Mother Jones*, Nov 23; last accessed on April 30, 2016; www.motherjones.com/kevin-drum/2015/11/hillary-clinton-strongly-trusted-national-security; Kayyem, J. (2016). "How candidates can capture 'Security Moms'", *CNN*, April 6; last accessed on April 30 2016; www.cnn.com/2016/04/06/opinions/security-momstrump-clinton-kayyem/.

27 Clinton, H. (2010). Remarks at the TEDWomen conference, Washington, DC: U.S. State Department; last accessed on Feb. 25, 2016; www.state.gov/secretary/20092013clinton/rm/2010/12/152671.htm.

28 Clinton, H. (2014). *Hard Choices*, New York: Simon and Schuster, p. 562.

29 Le Gauchiste, (2015). "Anti-capitalist meetup: How neoliberal is Hillary Clinton?" *Daily Kos*, Jul 19; last accessed on Feb. 24, 2016; www.dailykos.com/story/2015/7/19/1403488/-Anti-Capitalist-Meetup-How-Neoliberal-is-Hillary-Clinton.

30 Clinton, H. (2015). "Hillary Clinton on National Security and the Islamic State: A Conversation with Hillary Clinton," Council on Foreign Relations; last accessed on Feb 24, 2016; www.cfr.org/radicalization-and-extremism/hillary-clinton-national-security-islamic-state/p37266.

31 Clinton, H. (2015). "Hillary Clinton: Smart power & foreign policy," Correct the Record, last accessed Feb 24, 2016; http://correctrecord.org/hillary-clinton-smart-power-foreign-policy/.

32 Clinton, H. (2011). *Smart Power Approach to Counterterrorism*, last accessed Feb 24, 2016; www.state.gov/secretary/20092013clinton/rm/2011/09/172034.htm

33 Clinton, H. (2014). *Hard Choices*, New York: Simon and Schuster, pg. 174.

34 Clinton, H. (2014). *Hard Choices*, New York: Simon and Schuster, pg. 44–45.

5

HILLARY RODHAM CLINTON AND THE 1995 BEIJING INTERNATIONAL CONFERENCE ON WOMEN

Gender and the Nexus of Global and Domestic Power Dynamics[1]

N'Dri Thérèse Assié-Lumumba

"If there is one message that echoes forth from this conference, let it be that *human rights are women's rights and women's rights are human rights*, once and for all" (Clinton, 1995, emphasis added). This speech echoed from Beijing to the world. The participants of the NGO Forum and UN Conference on Women held in Beijing, China (4–15 September 1995) represented a wide spectrum of the global human demographic. There were many women of humble origins but with powerful voices, extraordinary might and energies who shared their experiences. However, among the most prominent participants of the United Nations Fourth World Conference were, undoubtedly, First Lady Hillary Rodham Clinton of the United States and the Honorable Winnie Nomzamo Mandela of South Africa.[2]

The year 2015 marked anniversaries and deadlines of the United Nations' global engagements toward gender equality and equity, including Education for All (EFA) and the Millennium Development Goals (MDGs). Of great significance is the celebration of the 20th anniversary of the Beijing Conference, Beijing +20, which was held in New York City at the headquarters of the United Nations.

The role of the First Ladies of the United States in the United Nations started from the founding of this international organization at its inception with active involvement of First Lady Eleanor Roosevelt. She played prominent roles, including her appointment by President Harry Truman to serve as the first American delegate to the United Nations. She held this position from December 31, 1945 to December 31, 1952. Since that initial stage, the level and extent of her substantive engagement in the United Nations has been unparalleled. The involvement and visibility of individual First Ladies as heads of the United States delegations and/or prominent speakers at the United Nations international conferences on women has varied considerably since then.

Nevertheless, the White House has accorded importance to the United Nations and its major events, even when the First Ladies do not play prominent roles in them. For instance, the official American delegation to the 1985 Nairobi conference celebrating the end of the United Nations Decade for Women was headed by Maureen Reagan, the daughter of then president Ronald Reagan. Thus, given the political and ideological background, the world-renowned scholar and activist Angela Davis articulated that Maureen Reagan did not represent her at the Nairobi Conference, ten years before Beijing.

The theme of the Beijing Conference was "Action for Equality, Development and Peace." With the state of the world in this present time of in the second decade of the 21st century, it is important to note how the theme remains relevant. The Beijing Conference has been a critical historical point of reference. All the UN conferences since Beijing have been numbered using Beijing as the initial marker: Beijing +5 in 2000, Beijing +10 in 2005, Beijing +15 in 2010, and Beijing +20 in 2015.

My reflections on various aspects of the Beijing Conference have been shaped by the different angles from which I took part in this major international event. I participated in the preparation of several activities, including playing a role in both the UN[3] and NGO[4] dimensions. To better locate First Lady Hillary Rodham Clinton's participation in the Conference, it is important to note that in the month preceding the Beijing Conference, in August 1995, President Clinton created the President's Interagency Council on Women (PICW) with the goal of ensuring that the resolutions to be adopted in Beijing would be implemented in the United States as well. As part of its coordinating role toward the implementation of the Beijing Platform for Action, PICW organized many activities.

At the time, First Lady Hillary Rodham Clinton served as its honorary chair. Prominent women in the political arena who served as PICW successive chairs included Secretary of State Madeleine Albright and Donna Shalala, who served as secretary of Health and Human Services. The members of the Council included an impressive and comprehensive list of high-level officials from executive branch agencies of the United States government ranging from the Departments of State, Treasury, Defense, Justice, Interior, Agriculture, Commerce, Housing and Urban Development, Transportation, Education, Energy, and so forth.

As part of its evaluation of post-Beijing activities, in September 1996, the White House, specifically PICW, organized a satellite conference. I was invited to contribute to this evaluative exercise. For the same event, I was also invited to Washington, DC, by the President Council on Cornell Women (PCCW) to make a presentation on the Beijing Conference to assist the PCCW members in their participation in the post-Beijing assessment.

My perspectives on the Conference in general, especially in this paper are shaped by intellectual positions, as I attended the Beijing Conference as an academic, teaching at Cornell University. I traveled to Beijing also as a member of the delegation of the United Nations Economic Commission for Africa (UN-ECA) as well as a member of the executive committee of the then leading African NGO, the Association for the African Women for Research and Development (AAWORD). My reflections in this paper are a continuation of other post-Beijing activities that I have been engaged in.[5]

When then First Lady Hillary Rodham Clinton attended the Beijing Conference, she already had a full life and a track record as an assertive, articulate, and educationally and professionally accomplished person. However, she was mainly known, especially to the rest of the world, as the First Lady of the United States, a recently acquired title after the election of her spouse, Bill Clinton, to the office of the president of the United States in 1992. At the time, despite her previous accomplishments, even on the domestic front, she had not yet built her own clearly articulated and autonomously earned political power base at home to give more credibility to her international stature. Her very productive and active participation in the Beijing Conference contributed to confirm her autonomous image.

In the American national context, several years after Beijing, there was neither much recognition nor acceptance of her independent political ambition. This was in spite of her additional credentials acquired in serving a full term as senator of New York. When in her second term as senator, she decided to run for the 2008 presidential election, she was still perceived as not having sufficient credentials of her own and rather banking on her husband's political achievements and clout. However, she has since acquired more credentials as former secretary of state, thus further affirming her individual prominence at home and abroad.

The purpose of this article is to reflect on the dimensions of Hillary Rodham Clinton's presence and engagements in the Beijing International Conference on Women, paying particular attention to the critical intersection of gender and power dynamics on both the domestic and global fronts, as well as understanding the meanings of the various activities that she was involved in, with a focus on her public speeches during the Conference.

The first section of this paper will briefly present the United Nations and its role in addressing key gender issues leading to the Beijing Conference. The second section focuses on an analysis of the activities, especially the speeches delivered by First Lady Hillary Rodham Clinton at the Beijing Conference. The third section deals with the global dynamics of gender and power. The conclusion is a forward-looking reflection on a resolute former secretary of state Hillary Rodham Clinton, with her eyes on the presidential election this year.

The United Nations, Gender and the Road to Beijing

The idea and conceptualization of the United Nations, following the obvious and notorious ineffectiveness of its forerunner, the League of Nations, and amidst World War II, was a long process. The term appeared for the first time in a document that was co-signed on January 1, 1942, by President Franklin Delano

Roosevelt of the United States, Prime Minister Winston Churchill of the United Kingdom, Maxim Litvinov of the USSR, and T.V. Soong of China, with 20 more co-signers joining on January 2 with the aim of increasing their war effort and pledging not to make separate peace deals.

After several other momentous events toward the actualization of the idea, subsequently at the end of the war and at the conclusion of the United Nations Conference on International Organization, the Charter of the United Nations as it is known today was signed in San Francisco on June 26, 1945. It stipulated that it would promote "social progress and better standards of life" as well as encourage "respect for human rights and for fundamental freedoms for all without distinction as to race, sex, language or religion."

Despite these ideals, the launching of United Nations was marked by glaring contradictions. Indeed, while the Charter was being signed, large parts of Asia and almost the entire African continent were still under colonial rule, and racial segregation prevailed in the United States. When in 1948 the United Nations proclaimed its Universal Declaration of Human Rights, India, for instance, had just acquired its independence, and European colonial domination of Africa with its dehumanizing policies was prevalent. That same year the white minority in South Africa began to reinforce and elaborate new apartheid laws. This is to recall the long history of global contradictions despite the idea and ideals imbedded in the United Nations.

The question of gender inequality in all spheres of life was raised at the inception of the United Nations. While in the beginning of the preamble of the Charter, there is use of a gender-insensitive term of "mankind" in reference to humanity, it was also immediately stipulated that it aims "to reaffirm faith in fundamental human rights, in the dignity and worth of the human person, in the equal rights of men and women and of nations large and small." Subsequently, the Commission of the Status of Women (CSW), which is functional unit of the Economic and Social Council (ECOSOC), was established in 1946, an held its first meeting in 1947 at Lake Success (New York). This inaugural meeting was attended by women representing 15 governments. CSW became immediately active, and has remained so, within the UN, playing leading roles, for instance in working on numerous declarations and conventions on gender equality. Thus, with the work of CSW, for example, the Convention on the Political Rights of Women in 1953 was adopted and the General Assembly in Resolution 2263 (XXII) of 7 November 1967, adopted the Declaration on the Elimination of Discrimination against Women.

The United States, as the leader of the Western world, played a determining role in the outcome of World War II and the reconstruction of Europe through the Marshall Plan in the late 1940s and into the 1950s. It also took leadership in the development theories and policies to foster development despite the contradictions and prevailing disenfranchisement and marginalization of vast groups in society. The United Nations served as a global vehicle in promoting the actualization of the ideals enshrined in its Charter. Thus, for instance, during the sixteenth session of its General Assembly, on December 19, 1961, by Resolution 1710 (XVI), the decade of the 1960s was declared the "United Nations Development Decade." Several other resolutions aiming at global change and social progress, amid the Cold War, were adopted during the same and subsequent sessions.

Through the work of CSW and other units of the UN on women such as the former United Fund for Women (UNIFEM), it was concluded that gender inequality was still a persistent and major social human rights and socioeconomic development issue. Although this topic had national and local specificities, it was also a global issue and thus needed to be addressed at the international level. In the 1970s, resolutions were adopted to tackle the problem. Thus, Resolution 2626 (XXV) of 24 October 1970, articulating the International Development Strategy for the Second United Nations Development Decade, aimed at promoting the full integration of women with a comprehensive development agenda. Subsequently, the year 1975 was declared the International Women's Year (IWY). It was the beginning of a series of activities and programs including the United Nations Women's Decade (1976–1985).

During that decade three major conferences known as the United Nations International Conferences on Women were organized. The inaugural conference was held in Mexico City in 1975 (19 June to 2 July) on the theme of "Equality of Women and Their Contribution to Development and Peace." This was followed by the midway Copenhagen Conference in 1980 (14 to 30 July) to assess the achievements toward "Equality, Development and Peace." Afterward was the conference marking the celebration of the end of the Women's Decade, the Nairobi Conference in 1985 (15 to 26 July) on "Forward-Looking Strategies" in reviewing and appraising the achievements of the "United Nations Decade for Women: Equality, Development and Peace."

Following a very long and complex process, just a year before the Copenhagen midway assessment of the UN decade for women, in 1979, the most known of the gender-focused equality conventions pressed by CSW, namely the Convention on the Elimination of All Forms of Discrimination Against Women (CEDAW), was adopted as a central international agreement on women's human rights. Generally, in the 1980s and 1990s, gender discourse and awareness gained momentum.

In addition to the three international conferences that focused on women, other major international meetings were organized following the 1975 Mexico City meeting, which also had women's issues on their respective agendas and in their deliberations and resolutions. It was the case with the Rio de Janeiro Conference on Environment and Development in 1992, the Vienna Conference on Human Rights in 1993, the Cairo Conference on Population and Development in 1994, and the 1995 Copenhagen World Summit for Social Development. The most common feature of the gender debates in such meetings and resolutions (all the documents produced) was the acknowledgement of its critical importance of women's and girls' rights, though there were major variations in this recognition across regions and among countries.

At the three aforementioned United Nations international conferences on women, considerable work was done toward producing well-articulated documents: the 1975 Plan of Action, the 1980 Programme of Action, and the 1985 Forward-Looking Strategies to the Year 2000, a few years later. However, it was unanimously recognized that the Nairobi Forward-Looking Strategies fell far short of its expectations. A critical examination of the determining factors of the failure was not really systematically done, in part because the representatives who, on behalf of their states, discussed these issues of the persistence of gender inequality were selected on the basis of their loyalty to the ruling governments headed by male leaders. Notably, those leaders were not known for their vision and benevolent and/or genuine commitment for the promotion of gender equality and social progress in general. A lot of internal UN criticism came from the units that focus on women's issues, such as CSW and UNIFEM and also NGOs, which had been growing in numbers and sharpened their analytical and activist capabilities.

When gender inequality, as a social issue, was raised at the United Nations, the world conferences were organized with the official goals of improving women's conditions and working to promote gender parity. Because the observation that the Nairobi Forward-Looking Strategies for the Advancement of Women was not followed by significant progress, critical areas of concern were identified for each region of the world for the next meeting: the 1995 Beijing Conference. These issues, which were addressed in regional pre-Beijing conferences, included women and poverty, women's access to education, their role in culture, the issues of access to health services with a focus on reproductive health, women's relationship to the environment, the involvement of women in the peace process, the legal and human rights of women, the need for mainstreaming gender-disaggregated data, women's relationships to communication and information, special concern for the girl-child, and women's political empowerment.

In the next section of this paper the role of First Lady Hillary Rodham Clinton at the Conference is analyzed, with a focus on the speeches that she delivered. The way the international conferences are organized, considering the various channels for making contributions (including interviews with media and in various sites), it is obvious that the formal speeches constitute only a component of her actions in Beijing during the Conference. However, they give an indication of the pattern of her interventions and the substance of her ideas.

Hillary Rodham Clinton at the Beijing Conference: Speeches and Engagements

Like the previous UN conferences, the momentous 1995 Beijing Conference was convened by the United Nations General Assembly. The United Nations

Commission on the Status of Women served as the Preparatory Committee, which made recommendations to member states to establish national committees in collaboration with NGOs, in order to ensure the coordination and promotion of actions at the national levels.[6]

Governments, various United Nations organizations, intergovernmental organizations, national liberation movements, nongovernmental organizations (NGOs), independent experts, and professional associations were the participants or observers of the Conference, as specified by the United Nations.

Under the themes and many other sub-themes that were selected for Beijing, a considerable number of officials representing nation-states as well as NGOs, grassroots groups, and individuals shared their thoughts, experiences, frustrations, hopes, visions, and plans with participants from around the world. There were indications of various levels of concern, commitment, and readiness to make contributions for future change. So many activities were simultaneously taking place, day and night, that it was always difficult to make a choice in sharing experiences; listening to the papers, testimonies, and proposals; or seeing the enriching documentaries, pictures, documents, and various forms of artwork about the various regions and countries of the world. However, given the status of the United States on the global scale, the speech of First Lady Hillary Rodham Clinton was prominent. In addition, at the time of the Beijing Conference it was clear that she had been positioning herself as an articulate and autonomous thinker on the various dimensions of gender equity at home and globally, asserting herself as a contemporary, politically savvy, and professional woman when she became First Lady of the United States.

In Beijing, the process for adopting the final official texts was similar to the usual UN procedures where member states have authority over every other entity. Thus, although in actuality these states have equal legal status within the UN, they possess unequal power and clout. Thus, the input of many well-intentioned and committed individuals, groups, and NGOs into the final platform had to be communicated through an intricate lobbying mechanism through member states. Eventually, the *Global Platform for Action* and also the *Beijing Declaration* were adopted by consensus. Before the diplomatic maneuvering and other processes led to the adoption, numerous panels and other spaces were organized for presentations and vigorous debates of experts and activists, and for delivering official speeches.

This is the context in which First Lady Hillary Rodham Clinton delivered several formal speeches at the Beijing Conference. In this article, I focus on four of such speeches, including the one in which she made her famous and now historic statement referred to in the introduction: 1) "Remarks by First Lady Hillary Rodham Clinton to the United Nations Fourth World Conference on Women Plenary Session" in Beijing on September 5; 2) "Remarks by First Lady Hillary Rodham Clinton to the NGO Forum" in Huairou on September 6; 3) "Remarks by First Lady Hillary Rodham Clinton to the World

Health Organization Colloquium 'Women and Health Security'" in Beijing on September 5; and 4) "Remarks by First Lady Hillary Rodham Clinton to the United Nations Development Fund for Women Panel Discussion 'Women's Economic Empowerment'" in Beijing on September 6 (Clinton 1995).

As the titles of the addresses suggest, each of the speeches was tailored to specific platforms and audiences. The remarks were designed as global messages that seemed to have been purposefully shaped for layers of domestic audiences as well, including Americans who were attending the Beijing Conference and political/politicized population segments as well as the general public. For this paper, selected themes in her addresses are analyzed, focusing on the following: the universal woman question; change and persistence of the location of women in society; regional, national, and local specificities; solidarity for common battle and support to different groups according to their needs; women's role in reshaping history; education to acquire critical knowledge for action; comprehensive health care needs; political empowerment; economic empowerment; strategic and necessary alliance with men; resolve toward irreversible change.

Regarding the universal woman question, it is worth indicating that her address at the plenary session was presented with a high note on contrasts while referring to the common history of marginalization and current locations in society of women across the globe. Her address is nuanced in shedding light on the history and objective situation of gender inequality while also refuting the argument that presents women as passive victims. She provides a balanced perspective on the positive and negative implications of women's roles. She articulates the idea of celebration of women from around the world meeting in Beijing as she refers to women "coming together, much the same way women come together every day in every country." She identifies with the women in Beijing as a space of global gathering in reiterating the "we," "our," and "us" in stating, for instance, "We come together." She acknowledges the diverse locations where women perform their roles in referring to "the contributions women make in every aspect of life: in the home, on the job, in their communities, as mothers, wives, sisters, daughters, learners, workers, citizens and leaders" (Clinton 1995).

A major criticism of Western/classical feminism widely articulated among scholars and activists on the situation of girls and women of the Global South and also historically oppressed groups in the Global North, such as African Americans, Native Americans, Latina women, working-class women, and so forth, is that there is no generic woman. Indeed, the argument goes, while gender inequality is global, its manifestations and impacts reflect the interface of many badges of identity that compound the marginalization based on gender. Scholars such as Angela Davis (1981), in *Women Race and Class*; Patricia Hill Collins (2000), in *Black Feminist Thought: Knowledge, Consciousness and the Politics of Empowerment*; Filomina Chioma Steady (1987); Rosalyn Terborg-Penn (1987); Chandra Talpade Mohanti (1991); and Oyèrónké Oyěwùmí (1997) have analyzed different identities and the concept of "intersecting oppressions" that captures the multiple factors that operate simultaneously and exacerbate gendered marginality. Such factors of oppression and marginalization include race, class, sexual orientation, and nationality, within nations and geographic locations.

First Lady Hillary Rodham Clinton recognizes the numerous grounds of differentiation in referring to the different angles from which women experience their lives. Thus, women of all walks of life in any country and national space of the world are acknowledged as she states, "However different we may be, there is far more that unites us than divides us" (Clinton 1995). She goes on to refer to some of these social locations that define the specificities of marginality when she states, "We come together in fields and in factories. In village markets and supermarkets. In living rooms and board rooms."

Despite these acknowledged differences, she articulates certain universal factors. She articulates the critical importance of education as the universal key determinant of life opportunities everywhere. Certainly, she acknowledges that education is not a sufficient condition, as women in many countries who have achieved equality of access to education still suffer from other forms of gender inequality. Indeed, as I have argued in various works, unequal educational opportunity cannot be reduced to the mere access or basic literacy, no matter how important they are. Inequality related to education has many other dimensions beyond access, such as unequal retention; the possibility to move from basic to secondary and higher education; gender-based disciplinary clusters at the higher education level, especially in the university, leading to unequal educational outputs and outcomes in terms of academic and professional attainment; and sheer gender bias against even women with impeccable academic achievements (Assié-Lumumba 2001, 2007). Bright women with stellar credentials and assertiveness can be actually perceived as threats for not respecting some expected demeanor considered to be more appropriate for women.

In her speeches, First Lady Hillary Rodham Clinton aims to speak with a voice that reflects her familiarity with the issues and compassion across the global community. She cites her experiences with women in diverse national contexts, referring to her meetings with many women facing various challenges in different geographic locations. They share the common gender-related constraints. She also refuses to portray women as passive victims. Indeed, despite the recognized obstacles, she refers to numerous actions women have been taking historically and in the contemporary era to find their niche and broader justice. For instance, she talks with admiration about the women who shared their experiences in the leading roles they played in toppling the apartheid system and their contributions in creating a new democratic culture in South Africa; she recalls the women in India and Bangladesh who, using the opportunities offered by a micro-credit scheme, are actively engaged in building life and opening possibilities; and women in medicine in Belarus and Ukraine working to save children following Chernobyl (Clinton 1995). She also cites social spaces that, in the world, offer models when she mentions her meeting in Denmark where parents have "comfort . . . in knowing that their children can be cared for in creative, safe, and nurturing after-school centers." It is worth adding on this matter that the United States was then and still is the industrial country with no such services, hence with continued responsibilities for women as having the primary responsibility for providing child care services.

Speaking to issues of the world, she also mentioned by name many other countries and cities to illustrate various arguments, either to identify the existing problems and/or to acknowledge hopeful and even inspiring solutions. She addresses issues that are specific to regions, especially the Global South, when, for instance, she cites the assistance from the United States "for girls so that they could attend school in Africa, Asia and Latin America" (Clinton 1995).

She submits that on aspects of the economic front, there are similar contrasts in industrialized countries, including the United States, such as constraints encountered by women who do not meet the requirements for loans they need for their businesses. She explains how some solutions in countries of the Global South can constitute a model in the most powerful economy. Thus, she refers to the microcredit scheme, the most known being the Grameen Bank of Bangladesh founded by Professor Muhammad Yunus. This credit system has inspired programs in the United States. She addresses other global issues, such as domestic violence that is global, and thus does not spare women in industrial countries.

Obviously, she did not miss talking specifically about the United States. She deplored the deep roots of patriarchal culture in the United States where, as she stated, "It took 150 years after the signing of our Declaration of Independence for women to win the right to vote" (Clinton 1995). At the same time she celebrates the perseverance of women and some men whose hard work led to the victory.

She analyzes the unequal educational opportunities, health disparities, and the burden on women who, while they are the main caregivers in families, do not receive enough broad education and adequate technical/specialized training, experience low representation in the political systems, and so forth. The First Lady captures the full meaning of the United Nations International Conference on Women held in Beijing, as she applies her analytical capacity to identify the determining factors and the mechanisms through which gender inequality is reproduced, with the key purpose of finding ways to change it. Thus, structural, cultural, and institutional changes are the goal.

Here First Lady Hillary Rodham Clinton sees women as having their full agency to change and rewrite history. There is a resolve in her tone toward irreversible change with a march for a new future. She introduces and returns to the theme of time, and the dynamics of movement in referring to the past and present condition yet also pointing to a promising and even bright future that women as agents of history will build, not for themselves but for humanity, as she states, "We share a common future. And we are here to find common ground so that we may help bring new dignity and respect to women and girls all over the world" (Clinton 1995).

She argues about the critical importance of alliances as she acknowledges that despite women's resolve and agency, men's contribution is important in building a new society in which everyone will be a winner. She argues that gender equality is not a goal that will restore women's rights only, as women's educational and socio-economic attainment constitute an investment that benefits families, communities, and nations. She states, "What we are learning around the world is that if women are healthy and educated, their families will flourish. . . . And when families flourish, communities and nations will flourish. That is why every woman, every man, every child, every family, and every nation on our planet has a stake in the discussion that takes place here [in Beijing]" (Clinton 1995).

What are the conditions and the local and global contradictions that must be addressed in working productively to the envisioned new future? In the next section some of these contradictions and factors that hinder or can enable gender equality are discussed.

Global Dynamics and the Nexus of Gender and Power

Beijing offered an opportunity to the participants to make contacts, exchange experiences, learn specific skills, identify funding agencies and meet their representatives, submit proposals, and develop new friendships. More important were strategies to tackle the entrenched and seemingly intractable patterns of global, national, and local structures of gender inequality and inequity. Besides the formal platforms, there were other opportunities for exchange between the UN system and the NGOs. Among various other meetings, it is worthwhile to cite the one between the NGOs and the president of the World Bank on September 15, 1996,[7] especially considering the destructive impacts of the Structural Adjustment Programs (SAPs) policies of the World Bank and the International Monetary Fund (IMF) in many countries of the Global South in the 1980s and 1990s, with more negative consequences for women.

After the 1990 decision to hold the Beijing conference, in subsequent UN annual sessions, the United Nations Commission on the Status of Women recommended that member states establish national committees in collaboration with NGOs. The official purpose of this move was to ensure the coordination and promotion of action at national levels in preparation for the conference and the subsequent implementations. Furthermore, it was recognized that NGOs play a vital role on the ground and thus constitute inevitable partners. Thus, NGOs and grassroots organizations were invited to collaborate among themselves and with governments to avoid duplication in the implementation of the platform. They were expected to play a key role in "popularization, information and promotional activities."

There is no doubt that the UN conference in Beijing was expected to offer, and indeed offered, an unprecedented opportunity for networking. However, the NGO Forum was held at Huairou, located at about 50 kilometers from Beijing, while the UN meeting was held at the Beijing Convention Center. This distance was not an enabling factor for optimal interactions, although the fact that the two meetings were held at different and consecutive dates mitigated the hindering factor.

Despite inevitable sources of frustration, there were numerous opportunities to share, learn, and develop networks. But fundamental questions, especially the following, remained and are still valid twenty years later, including the following: What was the actual effectiveness of yet another international conference in creating foundations and better conditions to foster and sustain permanent equality, development, and peace?

As mentioned above, I translated presentations by scholars, activists, policymakers, and others, from English to French and vice versa. These presentations were given in the form of well-researched papers, testimonies, extemporaneous talks, discussions among the participants, and speeches by various political figures and high-ranking bureaucrats of international organizations. Most of the speeches, particularly those delivered by professional politicians at top levels, did not provide any sign of actual commitment to undertake immediate, concrete, or specific actions in the critical areas identified. Despite talks by those who went through the ritual of listing the problems, women and people in general quickly pointed to the shrinking financial resources made available to fund projects and programs, which limits translation of good will into action. When pressed by the audience to become specific in terms of what they were prepared to contribute toward addressing the problems, they tended to remain vague. The Group of 77 and China expressed the need for more resources if the stated goals were to be met. The donor agencies and industrial countries emphasized the limited available resources. Yet, the world has more financial resources available now than ever before. It is matter of allocation of the resources to areas considered to be of priority by decision makers.

It is important to emphasize the genuine commitment of some high-profile political figures such as Winnie Nomzamo Mandela (affectionately referred to as Winnie). The power of her address was matched only by the incredible euphoria that was triggered by her mere presence at the African Tent in Huairou. As people in other regional tents and in Huairou in general realized what the source of the celebratory commotion was around the African Tent, they rushed to just get a glimpse of her. And she met the expectation in terms of the analysis what ought to be done. However, eventually she was to acquire the political position that would have enabled her to actualize some of the policies to impact South Africa where structural transformation for economic democratization is awaiting, and twenty years after Beijing.

Besides my translation of papers and messages delivered by young African girls in their plea for a better future, Winnie's visit was a most rewarding moment. To have the privilege of translating her message to all those who had come to the Tent was not simply a matter of honor, but the inspiration that Winnie was capable of providing. From the people's reaction to her speech, it was easy to understand that she was articulating what the ordinary and suffering people, especially women, everywhere would say and want to do if they had the forum to speak out and space to take action. Her speech (focusing on Africa) constituted a strong indication of her commitment to continue the struggle for liberation that, she argued, must include economic democratization. Powerful speeches without the spaces for actualization of visions remain as such: speeches, no matter how inspiring they might be.

While there was a discussion with the World Bank on the role of NGOs, grassroots organizations, and civil society at large, the impact of the globalization of the economy on the most disadvantaged sections of the world's population, particularly, was not properly addressed in the Beijing Conference.

On the whole, the actual world structure of economic and political power that dictates the rules at the international level was not altered by the Beijing Conference, no matter how powerful mere words could be. Under these conditions, besides some immediate gains and raised hopes, what could be objectively achieved that would be significant enough to contribute to set in motion a process of positive change in the living conditions and life course experiences of many people around the world did not happen.

Certainly the Platform for Action is, in principle, and in reality, to a certain degree, a compromise of different views. It is the final product of a work in which a certain popular input was made. But how has the Beijing Conference significantly contributed to positively affecting the curve of an increasing general poverty and its feminization?

***

For the secretary of state, the march to give meaning to some of the resolutions in the Beijing Platform for Action and Beijing Declaration has continued with a clear sense of purpose. Two decades after the Beijing Conference and on the occasion of the 2015 celebration, the new deadline for gender equality was set at 2030, with the following stipulation:

> We envisage a world where all women and girls have equal opportunities and rights by 2030. Step It Up asks governments to make national commitments that will close the gender equality gap—from laws and policies to national action plans and adequate investment. NOW is the time to Step It Up! (http://beijing20.unwomen.org/en/step-it-up; last accessed on December 17, 2015).[8]

Two decades after delivering her famous speech in Beijing, the celebration of Beijing +20 has coincided with the most critical campaign in the political career of Secretary of State Hillary Rodham Clinton, with her highest chance to become the first woman to lead the most powerful country in the world. When the factors that made it necessary to meet in Beijing are analyzed, they are still relevant about her own struggle to deal with both the "glass ceiling" and the "sticky floor." As Leslie Bennetts (2008: 230–231) argued:

> As we continue to dither over whether the United States is ready to elect its first woman president, the real problem is our own schizoid relationship with female gender roles—and the fact that we don't even recognize the true nature of what's bothering us. In many ways, Hillary's entire adult life can be read as one long struggle against the stereotypical roles that still pinion women to rigid, simplistic definitions, like butterflies under glass. As a brilliant young woman who came to age when burgeoning feminist movement was exploding the nation's understanding the roles women could play, Hillary seemed bold and fearless, nationally recognized as a comer before she arrived at law school.

Then First Lady Hillary Rodham Clinton's speech at the Beijing Conference back in 1995 resonated with women present in Beijing as well as those not attending the Conference who were longing and struggling for structural change toward gender and holistic equality locally, nationally, and globally. These in the struggle for gender equality are from a wide political spectrum in terms of views on nation-states and global affairs and their contradictions. Some may even be resigned to only the mere symbolism of just breaking the cycle of marginalization based on ascriptive factors such as race and gender. The election of a Black president has only started to dispel constructed myths and social structures that have reproduced historically skewed power on the basis of socially significant factors such as race, in this case. However, some of the outright resistance encountered by President Obama may be a prelude to what "President" Hillary Rodham Clinton might encounter, if or when elected, in terms of double standards in assessing effectiveness and plain resistance. Thus, the call for structural change still resonates. Nevertheless, her intelligence and stamina are consistent with what is needed to actualize at least one of the resolutions of the Beijing Platform for Action and the Beijing Declaration: Women's political empowerment everywhere. If she is elected President of the most powerful country in the world, the question remains how she will address the Beijing call for "Equality, Development and Peace."

Notes

1 Part of this article draws from earlier works including my article "Behind and Beyond Beijing: An African Perspective on the Fourth World Conference on Women," *CODESRIA Bulletin*, No. 3, 1996, adapted with permission from CODESRIA, and "Why Maman Went to Beijing" in Leon Knight (ed.) *Full Circle Twenty*, Robbinsdale, Guild Press, 1999, pp. 56–59.

2 This author had the honor of translating (from English to French) a powerful and inspiring speech delivered by the Honorable Winnie Mandela when she visited the African Tent in Huairou, and her presence attracted an exceptionally huge crowd as people continued to converge with indescribable excitement as words about her visit continued to spread.

3 Like in other regions of the world, for Africa there were pre-Beijing preparatory meetings that included: 1) the November 1994 Fifth African Conference on Women in Dakar (Senegal) in which I took part as an adviser to the United Nations Development Fund for Women (UNIFEM); and 2) the "Regional Forum of Women Leaders which was to Consider the Global Platform for Action in Preparation for the Fourth World Conference on Women," held in Addis Ababa in July 1995. Upon the invitation of the United Nations Economic Commission for Africa (UN-ECA), I served as a regional advisor to the UN-ECA in Addis Ababa (Ethiopia) on the Advancement of Women in Africa in preparation for the Beijing Conference. Part of my responsibilities toward the UN-ECA in Beijing was to help facilitate communication, mainly conducting simultaneous translation (English to French and vice-versa) of some events, especially organized by African NGOs during the NGO Forum in Huairou, including speeches of several African officials who visited the African Tent. I presented a paper "Women in the Democratization Process" under the African NGO theme "Democratization and the Economic Status of African Women."

4 As a member of the Executive Committee of AAWORD, I participated in the preparation of the Beijing Conference from an NGO perspective in serving as a member of the AAWORD Task Force (representing North America) for Beijing and also as a member of the NGO FORUM Beijing '95 "Task Force on Communication" working with the Planning Committee for the Preparation of the Beijing Conference. I attended the AAWORD General Assembly and seminar on "Women and Democratization in Africa: Challenges and Prospects" held in Pretoria (South Africa) in April 1995 and presented a paper on "Democratic Culture and Practice."

5 Since the Beijing Conference I have participated in numerous post-Beijing conferences, including invited presentations at Cornell, the UN Beijing +5 International Conference on Women as a member of the Executive Committee of the AAWORD, at the UN headquarters in New York, June 2000. Invited presentation on "ASSESSING BEIJING +20: An African perspective on Gender and Health Challenges Including HIV/AIDS, Ebola, Malaria" to a panel organized by the Voices of African Mothers (VAM) for the 59th Session of the United Nations' Commission on the Status of Women (CSW) and the Celebration of Beijing +20, New York, New York, March 2015.

6 In the case of Africa, in which I had more involvement, the UN-ECA was selected as the facilitator in charge of the regional preparatory meetings representing the UN and African member states. The African Women's Development and Communication Network (FEMNET) was selected as the African focal point whose role was to facilitate the coordination of NGO activities and their collaboration with the UN and governments. The UN-ECA and FEMNET were in charge of the regional preparatory meetings. In collaboration with the other NGOs, specific responsibilities were assigned for the planning and coordination of Beijing activities around major themes and subthemes such as "Women, Violence and Legal Rights," "Education," "Gender Planning and Training," "Health," "The Girl Child," "Poverty and Economic Empowerment," "Peace and Women in Conflict," "Media," and "Art, Culture and Sports." Various activities were coordinated by different specialized NGOs, such as the Environment

Liaison Center International (ELCI) and the Network of Rural Women Associations (NARWA/WEDO). The Association of African Women for Research and Development (AAWORD), which was joined later by Le Réseau des Femmes Africaines pour le Développement (REFAD-Network of African Women for Development), coordinated the theme of "Women in the Democratization Process" with a particular attention given the issue of political empowerment.

7 Under the motto of "Women's Eyes on the World Bank," the NGO-World Bank meeting was opened. The AAWORD executive secretary was selected by the NGOs of the world to read their statement and submit the signatures of participants protesting World Bank policies.

8 Copyright © 2016 by the United Nations Entity for Gender Equality and the Empowerment of Women (UN Women). All worldwide rights reserved.

References

Assié-Lumumba, N'Dri T. 2001. "Gender, Race and Human Capital Theory: Research Trends in the United States from the 1950s to the 1990s," *Journal of Comparative Education and International Relations in Africa*, Vol. 4, Nos. 1–2, December, pp. 1–25.

Assié-Lumumba, N'Dri T. 2007. *Women and Higher Education in Africa: Reconceptualizing Gender-Based Human Capabilities and Upgrading Human Rights to Knowledge*, Abidjan: CEPARRED.

Bennetts, Leslie. 2008. "Beyond Gender: The Revenge of the Postmenopausal Woman," in Susan Morrison (ed.), *Thirty Ways of Looking at Hillary: Reflections by Women Writers*. New York, NY: Harper Collins Publishers, pp. 230–247.

Clinton, Hillary Rodham. 1995. *United Nations Fourth World Conference on Women*, September 5–6, 1995, China. Retrieved from http://clinton3.nara.gov/WH/EOP/First_Lady/html/China/.

Davis, Angela Y. 1981. *Women, Race and Class*. New York: Random House.

Hill Collins, Patricia. 2000. *Black Feminist Thought: Knowledge, Consciousness and the Politics of Empowerment*. 2nd edition. New York: Routledge.

Mohanty, Chandra Talpade, Ann Russo, and Lourdes Torres. 1991. *Third World Women and the Politics of Feminism*. Bloomington and Indianapolis, IN: Indiana University Press.

Oyěwùmí, Oyèrónké. 1997. *The Invention of Women: Making an African Sense of Western Gender Discourses*. Minneapolis: University of Minnesota Press.

Steady, Filomina Chioma. 1987. "African Feminism: A Worldwide Perspective" in Terborg-Penn, Rosalyn, Sharon Harley, and Andrea Benton Rushing (eds.), *Women in Africa and the African Diaspora*. Washington, DC: Howard University Press, pp. 3–24.

Terborg-Penn, Rosalyn. 1987. "African Feminism: A Theoretical Approach to the History of Women in the African Diaspora," in Terborg-Penn, Rosalyn, Sharon Harley, and Andrea Benton Rushing (eds.), *Women in Africa and the African Diaspora*. Washington, DC: Howard University Press, pp. 43–63.

6

SEEING RED

Republicans and Democrats in Alaska View Hillary Clinton and Sarah Palin

Grant J. Rich

Being female and a politician in the United States represents a combination of identities that remains replete with controversy and lack of clarity, perhaps not surprisingly for a nation in which women were granted the right to vote less than one hundred years ago, in 1920, with the 19th Amendment to the U.S. Constitution. The case of Alaska, which became the 49th of the 50 U.S. states in 1959, is especially relevant to discussions of women in politics, as it has been closely associated with Republican politics since at least statehood, and recently attracted widespread attention with the nomination of then Alaska governor Sarah Palin as the Republican Party nominee for vice president in the 2008 U.S. presidential election.

Though numerous other psychology publications have detailed factors related to gender in the workplace (e.g., Hyde, 2004; Valian, 1998), including women in leadership in general (e.g., Crosby, 2008; Hollander, 2009), this chapter offers insight into what it means to be a female politician in the USA today, through the lens of a close examination of how two eminent female politicians in particular— Sarah Palin and Hillary Clinton—have been viewed in the unique political test laboratory of Alaska. How can one female candidate have been so popular, at least for a time, whereas another female candidate has been so popularly reviled? How can one reconcile the relative popularity of these figures in Alaska with their backgrounds and qualifications?

Perhaps several of the main differences between the candidates involve their personal, educational, and career backgrounds, as well as their values and beliefs. In terms of education, Idaho-born Palin attended six colleges (including community college) before graduating, then worked as an Anchorage sportscaster, later helping her husband, Todd, with his fishing business. Todd, her high school sweetheart, is perhaps best known as the four-time champion of the Iron Dog, the world's longest snowmobile race, which follows a course similar to that of the famous 1,100-mile-long Alaskan Iditarod sled dog race. Despite this rather unusual set of qualifications and choices, in 2006, Sarah Palin became the first woman elected Alaska governor, and polls taken in 2007 showed her with extraordinarily high approval ratings: 89% and 93% popularity among all voters. In contrast, Illinois-born Hillary Clinton has impeccable academic credentials, including an undergraduate degree from famous Wellesley College in political science and a J.D. in law from the prestigious Yale Law School. *The National Law Journal* has listed her more than once among the one hundred most influential lawyers in the USA. In her political career she has served as United States secretary of state, and as a United States senator. Of course, in her personal life, she married a very different man than Todd Palin, when she wed Bill Clinton, the future governor of Arkansas and future president of the United States. Yet Clinton appears to be a very unpopular politician among Alaskans, despite (or because) of this background and these credentials.

This chapter also explores the reasons behind why these politicians are received so differently in Alaska, referencing their backgrounds in the context of the special state of Alaska. In addition to the usual differences between Republican and Democrat candidates in terms of topics such as "God, Guns, and Gays," these two candidates also share different philosophies and beliefs on such topics as health care and religion (such as Palin's opposition to abortion, even in cases of incest and rape, and her advocacy for teaching creationism in the public schools).

Among the points for discussion will be the history and present demographics of Alaska, the largest state in the USA geographically, but the least densely populated state, with under one million residents. One issue relevant to political views of the population is the education level and the educational opportunities for Alaskans. The state has no medical or law school, and a 2008 report from the Alaska Commission on Postsecondary Education reports that 38% of ninegraders will not have high school diplomas ten years from now. The commission noted then that Alaska ranked last (50th) in numbers of ninth graders likely to have a bachelor's degree in ten years. Social problems also plague the state, and Alaska has ranked in the top worst states for domestic violence, the worst state for rape per capita in 1993 (and since 1976, it has ranked in the top five states in the nation for the highest rate of reported rape per capita). Some studies find that Alaska has the highest rate per capita of alcoholism in the USA, and in 2006, NAMI ranked it the number two worst state for suicide per capita. Finally, 2008 data from the Violence Policy Center found that Alaska led the nation in per capita gun deaths (Rich, 2010).

In sum, Alaska is unique in many ways among other states. While its beauty is truly extraordinary, drawing thousands of tourists annually, and its natural resources are abundant, its special characteristics and history lead to political views in the population that merit careful exploration. In addition to the quantitative data, one must also point to the special Alaskan spirit of independence and self-reliance, a quality that makes many Alaskans skeptical and indeed angry when it comes to what is disparagingly referred to as the lower 48 states. There is a feeling that federal policy-makers in places such as Washington, D.C., may not have the faintest idea what policies may or may not fit or be appropriate to the special state of Alaska. A bridge to nowhere for someone in Washington, D.C., is most definitely a bridge to somewhere for someone in Alaska.

Therefore perhaps it is no contradiction at all that a state can revere a female winner of the Iditarod, the grueling, and sometimes dangerous, thousand-mile-long sled dog race, and celebrate its first female governor and her fondness for moose burgers, but revile an Ivy League–educated, well-traveled politician such as Hillary Clinton. Thus, an aim of this chapter is to clarify how such a political reality makes sense in Alaska and what the implications may be for other female politicians elsewhere as well. Data for the chapter include memoirs by Palin and Clinton (such as Palin's *Going Rogue* and Clinton's *Living History*), as well as academic scholarship, some journalistic accounts, and survey data.

Alaska versus New York

To understand the reasons behind why these politicians are received so differently, it is valuable to reference their backgrounds in the context of the special state of Alaska, where Palin served as governor, versus New York, where Clinton served as U.S. senator.

Alaska is geographically the largest state in the USA, and is about two-and-one-half times the size of the next largest state, Texas. That said, it is the fourth least populous state in the USA, with slightly under 750,000 people. It is the least densely populated state in the USA, and in fact if New York City had the population density of Alaska, there would be just about only 16 people living in that city. Along with Hawai'i, it was one of the last two states to be admitted to the USA, in 1959. Its economy is largely based upon oil, gas, and fishing, along with seasonal summer tourism. Demographically, according to the 2010 U.S. Census, it is about 64% non-Hispanic Caucasian, 15% Native Alaskan/Native American, 6.4% Asian/Pacific Islander, 3.3% African-American, 5.5% Hispanic/Latino (of any race), and 7% mixed race. Since statehood, Alaska has reliably voted Republican in most national elections. For instance, its electoral votes went Republican in all elections except 1964. Barack Obama lost Alaska in both 2008 (59.49% to 37.83%) and in 2012 (when he earned 40% of the vote). Given its small population, Alaska has only one member of the House of Representatives, Don Young, and the congressman has won 22 consecutive terms, most recently in 2014, and he is the most senior Republican in the House. His position, with over four decades as Alaska's lone congressman, seems very secure, and thus he has been able to continue to easily win election despite controversies such as his use of a racial slur in a radio interview in 2013, when he commented that his father "used to hire 50 to 60 wetbacks to pick tomatoes" on his farm (Milbank, 2013).

In contrast to Alaska, New York, where Hillary Clinton has served as U.S. Senator, reflects a much different reality. New York State is the fourth most populous state and seventh most densely populated state in the USA. In addition, its location in the Northeast/Mid-Atlantic region of the contiguous USA, places it geographically more centrally to much of the USA population, as is reflected in the fact the most locations in Alaska are a four hour time difference from New York. New York City itself, where the Clintons maintain a home, has a population of close to 8.5 million, a significant contrast to the population of about 301,000 of Anchorage, Alaska's largest city, or to the approximately 32,000 population of Juneau, Alaska's state capital, or to Wasilla, the town where Sarah Palin served as mayor, which has a population of under 8,000 according to the 2010 Census. Economically, New York State dwarfs Alaska, and it ranks third behind California and Texas; notably, if New York State were a country, it would rank as the 15th largest economy internationally. New York City includes Wall Street in the financial district, but New York State also ranks high in agriculture, and among the top five states in agricultural production, including apples, dairy, potatoes, and grapes. Demographically, according to the 2010 U.S. Census it is about 65.7% non-Hispanic Caucasian, 16% African-American, 7% Asian, 3% mixed race, 0.6% Native Alaskan/Native American, 7.5% other race, and 17% Hispanic/Latino (of any race). New York State much more closely resembles the USA as a whole demographically, than does Alaska: the Census reports that for the USA as a whole, one counts about 77% Caucasians, 13% African-Americans, 5.5% Asian/Pacific Islanders, 1.2% Native Alaskans/Native Americans, 2.4% mixed race, and 17% Hispanic/Latino (of any race). In recent decades, New York State as a whole has tended toward Democrats, though there is Republican support, especially upstate, outside of urban regions. Barack Obama won the state in 2008 and 2012, with roughly 63% of the vote in each election. In contrast to Alaska's one member, New York State has 27 members of the House of Representatives, of which 18 are Democrats.

Though Alaska offers much in terms of natural beauty, a notable feature of the state has been the persistence and severity of a number of enduring social problems. For instance, its suicide rate is consistently one of the highest in the USA (in 2002, it was double the national rate). For six major types of crimes it has ranked 43rd worst of 50 states, and since 1976 it has ranked among the five worst states for rape. Recent polls have also shown Alaska among the five worst states for both domestic violence and for assault. Alaska's school drop-out rate, remains high, double the national average in 2005–2006, and in 2006 an Alaskan Commission found Alaska ranked last among the 50 states in the number of ninth graders who will likely have a bachelor's degree in ten years. In addition, recent polls listed three Alaska cities (Anchorage, Fairbanks, and Juneau) as among the top ten most expensive cities to live in the USA, and in 2006 Alaska topped the nation in median credit card debt (Rich, 2010; 2014). Though New York State faces challenges as well, in comparison to Alaska they proportionally seem, in general, less persistent and severe.

Childhoods and Backgrounds of Palin and Clinton

Given that both Palin and Clinton have been successful female politicians, but reflect such different values and are both polarizing figures, what may be learned through analysis of their childhoods and backgrounds? Even a cursory examination reveals significant differences between the two women, differences that can be linked to their receptions by their associated constituents. Of course, a long history in psychology has utilized examination of childhood experiences to illuminate adult behavior and achievement of eminent figures. For instance, the psychoanalytically influenced Erik Erikson (2013/1958) famously wrote a psychobiography on Martin Luther's youth, and creativity researchers, utilizing both psychometric approaches (e.g., Simonton, 1994), and case study approaches (e.g., Gardner, 1996) have emphasized the role of early experience on later life. Thus exploration of the present politicians' backgrounds is supported by a significant research tradition.

Sarah Palin (b. 1964) was born in Idaho, to a mother who worked as a school secretary and part-time lunch lady, and a father who worked as a science teacher, track coach, and occasional bartender for tourists. She was the third of four children. The Palins moved to Skagway, Alaska, when Sarah was still an infant, then relocated to Eagle River, Alaska, in 1969, and finally to Wasilla in 1971. Wasilla is probably best known as both the "Duct Tape Capital of the World" and as the home of the original official restart of the famous Iditarod sled dog race (Brown, 2006; Palin, 2009, pp. 64–66). In her memoir, Palin (2009) emphasizes the religious focus of her family upbringing; her mother, especially, was active in church, becoming evangelical after time in the Catholic Church. Palin's mother would read her the Bible, and religiously minded fiction such as *Jonathan Livingston Seagull* and works by C. S. Lewis, as well as poems by secular Alaskan poet Robert Service (Palin, 2009, p. 14), known for poems such as "Bessie's Boil" (Service, 2002), formative experiences for Sarah. As television programs could be delayed up to a week in the 1970s in Alaska, much activity was centered on the outdoors, and Sarah recounts joyous memories of time spent "bagging a moose" before school with her father (Palin, 2009, p. 31), experiences probably quite unusual for many outside of Alaska. In school Palin was active playing flute in band and in sports, especially basketball (she was team co-captain for the team that won the Alaska state championship), and served as the head of the Fellowship of Christian Athletes. As Palin notes, "Everything I ever needed to know I learned on the basketball court" (p. 41). After high school, Palin attended several colleges, including the University of Hawai'i in Hilo and Hawai'i Pacific University in Honolulu in 1982, then North Idaho College in 1983, then the University of Idaho in 1984, then Matanuska-Susitna College in Alaska in 1985, before returning to the University of Idaho in 1986, ultimately graduating with a bachelor's degree in communications in 1987. While in college, notable among her accomplishments, she earned money toward her education by participating in beauty pageants (Palin, 2009), winning the Miss Wasilla pageant in 1984 and finishing third for Miss Alaska. She played flute in the talent part of the competition. As for role models, Sarah mentions that while "other college students had had posters of Metallica or Michael Jordan on their dorm walls, mine had been plastered with a *Vogue* magazine spread of Libby Riddles," the first female winner of the Iditarod sled dog race, and a figure Palin views as an "outsider," shattering an "ice ceiling" (2009, p. 122). Palin reports she voted Republican beginning with her first election in 1982 at age 18, and points to Republicans' views on the military and free market as reasons, as well as her view that Jimmy Carter was letting the USA be "pushed around" in the Iran hostage crisis, and was retreating from the Soviets in "embarrassed pacifism" (p. 46). Upon graduation, her early jobs included working as a sportscaster in Anchorage, and ample work in her husband's commercial fishing business.

Hillary Clinton (b. 1947), was born in Chicago, Illinois, and raised in the nearby suburbs, to a mother who was a homemaker and a father who managed a small business. She has two younger brothers. In school Clinton was active in several sports, including baseball, and in Brownies and Girl Scouts. In her commitment to social justice and social change, she was influenced by her United Methodist youth minister, and with him she met Martin Luther King Jr. in 1962. She was also active on student council, with the student newspaper, was a member of the National Honor Society, and was honored as a National Merit Finalist, a national recognition. In 1965, she entered prestigious Wellesley College and majored in political science, also serving as president of the College Republicans. Though she had volunteered for the 1964 presidential campaign of Republican Barry Goldwater, her thinking changed in college, especially in light of Republican views of the Vietnam War and the civil rights movement (Clinton, 2003). In college, she interned at the House Republican Conference and attended the 1968 Republican National Convention. She graduated with departmental honors and offered Wellesley College's first student commencement address, and was written about in *Life* magazine. Like Sarah Palin, she worked in the fishing industry in Alaska; however, Clinton worked just one summer in a salmon cannery, also working as a dishwasher in the state. Afterward, Clinton entered the prestigious Yale Law School, serving on the editorial board of the *Yale Review of Law and Social Action*, and volunteering for New Haven Legal Services to assist the poor. In 1970 she began work with Marian Wright Edelman, the iconic leader of what would become the Children's Defense Fund. Clinton published her first scholarly article (on children and the law) in 1973 in the well-respected *Harvard Educational Review* (Rodham, 1973), and during her postgraduate study at Yale's Child Study Center worked as an attorney for Edelman's organization. On her move to Arkansas, she become one of only two female law faculty at the University of Arkansas, and continued publishing scholarly articles on children and the law.

Choice of Husbands and Political Impact

Many scholars have noted the importance of relationships with quality significant others for developing extraordinary professional accomplishments, such as great creative, career, or scholarly achievements (e.g., John-Steiner, 2006). Thus it is worth exploring the nature and influence of Palin and Clinton's choices of spouses, and what that may suggest about values, personalities, and professional and career development.

In her memoir, Palin (2009) describes how she met her future husband, Todd, while both were high school students in Wasilla. Sarah recounts how impressed she was with Todd, who was considered the best ball player in school (p. 33) and how awed she was that he owned not one, but two vehicles, a Mustang and a Ford pickup. Sarah describes how she was struck by Todd's comparative wealth and work ethic, how he liked the environment, respected the land, and hated prejudice, and that the "clincher" for Sarah was when Todd was baptized at sports camp (p. 37). Sarah reports that she learned about social diversity from Todd, and his "exotic" family (p. 35), as Todd was part Yupik eskimo. Todd's grandmother was among the first female commercial fishermen and Sarah emphasizes her traditional background, such as her ability to weave grass baskets and sew squirrel skins into garments (p. 118). Todd's grandfather was a boat builder and fisherman. Sarah reports being impressed with the successful business of Todd's family, and that it strengthened her beliefs in related Republican values regarding supporting government policies that promoted worker motivation, rather than government handouts. Though Todd graduated high school and took some college classes, he did not graduate college. In 1988, Sarah married Todd by eloping. Todd worked as a baggage handler for the airlines and plowed snow at nights. Later he would work one week on, one week off, on Prudhoe Bay. Palin describes Todd as a "blue collar union hand, a production operator wearing a hard hat and steel-toe boots . . . he's not in management. He actually works" (Palin, 2009, p. 95). Their children's names reflect some of the family's values: for instance, Track is named after the sport; Bristol is named after both the Alaska community and the Bristol, Connecticut, hometown of ESPN, the sports channel (p. 57); and Piper is named for the type of airplane Todd flies (p. 75). Among Todd's other work was a snow-machine/ATV business. Perhaps Todd's most notable achievement is that he is a four-time champion of the Iron Dog snowmobile race, which runs approximately 2,000 miles, and, though the trail varies, typically runs from near Wasilla through Nome, the endpoint of the Iditarod sled dog race. Though Todd has never been a registered Republican, he did register to vote for the first time in 1989, when he was about 35 years old (Palin, 2009).

Hillary Clinton married a very different man than did Sarah Palin. Hillary met Bill Clinton in 1971 when both were law students at Yale University, and both campaigned together for Democratic presidential candidate George McGovern. Bill had already graduated from Georgetown University and earned a prestigious Rhodes Scholarship to Oxford University. Hillary followed Bill to his home state of Arkansas, where career options were more bountiful than on the East Coast, and they married in 1975. Bill Clinton ran but lost a congressional race in 1974, but was elected Arkansas attorney general in 1976. In 1978 Bill Clinton was elected governor of Arkansas, though in 1980 Bill Clinton lost his re-election attempt. Daughter Chelsea was born in 1980, and during these years Hillary remained very active professionally, especially in legal matters relating to children, poverty, and health care. For instance, she was named first female chair of Legal Services Corporation in 1978. Bill was re-elected governor in 1982 and held the position for ten years. In 1992 he earned the Democratic nomination for U.S. president, ultimately serving two terms in the White House (Clinton, 2004). Since leaving the Oval Office, Bill Clinton has remained enormously active, especially with fundraising, public speaking, and work with charitable groups (including his own Clinton Foundation) and humanitarian organizations, such as for the 2004 Asian tsunami, the 2005 Hurricane Katrina, and the 2010 Haiti earthquake (he was named UN special envoy to Haiti in 2009).

When one compares the backgrounds of Todd Palin and Bill Clinton, one is struck by the different intellectual, cultural, and political worlds the two men inhabit. While too much speculation is beyond the scope of an academic psychology chapter, one wonders what dinnertime conversations at the two households must have been like over the past several decades. Are the Palins' conversations focused on salmon fishing, snow-machining, moose-meat, and Bible study? Are the Clintons' conversations focused on international events, public policy, and matters of national concern? What is the impact of years of daily conversation in such disparate sociocultural milieux? What effect does such an environment have on both personality development and on public perceptions?

Adult Political Experiences

Sarah Palin's first political role was her election to Wasilla City Council in 1992. Wasilla has grown to nearly 8,000 people by 2010, and is the largest city in its borough, and Palin won the election 530 to 310 votes. As Palin (2009) notes, her constituents included neighbors, family, friends, and people she would see at the hockey rink, post office, and grocery store. In 1996 she ran for Wasilla mayor at age 32, defeating the incumbent, 651 to 440 votes. She worked for less government and more individual control, and sought power, noting, in a sports metaphor comparing political leadership to dog mushing, that "if you're not the lead dog, the view never changes" (2009, p. 70). She ran and won again in 1999, 909 to 292 votes. Among her activities while mayor, she cut property taxes and stopped property and business inventory taxes, reduced the museum budget, and facilitated the creation of bicycle paths, as well as increased funding for the police and sewers. In her second term, she led the initiative for a municipal sports center to be financed by a sales tax and a close to $15-million-dollar bond issue; voters approved the measure. The center was built, though Wasilla's debt increased due to the sports complex, water, and streets projects (Phillips, 2008).

After serving her terms as mayor, Palin entered state level politics with an unsuccessful bid for lieutenant governor in 2002. In 2003 she was appointed to the Alaska Oil and Gas conservation commission, which works on issues related to integrity and safety. She resigned in 2004. In 2006 Palin beat incumbent Alaska governor Frank Murkowski in the Republican gubernatorial primary, and defeated the former Alaska governor, Democrat Tony Knowles, in the overall election for governor. In the election she had positioned herself as someone who was not part of the Juneau "good old boys' club" and an outsider, a position also reflected in the title of her memoir, *Going Rogue* (2009, p. 85).

In 2008, John McCain offered Palin the position of vice presidential candidate as his running mate on the national Republican presidential ticket. Palin (2009) opens her memoir with an account of how she was at the Alaska State Fair at the Alaska Right to Life booth (Sarah's daughter Piper was the poster child for this group), when McCain called to make the offer. Palin notes her approval rating since her election as governor in 2006 had reached 88 percent, though she "didn't put much stock on fickle polls" (p. 6). Though McCain and the Republicans may have thought Palin's high polls numbers, her potential attraction to the religious right, and her gender, as well as her status as Washington outsider would assist in the election, Palin soon faced many questions from the media, the Democrats, and some Republicans about her experience, views, and qualifications. Palin faced some tough interviewers (such as Katie Couric of CBS News) and was parodied by pundits and late-night comedians (such as Tina Fey of *Saturday Night Live*), and Republican poll numbers declined, with Barack Obama the winner in the November 2008 presidential election. Since that election Palin resigned as Alaska governor (in July 2009), has worked in journalism, such as for *Fox News*, has written her best-selling memoir and two other books (Palin 2013a, 2013b), and has advocated for the Tea Party movement as one of its major leaders. Several times since the 2008 election, she has mentioned a possible run for U.S. president.

In contrast to Palin, Hillary Clinton has held many more state level and national level political positions. While she was First Lady of Arkansas she served as chair of the Arkansas Educational Standards Committee, practiced law with the Rose Law Firm (where she was first female partner), was named the first chair of the American Bar Association's Commission on Women in the Profession, was named Arkansas Woman of the Year in 1983, and was named more than once by the *National Law Journal* as one of the one hundred most influential lawyers in the USA. She also served on the boards of Children's Defense fund, and TCBY and Wal-Mart Stores (these last two companies are Arkansas based). She was the first female member of the Wal-Mart board. When Bill Clinton became U.S. president, Hillary became the first First Lady to hold an advanced degree. Among her activities was heading the National Health Care Reform starting in 1993, and helping to lead the passage of federal State Children's Health Insurance Program in 1997. She also helped Attorney General Janet Reno institute the Office on Violence Against Women, and in 1997 she spearheaded the Adoption and Safe Families Act. Hillary Clinton traveled broadly as First Lady, and visited close to eighty nations, mostly working on women's issues, as in her speech in the 1995 World Conference on Women, in China, when she described "women's rights" as best characterized as "human rights" (Clinton, 2003). Unlike Palin, who worked to decrease the museum budget while she was Wasilla mayor, Clinton advocated to preserve the history and heritage of the USA, serving as founding chair of the Save America's Treasures program, which worked to save items such as the flag that inspired the U.S. national anthem. In 2000, she ran for U.S. senator in New York, and won with 55% of the vote, on a platform that included a plan for tax credits for job creation and tax cuts for college tuition. She was the state's first female U.S. senator. In 2006 she won re-election with 67% of the vote. Though she ran for the 2008 Democratic presidential nomination, she lost to Barack Obama, though in November 2008 she accepted Obama's offer to become U.S. secretary of state, and near confirmation time in early 2009 her approval ratings hovered around the mid-60s percentile. Clinton's approach as secretary was to work to repair damages she saw to the international reputation of the USA, damages that in part resulted from U.S. foreign policy in Iraq and Afghanistan, and later, in 2010, from the leaked WikiLeaks diplomatic cables. She also utilized her leadership position to continue to advocate for women, such as empowering women economically and health-wise, as in her work to offer cooking stoves to women across the globe. Echoing her 1995 comments on women, in 2011 Clinton spoke before the United Nations and affirmed that "gay rights are human rights." Her other accomplishments as secretary included work on an agreement to establish diplomatic relations between Turkey and Armenia, and responding to the Arab Spring protests and political developments beginning in 2011. After noting she was not interested in serving a second term, Clinton left the position in early 2013, after John Kerry had been named her successor. After leaving that role, she has served the Clinton Foundation, especially focusing on early childhood development, and also partnered on projects with the Gates Foundation on advocating for women and girls around the globe. In April 2015 she announced her candidacy for U.S. president in the 2016 campaign, and is widely considered the Democratic front-runner.

Palin and Clinton have had adult political experiences that differ enormously. Palin has held municipality-level positions for a small community, and served part of a term as governor of a state with a population of under one million, and run unsuccessfully once for national office. Clinton, in contrast, has lived much of her life in the national spotlight, both as a First Lady of a state (Arkansas) and of the USA, and as a leader in her own right as U.S. senator and as U.S. secretary of state. Their international experiences also differ dramatically, with Palin receiving her passport in 2006 and visiting a handful of nations (Kuwait, Iraq, Germany, India, and Israel) on brief visits, while Clinton visited 112 nations as U.S. secretary of state, more than any other person in that position (in addition to meeting many world leaders in her extensive international travels while U.S. First Lady)

(Clinton, 2003). Later in the chapter these disparate experiences will be compared in terms of how they help form public perceptions of the two politicians.

Political Positions

Politically, perhaps it is not surprising that Palin and Clinton largely follow party lines for the vast majority of their political positions, though it can be argued that Clinton is a more moderate Democrat in many of her views than Palin is a moderate Republican.

In brief, in terms of social issues, Palin opposes same-sex marriage (favoring a traditional definition of marriage, Palin, 2009, p. 143), supports capital punishment, and opposes abortion, even in cases of rape, incest, and embryonic stem cell scientific research. For instance, she describes how she was appalled when her 17-year-old son, Track, injured in a hockey game, could not even get a glass of water at the hospital without parental permission, but that a "thirteen-year-old girl could undergo a painful invasive and scary abortion and no parent even had to be notified" (Palin, 2009, pp. 168–169). She supports sex education in schools that includes discussion of contraception but encourages abstinence. She supports discussion of creationism in public school lessons on evolution. In her memoir, Palin discusses the "nonsense" of gun bans (2009, p. 133) and reports she is a life-long NRA member; in fact, as she notes, Alaska has the highest per capita NRA membership in the USA. Palin has reported she had "plenty of backup when telling Hollywood liberals what [she] thought about their asinine plans to ban guns . . . we had to control predators, such as wolves" (p. 134). Palin also reports personally enjoying guns as when she describes clay shooting while pregnant with Piper, and "in a nod to our Second Amendment," having her baby shower at a shooting range (pp. 75–76). Though Palin considers herself a conservationist, and spends ample time in her memoir (2009) discussing how she and her family enjoy and love the Alaska outdoors, Palin supports offshore drilling in ANWR (Arctic National Wildlife Refuge) and is skeptical about global warming, unsure if it is part of nature's cycles or partly caused by humans. Though, besides her run for U.S. vice president and Tea Party leadership roles, most of Palin's experience has been in Alaska, in foreign policy, she has made statements strongly supporting Israel. Before 2007, she had not been outside North America, though after obtaining a passport in 2006, she was able to visit Kuwait and Iraq, and even make a stop at Landstuhl Regional Medical Center in Germany, two summers later visiting "our Guard in Kosovo and [spending] another day visiting the wounded at Landstuhl" (2009, p. 166). Later, in 2011, she increased her international experience with brief travel to India and Israel.

In brief, in terms of social issues, on abortion Clinton is pro-choice, but has stated she hopes that abortions would be safe and rare, and the women had other options, such as adoption and foster care, and has worked for reductions in teenage pregnancy rates. Clinton supports the death penalty but was a co-sponsor of the Innocence Protection Act, which became the Justice for All Act in 2004 and offers funding for DNA testing post-conviction for those sentenced under federal law to the death penalty. Like many Americans, her views on GLBTQA (gay, lesbian, bisexual, transgender, questioning, and allied) issues have evolved over time. About ten years ago, though she indicated she would not oppose efforts for same-sex marriage in New York State, she did support the Defense of Marriage Act and had said she personally opposed gay marriage, and in 2008 she supported civil unions as an alternative to same-sex marriage. However, in 2015 she offered her support for same-sex marriage. Earlier she has shown other types of support for the gay and lesbian community. For instance, in terms of integrating troops in the military, she noted that "you don't need to be straight to fight and die for your country. You just need to shoot straight" (Clinton, 2003, pp. 241–242). On gun control, Clinton has expressed respect for the Second Amendment, and has noted the need to balance the right to own guns with the importance of keeping guns from criminals. She has favored tough gun control laws. Planned Parenthood has commended Clinton for her work as U.S. senator on sex education and has welcomed her candidacy for 2016 U.S. president (Planned Parenthood, 2015). In an earlier section of this chapter, Clinton's extensive experience in foreign policy was discussed, as reflected in a number of her roles, from First Lady of the USA to U.S. secretary of state. Though these politicians' political positions diverge widely, they help explain the reception of the two politicians in their respective communities and among their respective constituents, as will be discussed later in this chapter.

Why Palin and Clinton Are Polarizing: Love and Hate but Not Love-Hate

Both Palin and Clinton tend to elicit strong emotional reactions; voters tend to love or hate each of them, but not simultaneously love and hate them. It is worth exploring why such disparate female politicians as these two women elicit strong reactions.

Palin is an interesting case, in that initially part of her attraction to John McCain and the Republicans for the 2008 presidential campaign was that she had enormously high approval ratings in Alaska as governor. For instance, in her memoir, Palin (2009, p. 6) notes her approval ratings had been as high as 88 percent. However, while Palin was known in Alaska since her 2006 election as governor, two years earlier, nationally she was largely unknown. Soon after being selected as the vice presidential candidate she scored very high in the polls, especially with Republicans, and in early September 2008, she even polled more favorably than McCain (Rasmussen Reports, 2008a). However, as the 2008 presidential campaign progressed, Palin's favorability ratings declined, as a response to a *USA Today*/Gallup poll question asking if she was ready to serve as president if needed revealed that 39% of respondents said she was ready, 33% said she was not, and almost a third (29%) had no opinion, an intriguing result that perhaps is indicative of how little many in the lower 48 states knew about this vice presidential candidate (Page, 2008). Notably, these low poll numbers are comparable to the lowest Hillary Clinton received in the White House (in 1994). The general public quickly developed polarized views of Palin; for instance, one month after she became McCain's running mate, Palin was viewed as both more favorably and less favorably than the Democrat's choice for vice president, Joe Biden (Rasmussen Reports, 2008b). In general, those potential voters skeptical of Palin voiced concern over what they perceived to be her lack of experience, especially at the national and international levels; their general lack of knowledge about her; and their concerns over some of her socially conservative views, such as on abortion, teaching creationism, and rights for the LGBTQ population. An interview with Katie Couric (2008) of *CBS News* led to declines in Palin's poll numbers, as skeptics felt Palin was uninformed about national and international events. For instance, when Couric asked Palin what newspapers and magazines she regularly read to establish her "worldview," Palin responded vaguely that she "read most of them, again with a great appreciation for the press, for the media." When Couric pressed, and asked what specifically Palin had read, Palin answered, "All of them, any of them that have been in front of me all these years." In her memoir, Palin (2009, p. 207), writes that she was "shocked" when Couric asked this question, and that she "should have asked her what *she* reads." Other media began parodies of Palin, perhaps most notably Tina Fey on *Saturday Night Live*. While some of the parodies focused on Palin's perceived lack of qualifications to be a "heartbeat away from the Presidency," at times the parodies poked fun at Alaska, including Alaska natives, in sketches that a number of Alaskans found offensive and morally repugnant.

As evidence that while Palin has drawn intense criticism, and elicits strong negative emotions among some voters, others have had enormous respect for her; one may note, for instance, that in 2009, Sarah Palin came in second in the Gallup poll of "most admired women." There, she placed behind Hillary Clinton, with Michelle Obama and German Chancellor Angela Merkel also in the top ten. However, rankings seem to show Palin's power waning since 2008. For example, though she featured in the 2010 *Time Magazine* list of the 100 most influential people in the world, she was not on its 2011 list (Goudreau, 2011). Similarly Palin was not on the 2015 *Forbes* list of the 100 most powerful women in the world, a list on which Hillary Clinton placed second (Howard, 2015). Indeed, a recent Public Policy Polling survey found that among Alaskans, Palin was the only candidate of all the Republican candidates in the poll that could not beat Clinton in a hypothetical one-on-one comparison; additionally, Palin ranked sixth from the top when the choices were confined to Republican candidates, behind the now more popular conservative Republicans Ted Cruz and Rand Paul (Public Policy Pollint, 2014).

Hillary Clinton also has long been considered a politically polarizing figure. In fact, one historian argued Clinton "has been uniquely controversial and contradictory since she first appeared on the national radar screen" (Troy, 2006, p. 4).

For instance, several factors appeared to impact her approval ratings as First Lady of the USA. Gallup poll numbers during these years tended to follow party lines, with about 70–90% of Democrats but just 20–40% of Republicans viewing her favorably; in addition, women tended to rate Clinton more favorably by approximately ten points (Burrell, 2000). Clinton's involvement with health-care reform also was associated with a decline in her numbers, which began in the high 50s percentile in her first year as First Lady but fell to the mid-30s percentile in 1994. Interestingly, despite all of Clinton's professional activities as First Lady, her approval numbers were highest in the wake of the Lewinsky investigation, perhaps reflecting public sympathy rather than understanding of the highly technical and political public policy, legal, and health-care work in which Hillary Clinton had been immersed for years (Burrell, 2000). The famous Ivy League communications professor Kathleen Hall Jamieson has written that Clinton, as a female politician, unlike male politicians, has had to publicly juggle the worlds of career and family, challenging and mirroring public attitudes about women and women's roles. As a woman, Clinton was especially subject to disparaging and degrading public comments, above and beyond what is typical of public figures in general, and these comments included misogynistic comments posted on the Internet, including sexual humiliation. Regarding the double bind faced by Clinton, Jamieson notes that public perceptions of this leading politician serve as a sort of Rorschach test for societal views on gender and can function as a gauge of social change and progress as people project their general views of the issues upon her specifically (Jamieson, 1995; 2007). Jamieson (2007) also notes that the unflattering and demeaning views of Clinton over the decades reflect a "long-lived fear of women in politics. For example, we know that there's language to condemn female speech that doesn't exist for male speech. We call women's speech shrill and strident. And Hillary Clinton's laugh was being described as a cackle." Despite such evidence of strong emotions, indeed hatred on the part of some persons, Clinton also has many admirers and indeed true believers and devotees to her cause and to her personally. For instance, Clinton has been assessed as "most admired woman in the USA" in the respected Gallup poll nineteen times.

***

While some in the lower 48 states may be dumbfounded at how Sarah Palin could be selected as the U.S. vice presidential candidate for a major political party, many Alaskans are just as dumbfounded about how such an "out of touch" egghead (think Adlai Stevenson) as Hillary Clinton could possibly represent their interests. Alaska is not New York State, and it is not the USA as a whole either. In many ways it is special, and unique.

Thus when Alaskans hear Sarah Palin talk about some local passions, such as dog mushing or snow-machines, they are excited. Locals could connect approvingly with her reports of serving moose chili to her children or seeing black bear and cubs from the governor's mansion. When Katie Couric or Tina Fey put Palin under pressure, and caused her embarrassment, for many Alaskans, this seemed like a personal attack on Alaska and the Alaskan way of life. Such emotional responses, gut instincts, and moral intuitions to political decision making are in keeping with much psychological research, such as classic work on the peripheral route of persuasion (Petty & Cacioppo, 1996) and recent work on moral and political psychology by Haidt (2012). It must be remembered that no sitting president of the USA has even visited the state of Alaska, other than brief refueling stops while en route to other, usually international destinations. For many Alaskans, the fact that Hillary Clinton has been to many of the capitals of the world in her international travels counts for far less than the fact that Sarah Palin lives close by, in Wasilla, the duct tape capital of the world. While some in the contiguous United States may be stunned that Todd Palin was well into adulthood before registering to vote, in Alaska, politics, even state politics, let alone national or international politics, often seems irrelevant to lives in many rural communities, many of which are accessible only by air or by sea. When Palin refers to John Kerry as an "elitist loon" (2009, p. 181) it resonates with many Alaskans, who fail to see the value of this French-speaking politician for diplomacy, in a state where, aside from English, a number of indigenous languages are spoken. A telling example of this local perspective came when Sarah Palin called to congratulate Lance Mackey on winning the 2007 Iditarod sled dog race. Mackey, a hero for many Alaskans, picked up the phone, asking "Hey! How ya doing, sir?" unaware that the governor was a woman. The following year, Mackey also was victorious—and ready for his call from the governor: to help him remember her name, he had named one of his sled dogs "Sarah" (Palin, 2009, pp. 190–191). In Alaska, one's dogs are often more important than politician's names.

Ample research in social psychology, especially the social psychology of persuasion and attraction, supports the view that similarity is closely associated with liking (e.g., Cialdini, 2006; Myers, 2012; Pratkanis & Aronson, 2001). We like—and are persuaded by—who we perceive to be similar to ourselves. Few psychological concepts are as simple, at least in basic form, and as well supported by research, as this one. When Palin and Clinton are viewed through this lens, the polarizing nature of their reception among disparate groups of voters largely disappears. Are you one of us? Come election time, this question is one about which voters will be thinking—and feeling.

Postscript

As this chapter goes to press, results of the March 2016 Alaska caucuses and April 2016 New York primaries are available. In Alaska, the Democratic candidate perceived more as a Washington outsider, and as a rogue/rebel/renegade candidate was victorious. Thus, in the Democratic Caucus Bernie Sanders won by a landslide with 81.6% of the vote to Hillary Clinton's 18.4%. For the Republican Caucus, Ted Cruz defeated Donald Trump (36.4% to 33.5%). Notably, in January 2016 Sarah Palin offered her endorsement of Donald Trump. In the New York Democratic primary, Clinton, with her close connections with the state and more moderate positions, won with about 57% of the vote compared to approximately 42% of the vote earned by Sanders. In the Republican primary, New Yorker Trump was able to marshal his local support and won with about 60% of the vote. These data support the arguments, evidence, and conclusions presented in this chapter, which was originally written in May 2015. As an additional update to the chapter, it should be noted President Barack Obama visited Alaska in September 2015; among his activities was a visit with 2011 Iditarod champion John Baker and his dogs in Kotzebue.

References

Brown, T. (Ed.). (2006). *Iditarod fact book* (2nd ed.). Kenmore, WA: Epicenter Press.

Burrell, B. (2000). Hillary Rodham Clinton as first lady: The people's perspective. *The Social Science Journal, 37*(4), 529–546. doi:10.1016/S0362-3319(00)00094-X.

Cialdini, R. B. (2006). *Influence: The psychology of persuasion* (Revised ed.). New York: Harper Business.

Clinton, B. (2004). *My life*. New York: Knopf.

Clinton, H. (2003). *Living history*. New York: Scribner.

Clinton, H. (2011, December 6). Remarks in Recognition of International Human Rights Day. U.S. State Department. Retrieved from www.state.gov/secretary/20092013clinton/rm/2011/12/178368.htm.

Crosby, F. (2008). Sex discrimination at work. In J. C. Chrisler, C. Golden, & Patricia D. Rozee (Eds.), *Lectures on the psychology of women* (4th ed.) (pp. 43–57). New York, NY: McGraw Hill.

Erikson, E. (2013). *Young man Luther*. New York: W.W. Norton (Original work published 1958).

Gardner, H. (1996). *Leading minds*. New York: Basic Books.

Goudreau, M. (2011). Sarah Palin missing from *Time's* most influential list. *Forbes*. Retrieved from www.forbes.com/sites/jennagoudreau/.

Haidt, J. (2012). *The righteous mind: Why good people are divided by politics and religion*. New York: Vintage Books.

Hollander, E. P. (2009). Women and leadership. In E. Hollander (Ed.), *Inclusive Leadership* (pp. 73–80). New York, NY: Routledge.

Howard, C. (2015, May 26). 100 Women who lead the world. *Forbes*. Retrieved from www.forbes.com/power-women/.

Hyde, J. S. (2004). *Half the human experience* (6th ed.). Boston, MA: Houghton Mifflin.

Jamieson, K. H. (1995). *Beyond the double bind*. New York: Oxford University Press.

Jamieson, K. H. (2007, December 7). *Bill Moyers Journal: Interview transcript with Kathleen Hall Jamieson*. Retrieved from www.pbs.org/moyers/journal/12072007/transcript1.html.

John-Steiner, V. (2006). *Creative collaboration*. New York: Oxford University Press.

Milbank, D. (2013, April). Rep. Don Young faces backlash for 'wetback' slur. *Washington Post*.

Myers, D. (2012). *Social psychology* (11th ed.). Boston, MA: McGraw-Hill Education.

Page, S. (2008, August 30). Poll: Voters uncertain on Palin. *USA Today.* Retrieved from http://usatoday30.usatoday.com/news/politics/election2008/2008-08-30-palin-poll_N.htm.

Palin, S. (2009). *Going rogue.* New York: Harper Collins.

Palin, S. (2013a). *Good tidings and great joy: Protecting the heart of Christmas.* New York: HarperCollins.

Palin, S. (2013b). *American by heart: Reflections on family, faith, and flag.* New York: HarperCollins.

Petty, R., & Cacioppo, J. (1996). *Attitudes and persuasion.* Boulder, CO: Westview Press.

Phillips, M. (2008. September 6). Palin's hockey rink leads to legal trouble in town she led. *Wall Street Journal.*

Planned Parenthood. (2015, April 12). Planned Parenthood Action Fund welcomes Hillary Rodham Clinton to presidential field. Retrieved from www.plannedparenthoodaction.org/.

Pratkanis, A., & Aronson, E. (2001). *Age of propaganda: The everyday use and abuse of persuasion.* New York: Holt Paperbacks.

Public Policy Polling (2014, August 12). Alaskans remain down on Palin. Retrieved from www.publicpolicypolling.com/main/2014/08/alaskans-remain-down-on-palin.html#more.

Rasmussen Reports (2008a, September 5). Palin power: Fresh face now more popular than Obama, McCain. Retrieved from www.rasmussenreports.com.

Rasmussen Reports. (2008b, September 24). Palin still viewed more favorably and unfavorably than Biden. Retrieved from www.rasmussenreports.com/.

Rich, G. (2010). *The state of psychology in Alaska.* Paper presented, International Congress of Applied Psychology, Melbourne, Australia.

Rich, G. (2014). Positive institutions, communities, and nations: Methods and internationalizing positive psychology concepts. In H. Agueda Marujo & L. Miguel Neto (Eds.), *Positive nations and communities: Collective, qualitative, and cultural-sensitive processes in positive psychology* (pp. 17–34). New York, NY: Springer.

Rodham, H. (1973). Children under the law. *Harvard Educational Review, 43*(4), 487–514.

Service, R. (2002). *The very best of Robert Service.* Anchorage, AK: Todd Communications.

Sharma, D. (2011). *Barack Obama in Hawai'i and Indonesia.* Denver, CO: Praeger.

Simonton, D. K. (1994). *Greatness.* New York: Guilford.

Troy, G. (2006). *Hillary Rodham Clinton.* Lawrence, KS: University Press of Kansas.

Valian, V. (1998). *Why so slow? The advancement of women.* Cambridge, MA: MIT Press.

7

HILLARY'S SOFT POWER IN FRANCE AND GERMANY

Donald Morrison

To understand Hillary Clinton's considerable popularity in France, it helps to know something about her background. More than any American public figure in recent memory she is, quite literally, a child of France. Her great-great-great-great-grandmother (give or take a "great"), Marie Madeleine Plouart, was born in France in the mid-17th century. Plouart was not just any French citizen but one of the "King's Daughters," a group of 800 or so young women sent by King Louis XIV to help populate New France, as the kingdom's North American territories were known. She found a husband there and settled in Detroit, which later became part of the United States.

Clinton can claim a number of other illustrious French ancestors, including Louis Hébert, a Paris apothecary who charted the eastern coast of the New World in 1606 along with the explorer Samuel de Champlain; Nicolas Gode, who came to Quebec in 1642 and headed one of Montreal's founding families; and Guillaume Cuillard and Louis Henri, who were among the first permanent residents of Quebec City. Clinton is also related to the francophone 20th century Canadian prime minister Pierre Elliott Trudeau.

Despite that lineage, Clinton exhibits few visible traces of France. Her family has roots almost as deep in Britain (Prince Charles's wife, Camilla Parker-Bowles, is a distant relative), and her parents named her in admiration of New Zealand–born mountaineer Sir Edmund Hillary. She rarely visited France before becoming secretary of state and even now barely speaks French—unlike her successor John Kerry, whose fondness for the "language of diplomacy" has led him to negotiate directly with French counterparts in that tongue, to the alarm of aides. Indeed, being perceived as French in any way is a drawback in American politics. Conservative U.S. politicians have for decades pilloried France as a socialist hell, mired in low economic growth and high unemployment and hamstrung by an intrusive state. The elegant Kerry was criticized by opponents in his unsuccessful 2004 presidential campaign as "looking French," and Barack Obama was faulted in 2008 for allegedly wanting to bring the French economic model to the U.S.

Nonetheless, Clinton has developed both a persona and a world view that make her seem familiar and sympathetic to many people in France. More so than Obama, who remains an admired if somewhat distant figure in the French imagination (and certainly more than George W. Bush, whose French approval ratings have long been in the low double-digits), Clinton embodies qualities that the French admire in America and several that they see in themselves. Among the former are openness, energy, and ambition. The latter include seriousness, glamor, and a sense of responsibility for improving—and policing—the world.

Clinton's popularity in France is abundantly documented. She came in first in a 2007 Harris poll of French adults about their preference for the next U.S. president. Though she lost that election to Barack Obama, who was No. 2 on the Harris list, she continued to perform impressively in other French opinion surveys.[1] In a 2012 Pew Research poll, for instance, 61 percent of French respondents expressed confidence in her, while only 31 percent did not; That was in line with her ratings throughout Europe, and nearly as high as those in the U.S.[2] She was the only American politician on a list of the 10 "most admired" people in France, as determined by a 2015 YouGov survey.[3] (Barack Obama did not make the cut, though his wife Michelle did.) When pollsters start measuring French attitudes toward various U.S. presidential candidates closer to the 2016 elections, it is likely that Clinton will maintain her lead position. She has long been a fixture in the French popular press, where her travels and utterances have been chronicled with the close attention accorded to entertainment celebrities. The 2014 birth of her first grandchild, Charlotte, received lavish attention in the country's newspapers and magazines, along with photos of a beaming Hillary and Bill Clinton holding the infant.

Popular and elite opinion often diverges in France, as elsewhere, but not so much when it comes to Clinton. French officials are prominent among her fans, and they fell all over themselves to signal their approval after she launched her presidential candidacy in April 2015. In tweeted responses to her announcement, Prime Minister Manuel Valls wished her "good luck," and Health Minister Marisol Touraine declared, "Go, Hillary!" Dozens of newspapers reported a tweet from Justice Minister Christiane Taubira: "@Hillary Clinton running, good news! Could fair winds strengthen your sails and give you wings." All of those well-wishers were members of France's Socialist Party, whose policy positions are broadly similar to those of Clinton's Democrats. Yet former president Nicolas Sarkozy, leader of France's center-right Republicans, also offered his felicitations: "Good luck @Hillary Clinton. I know how strong your passion is for the United States." A few months earlier he had tweeted a photo of himself with Clinton on a 2014 visit to New York, with the words, "Friend of France."

Sarkozy's dealings with Clinton have been unusually friendly. She initially disappointed his government by skipping France—and the rest of Europe—on her first foreign trip after becoming secretary of state and traveling instead to Japan, Indonesia, China, and South Korea as part of the Obama Administration's "pivot to Asia." But on a visit to Paris a few months later, Sarkozy greeted her with characteristic exuberance. Rushing to meet him, she tripped on the steps of the presidential Elysée Palace and lost her right shoe, leaving her to hobble barefoot in front of laughing reporters and photographers. Sarkozy gallantly rushed to steady her, helped retrieve the errant footwear, and walked her to her car. Shortly afterward she sent him a photo of the incident inscribed, "I may not be Cinderella, but you'll always be my Prince Charming." (He kept the souvenir in his Elysée office until he vacated it in 2012.) As he told her during a bilateral talk some months later, "Hillary, I always like being with you. You are tough. You are smart. You are a good person."[4]

In her 2014 memoir *Hard Choices* (*Le temps des decisions* in its French edition), Clinton returned the favor, depicting Sarkozy as an endearing if slightly excitable companion. "Most foreign leaders are calmer in private than in public," she wrote. "Not President Sarkozy. He was even more dramatic—and fun—in person. Sitting in a meeting with him was always an adventure. He'd jump up and gesture dramatically as he made his points . . . Despite his exuberance, he was always a gentleman."[5]

Sarkozy's enthusiasm for Clinton was not shared by everyone in his government. Valérie Pécresse, who served as Minister for Higher Education, scoffed at a 2015 public meeting that Clinton was "not my model because, so far, she hasn't yet held real responsibilities." For Pécresse, evidently, serving as U.S. First Lady, senator, and secretary of state did not qualify. Dominique Bussereau, a cabinet minister under both Sarkozy and his predecessor Jacques Chirac, greeted the news that Clinton was running for president by tweeting that he "normally prefers modern Democrats to conservative candidates, but in this case I don't have confidence."

Sarkozy's successor, François Hollande, has interacted cordially with Clinton, though not nearly as enthusiastically as her "Prince Charming." Things got off to a rocky start when Hollande, during his ultimately successful 2012 election campaign against Sarkozy, canceled a trip to Washington after learning that he would be formally received by Clinton and not by President Obama. (U.S. presidents generally avoid meeting with foreign office-seekers in mid-campaign to avoid the appearance of meddling in another country's electoral process.) Hollande made up for that snub over a congenial breakfast with Clinton at the State Department on his first visit to Washington after his election victory. Clinton resigned as secretary of state a few months later, so her dealings with Hollande were not as extensive as they were with Sarkozy. But it is interesting to speculate, as some French journalists have, that Clinton and Hollande bonded over their shared experience as partners in a rocky "power couple" relationship. Hollande separated in 2007 from his longtime partner Segolène Royale, mother of his four children and a former presidential candidate herself. Though they remained apart, she joined his cabinet in 2014 as Minister for Energy and the Environment.

If Clinton's dealings with Hollande's government had any real warmth, it was supplied by Foreign Minister Laurent Fabius. He and Clinton worked together closely on Syria and Iran, among other issues. In July 2014, more than a year after she stepped down as secretary of state, Fabius praised her "leadership" and "natural authority" at an unusual dinner he organized for her at the Quai d'Orsay, France's Foreign Ministry headquarters. The event was attended by a half-dozen former foreign and defense ministers, along with French movie stars, sports heroes, rap musicians, and other nongovernmental celebrities. *Le Figaro*'s story on the evening was headlined, "*Hillary Clinton, superstar du Quai d'Orsay.*" When Clinton announced her presidential candidacy a few months later, Fabius parted with diplomatic protocol by becoming one of the few sitting foreign ministers (along with Germany's Frank-Walter Steinmeier) to effectively endorse a U.S. presidential candidate. In a press statement, he praised her as "an exceptional woman for a job that requires exceptional qualities."

U.S. presidential election campaigns are closely covered by the French press, which has largely followed its American counterpart's lead in speculating about the strengths and weaknesses of various 2016 candidates. Clinton was, French journalists mostly agreed, the clear front-runner, though she faced questions about her age, her chaotic 2008 campaign, her use of a private e-mail account as secretary of state, and the financing of the Clinton Foundation. At the same time, however, her experience and competence were rarely questioned. "She always arouses ambivalent reactions," said Anne Deysine, a U.S. specialist at the University of Paris-West-Nanterre, on a France24 website. "She has all the qualifications and all the knowledge of domestic and foreign affairs, but also all the scandals attached to the presidency of her husband—Travelgate, Troopergate, Monica Lewinsky—that Republicans have tried to make so much of."

One point of departure between U.S. and French commentators was Bill Clinton, who was still immensely popular in France and viewed there as a valuable asset, not a potential problem, for his wife. As Vincent Michelot, a historian of American politics at the Institute for Political Studies (Sciences Po) in Lyons, said on a France24 website, "As for distancing herself from the presidency of Bill Clinton, the negative elements of his two terms are fading into the distance, giving way to a more romanticized vision of years of strong economic expansion, a balanced budget and a period of peace marked by the end of the Cold War."

One of Clinton's biggest attractions in France is her gender. Many French would like to see a woman in the White House to complement the election in 2008 of America's first black president. And Clinton has received considerable praise from French women for her focus, as secretary of state, on women's issues. Historically, France has not been especially hospitable to women. They received the right to vote only in 1945, with access to contraception in 1967 and to abortion in 1975. Until 1965, wives could not have their own bank accounts or work outside the home without permission of their husbands. In recent years, however, lost time has been made up. A woman, Edith Cresson, served from 1991 to 1992 as prime minister, second-in-command to the president in the French system. A 1999 law requires political parties to ensure that 50% of their candidates for office are women. Partly as a result, women accounted for more than 27% of National Assembly members in 2015 (compared with fewer than 20% for both houses of the U.S. Congress). Women also made up about half of President Hollande's cabinet. Blacks, by contrast, held fewer than 2% of Assembly seats. Anne Hidalgo in 2015 became the first woman elected as mayor of Paris, and, more significantly, François Hollande's ex-companion Segolène Royale in 2007 became the first woman to make it to the second round of France's two-step presidential election, winning 47% of the vote to Nicolas Sarkozy's 53%.

The idea of a woman president incites little controversy in France, where television dramas featuring female political leaders have been numerous and popular in recent years. Denmark's acclaimed series *Borgen*, about the travails of a female Danish prime minister, was widely discussed in the French press, as were such American imports as *Commander in Chief, Veep, Madam Secretary* and *Political Animals* (in which, intriguingly, a former First Lady becomes secretary of state). A home-grown entry, *Les hommes de l'ombre* (*Shadow Men*), involved a female cabinet minister who, in a characteristically French twist, decides to run for the presidency after the death of the incumbent, who happens to be her lover. Another, *L'école de pouvoir* (*School of Power*), featured a character apparently modeled on Segolène Royale. "These series have gotten voters used to the idea that electing a woman is normal," observed Joseph Belletante, a French political scientist who studies culture and politics, in *Le Figaro*. The phenomenon was similar in the U.S., he said, where *The West Wing* may have helped acclimate Americans to the idea a black chief executive.

The marital and other scandals that have long clouded Clinton's image in the U.S. are casually accepted in France, where a politician's after-hours life is not considered especially relevant to his or her fitness for office. And in France, politicians have interesting personal lives. Consider Nicolas Sarkozy, who was twice divorced—messily, in the case of his second wife, Cecelia, who was his closest political adviser; shortly after the disclosure of her affair with an American public relations executive, the Sarkozys separated. Nicolas won the presidency and he promptly married Carla Bruni, a singer, actress, and fashion model with a rich and highly public romantic history of her own. As for the kind of corruption scandals that in the U.S. acquire the suffix "-gate," Sarkozy has been the subject of numerous official inquiries and court proceedings, many of them serious and at least one of them still under way four years after he left office. His successor, Hollande, can boast of fewer investigations but an equally complex love life. In 2014, he was photographed being ferried on the back of a motorcycle from the Elysée Palace, where he lived with his unmarried companion, journalist Valerie Trierweiler, to a late-night tryst at the apartment of the movie actress Julie Gayet.

Trierweiler soon left him and wrote a best-selling book about the betrayal. For the French, any Clinton-related saga, no matter how lurid, would likely pale in comparison to the domestic variety.

More to the point, Clinton's record as secretary of state encompasses a world view that coincides with the thrust of French foreign policy in recent decades, as well as Frances's longtime view of its role in the world. Though Clinton spent much of her time responding to largely unforeseen events—the Arab Spring movement; the uprisings in Syria, Libya, and Tunisia; the earthquake in Haiti— she did attempt to align American policy with the notion of "smart power." That term, popular among foreign policy experts for some years, connotes a deft mix of military, or "hard," power with such "soft" arts as negotiation, economic development, and cultural diplomacy. In 2009, at her first Munich Security Conference, an annual gathering of strategic policy makers, Clinton described this approach as "the ensemble of tools at our disposal: diplomatic, economic, military, political, legal and cultural—we must choose the right tool, or combination of tools, best adapted to each situation."[6]

To the French and other Europeans, that approach marked a welcome change from what the French website Nonfiction.fr described as the "messianic arrogance and the violence of arms of the Bush presidency, which seriously undermined the image of the U.S. in the world." Indeed, in the same week as Clinton's appearance in Munich, President Sarkozy and German prime minister Angela Merkel published a joint letter asserting that "no country today is capable of resolving by itself the problems of the world," hence the need to "review the manner in which we tackle the new threats, our partners and our structures." Clinton may not speak French (or German), but she was talking their language.

Comparisons between Clinton and Merkel are perhaps inevitable. The two can fairly be described as the most important politicians on either side of the Atlantic—especially now that Segolène Royale's march toward the French presidency has stalled and her rival, the far-right National Front's Marine Le Pen, appears stymied by France's complex electoral system. Both Clinton and Merkel have been on the international scene for decades and are immensely popular at home and abroad—though only Merkel has been named *Time* magazine's Person of the Year (in 2015). And, as the popular press around the world has noted, the two share a fondness for pantsuits. At a 2011 meeting in Berlin, Merkel presented Clinton with a framed copy of a *Frankfurter Allgemeine* front page, with a photo of the two women seen from the rear—one clad in a purple jacket, the other in a fuchsia jacket, both in black slacks—alongside the text: "Which one is Merkel and which one is Clinton?" (Clinton laughed heartily.) Clinton has been generous in her admiration of Merkel, once calling her "the greatest leader in Europe." Merkel, who is not given to such effusions, maintained their relationship even after 2014 revelations that the U.S. had eavesdropped on the chancellor's telephone conversations put a chill on German-U.S. relations. Clinton, rather than defend her own government over the wiretapping, denounced it.

Besides friendship and fashion, the two women share some interesting characteristics. Both are obsessed with policy details, as Clinton showed when she was in charge of health-care reform in her husband's White House—and as Merkel demonstrates almost daily. Both were once seen as heavy favorites to win their next elections—Clinton in 2016, Merkel in 2017—though events subsequently complicated their prospects. Both believe in dealing urgently with climate change and in developing alternative energy sources. Yet the two leaders are hardly identical in their approaches. Merkel, for instance, has launched a program to end Germany's dependence on nuclear power, to the chagrin of some European neighbors—and, possibly, Clinton, who has carefully avoided demonizing the nuclear industry. In addition, Merkel has long criticized Europe's expensive social safety nets, while Clinton continues to favor an expansion of such programs in the U.S.

When it comes to Europe, their differences are overshadowed by points of agreement. Both are firmly committed to the idea of a unified Europe. As Secretary of State, Clinton was an early backer of the Treaty of Lisbon, the 2009 agreement—orchestrated by Merkel—that reformed the structure and procedures of the European Union. Clinton's support for a strong Europe, shared by her boss Obama, was popular among French and German officials. It did not, however, endear her to Euro-skeptics and other political figures in Britain, which has long fancied itself as the beneficiary of a "special relationship" with the U.S. Clinton and Obama have been signaling the British to look to Europe, not the U.S., for its future. For the most part, however, American officials tend to view Europe's seemingly endless debate about the character and the internal policies of the Union as a matter best left to Europeans.

As secretary of state, Clinton supported Merkel's insistence on greater austerity as a condition for helping resolve Europe's fiscal crisis, once even calling austerity "chemotherapy" that would "give Greece a very strong economy going forward." But that tone changed once Clinton left the State Department and began preparing her presidential campaign. She started questioning austerity, lamenting the suffering of Greeks and urging the E.U. to do whatever it could to keep Greece and other ailing economies in the Euro system. Indeed, as Clinton moved from the tactfully worded world of diplomacy to the more voluble realm of presidential politics, a few other areas of apparent divergence with Merkel presented themselves. As a near neighbor of Russia, Germany's largest supplier of energy, Merkel has long taken a softer tone toward Russia than Clinton has. And as the leader of a country sensitive about its own military past, Merkel has been a minor and reluctant participant in the kinds of multi-lateral security efforts favored by Clinton. The chancellor did not offer to commit troops to the U.S.-led coalition fighting Islamic State militants in Syria until after the 2015 Paris terror attacks.

In her defense, however, Merkel can point to her decision to open Germany's borders to hundreds of thousands of Syrian refugees, who soon overwhelmed German social services and were blamed for a few high-profile criminal incidents.

Merkel's policy of generosity enraged and emboldened Germany's rising neofascist right, caused tensions within her governing coalition, and hung like a cloud over the 2017 federal elections. Germany's European neighbors were also not pleased. Greece and Italy complained that Merkel's gesture merely encouraged more refugees to come. Hungary, Poland, and even normally welcoming Sweden and Denmark imposed new barriers to the refugees. After the 2015 Paris terror attacks, France and other members even suspended the Schengen agreement, which allows for unimpeded travel within Europe. Yet on the refugee issue Merkel and Clinton were both essentially on the same side. The U.S. presidential candidate called on her government to admit 65,000 Syrians, more than six times the number it had earlier promised. She also denounced the Republican presidential candidates who called for a ban on admitting Syrians and, in in the case of Donald Trump, Muslims generally. Such behavior, she said, was antithetical to "who we are as Americans."

With the rise of ISIS and a spate of terror attacks in the U.S. and Europe, the issue of refugees became conflated with the problem of terrorism, much to the disadvantage of both Clinton and Merkel. Clinton's credentials on the domestic security had long been considered strong. Her tenure as secretary of state included an increase in domestic surveillance and a surge in prosecutions for espionage. She was one of the most outspoken critics of Edward Snowden after the former intelligence contractor's disclosure of U.S. surveillance activities. Yet a bungled State Department response to a fatal 2012 attack on the U.S. embassy in Benghazi by Islamic gunmen allowed Clinton's Republican opponents to question her commitment to combating terrorism. Meanwhile, Merkel was facing similar criticism in Germany. She admitted in 2014 that hundreds of Muslim immigrants had left Germany to join ISIS, and critics warned that some might return to carry out attacks at home. On the last night of 2015, gangs of men who were alleged to be asylum seekers harassed hundreds of females in several German cities. "If asylum seekers or refugees carry out these kind of attacks . . . it will bring their stay in Germany to an abrupt end," warned Andreas Scheuer, general secretary of Merkel's Bavarian ally, the Christian Social Union. As opinion polls showed rising anti-immigrant sentiment in both Germany and the U.S., Merkel and Clinton found themselves sharing yet another characteristic: a stubborn insistence on doing the right thing on behalf of refugees at a time when that course of action was increasingly unpopular.

Clinton did not have to deal with the global refugee issue as secretary of state. Indeed, she faced relatively few serious crises, aside from the upheavals caused by the Arab Spring. Her tenure was marked by attention to such "soft power" issues as economic development, women's empowerment, foreign aid, disaster relief, and the Ebola epidemic in Africa. On strategic matters, she shared President Obama's intention to avoid using American military power unilaterally and without clear goals—in other words, no more Iraqs. In a session with reporters, Obama colorfully described that approach as "Don't do stupid shit," and that phrase (substituting "stuff" for the final word) became an oft-repeated summary of his foreign policy. Clinton and Obama did intervene in regional conflicts—Tunisia, Libya, Syria—but typically as part of coalitions of allies within more clearly defined limits. Clinton herself initiated the direct talks between Iran and the P5+1 group of countries that ended, under her successor John Kerry, in the 2015 nuclear agreement. Those negotiations complicated the U.S. relationship with Israel, already strained over disagreements involving the Palestinians, and Clinton was in the thick of all those controversies. Yet the secretary of state had been a firm supporter of Israel even before her days as a senator from heavily Jewish New York, and she largely escaped the personal hostility that developed between Obama and Israeli prime minister Benjamin Netanyahu. That ability to avoid personalizing diplomatic differences no doubt resonated with citizens of such mature global powers as France and Germany.

Often during Clinton's tenure at the State Department, various U.S. efforts and interventions found her working alongside her counterparts in France, which had been a "smart power" practitioner for years without using the term. Since the days of Louis XIV, France has wielded its cultural prestige as a diplomatic tool and viewed its imperial ambitions as part of a "civilizing mission" to bring enlightenment to the world's more benighted corners. France today spends heavily to diffuse its language and culture around the globe. It also maintains the world's fifth or sixth largest military, depending on who's counting. It intervenes on a regular basis to maintain stability in former French colonies, as happened in the Ivory Coast, the Central African Republic, and Mali during Clinton's tenure in the State Department. France has also been a major participant in peacekeeping operations and in important multilateral negotiations, including the long-running talks with Iran over its nuclear program. But France sometimes goes its own way, as when President Charles De Gaulle in the 1960s made his country a declared nuclear power, pulled out of NATO's military command, and announced, with prickly independence, that France's nuclear missiles would henceforth be aimed not only at the Soviet bloc, but toward other countries as well.

Clinton sometimes found herself hastening to catch up with France's eagerness to take a leadership role in a foreign conflict. In 2011, Libya's Muammar Gaddafi launched attacks against rebels trying to overthrow him, and civilian casualties began to mount. Sarkozy led the charge to halt the conflict and unseat the dictator. He organized a hasty "summit in support of the Libyan people" in Paris, at which Clinton and a number of European and Arab counterparts agreed to join the fight. Less than two hours after the session ended, French warplanes were heading toward Tripoli, followed later by those of the U.S. and Britain. Sarkozy was eventually persuaded to seek a United Nations resolution to support the action. As Clinton noted in *Hard Choices*, Sarkozy led the charge. He had lobbied hard for military action, she said, and he welcomed an opportunity to demonstrate French leadership.

That role had been somewhat tarnished only months earlier, when Sarkozy underestimated the strength of the popular uprisings in Egypt and Tunisia. In the latter, a former French colony, his government had so misread the situation that his foreign minister at the time, Michèle Alliot-Marie, even offered security assistance to the reigning autocrat, President Zine Al Abidine Ben Ali, in suppressing the uprising. Ben Ali was toppled within weeks, Alliot-Marie was fired, and Sarkozy was determined never again to be caught on the wrong side of history.

Clinton was eager to help him with that intention. The two became leading advocates for arming moderate rebels trying overthrow another repressive strongman, President Bashar al-Assad, in yet another Arab nation, Syria. France eventually did begin sending weapons to Syria's moderate opposition. But President Obama, though willing to dump the dictator, had his doubts—and overruled Clinton. He was troubled by disarray among opposition forces and worried that any U.S.-supplied arms would end up in the hands of radical Islamic extremists who were also fighting Assad. "Wicked problems rarely have a right answer," Clinton wrote in her memoir, no doubt through clenched teeth. "In fact, part of what makes them wicked is that every option appears worse than the next. Increasingly that's how Syria appeared. The risks of both action and inaction were high, [but Obama]'s inclination was to stay the present course."[7] That meant maintaining sanctions against the Assad regime but not shipping weapons to the rebels.

Obama eventually agreed to intervene on a limited basis in Syria. By then, however, Clinton had left office, and the U.S. focus was less on toppling Assad's regime than on thwarting one of the factions trying to oust him: ISIS. As Clinton was preparing her presidential campaign in late 2014 and early '15, France and the U.S. began working together against this new threat. President Hollande convened a conference in Paris of two dozen nations, whose representatives vowed to use "any means necessary" to defeat the Islamic State. Soon, French and American planes were mounting air strikes in Iraq against the new joint enemy. "The French were our very first ally and they're with us again now," said General Martin Dempsey, chairman of the U.S. Joint Chiefs of Staff, at a June 2015 ceremony in Normandy honoring troops who died in World War II. "It just reminds me why these relationships really matter."[8] To many French, however, it seemed as if it were the Americans who had finally agreed to follow France's lead.

A Hillary Clinton presidency would likely make better use of the Franco-American relationship than she was able to do as secretary of state. Even in the U.S., she is widely believed to be more willing to project American power more forcefully than President Obama did—and more in the manner that Sarkozy did for France. Though she was a faithful executor of Obama's foreign policies, there were numerous points of divergence. Those involved not just Syria, but also a swap of Taliban prisoners for a U.S. serviceman (she considered the deal overly generous), her plans to visit the military regime in Burma (Obama opposed the trip as premature but later relented), his plans to close the U.S. military prison at Guantànamo (she wanted to move faster), and how long to support embattled Egyptian president Hosni Mubarak (Clinton wanted to give his regime more time to enact reforms, which turned out to be futile). In general, Clinton appeared to favor a more aggressive, less reactive U.S. approach to foreign policy, with lower barriers to military intervention than Obama had maintained—though with a similar insistence on broad coalitions and stipulated aims. She might also turn out to be more confrontational in dealing with rising rivals to U.S. power. She pursued President Obama's first-term "reset" of relations with Russia, an effort that was abandoned after that country's incursions into Ukraine. Just before leaving office, she urged Obama to not "flatter Putin with high-level attention." She also advocated allowing former East Bloc countries to join NATO in order to counter Russian expansionism. As for China, she would likely continue the Obama policy of seeking broader cooperation with Beijing, but she did not hesitate to criticize the Chinese over human rights and incursions into the South China Sea.

Sergio B. Gautraux, an analyst for *International Policy Digest*, waded through years' worth of quotes, policy papers, and other material to gain a picture of what a hypothetical President Hillary Clinton might be like on the world stage. She would, he concluded, "practice those beliefs espoused by such theorists as Robert Keohane [Princeton University], Joseph Nye [Harvard], and John Mearsheimer [Chicago], whereby various state actors remain engaged with the world through intergovernmental organizations and military force is used only in concert with the strong support of a prior-established alliance. This would be coupled with a strong dose of classically American, Jacksonian nationalism."[9] That approach, sometimes characterized as "neoliberal," is—like "smart power"—an idea beloved of French policy makers. The French defense issues newsletter *TTU* (which stands for *Très très urgent*) said, somewhat approvingly, that Clinton appears to share the world view of her husband Bill, whose presidency was marked by no major wars but several U.S. initiatives to contain lesser conflicts—in Bosnia and the Middle East, for instance. Said *TTU*: "Observers tend to predict a policy more "a la Bill" than "a la Obama."

That would likely suit the French, who prefer that the nation of Louis XIV and Charles De Gaulle remain an important player on the world stage—and that their leaders assert France's greatness at every opportunity. In that case, Marie Madeleine Plouart's great-great-great-great granddaughter would likely be viewed by the French as an American president they can call their own.

References

1 Chazyndec, J. (2007). Poll indicates how Europeans see U.S. election, and how some Americans see it, Dec. 6, 2007, last accessed on March 29, 2016 at www.nytimes .com/2007/12/06/world/americas/06iht-poll.4.8621752.html

2 Pew Research Center. (2012). Hillary Clinton's Career of Comebacks, last accessed on March 28, 2016 at www.people-press.org/2012/12/21/hillary-clintons-career-of-comebacks/

3 YouGov.us. (2015). Hillary Clinton: The most admired woman in America, last accessed on March 29, 2016 at https://today.yougov.com/news/2015/01/31/hillary-clintons-most-admired/

4 Alter, J. (2011). Woman of the world, June, last accessed on March 28, 2016 at www.vanityfair.com/news/2011/06/hillary-clinton-201106

5 Clinton, H. R. (2014). *Hard Choices*. New York: Simon and Schuster, p, 192.

6 New York Times. (2009). Senate Confirmation Hearing, Jan 13. www.nytimes.com/2009/01/13/us/politics/13text-clinton.html

7 Clinton, H. R. (2014). *Hard Choices*. New York: Simon and Schuster, p, 192.

8 Associated press. (2014). France joins U.S. airstrikes in Iraq, wipes out ISIS target, September 19; last accessed on March 28, 2016 at www.cbc.ca/news/world/france-joins-u-s-airstrikes-in-iraq-wipes-out-isis-target-1.2771357

9 Gautreaux, S. (2015). The Clinton Doctrine, *International Policy Digest*, April 24, last accessed on March 28, 2016, http://intpolicydigest.org/2015/04/24/the-clinton-doctrine/

8

CAN HILLARY CLINTON GET AFGHANISTAN RIGHT?

Prakhar Sharma

Despite the fact that many consider her a polarizing personality, it would be hard to find another woman in world politics who is as revered as Hillary Clinton. As the First Lady in the White House, Hillary unwaveringly stood by her husband, the then president Bill Clinton, at the height of the Monica Lewinsky scandal. As a senator of New York and, subsequently, the secretary of state, Hillary distinguished herself as a civil servant par excellence. She became the face of US diplomacy, traveled to more countries than any previous secretary of state, negotiated the challenges emanating from the uprisings in the Middle East, and even made an official—some may argue, premature—trip to Myanmar. Her domestic approval ratings as the secretary of state were consistently high.[1] By any yardstick, Hillary had a remarkable three decades in public service, culminating in a successful stint as the secretary of state in Washington, DC. Yet, if there is one country where the US foreign policy outcomes, despite enormous investment of blood and treasure, continue to elude larger goals of the US national security, it is Afghanistan.[2]

Despite Hillary's formidable reputation and her Herculean efforts to rally support for expanding US footprint in Afghanistan, one can argue that Afghanistan slipped away toward more uncertainty under her watch. Neither her efforts on reconciliation with the Taliban nor her impetus on the regional solution for Afghanistan translated into a tangible outcome. So, what is Hillary Clinton's legacy in Afghanistan? This chapter seeks to survey Hillary's engagement in Afghanistan, review her successes and missed opportunities, and make an attempt at understanding the nature of challenge that Afghanistan would pose to the next US administration.

The Beginnings: First Clinton Administration (1992–1996)

During the early months of the Bill Clinton administration, there was, perceivably, little interest or understanding in the White House about the political dynamics unfolding in Afghanistan. For an astute observer of the Cold War, this would not come across as a surprise; after the Soviet withdrawal from Afghanistan in 1989 and the subsequent collapse of the Soviet Union in 1991, Afghanistan did not offer much, geopolitically, to hold the curiosity of the Clinton administration. Dr. Barnett Rubin aptly wrote that between 1992 and 1994, the international community had no political strategy for Afghanistan.[3] The Afghan warlords fought one another for control over Kabul, while also representing conflicting regional interests.[4]

Until Kabul fell to the Taliban in 1996, some mid-level State Department officials hailed the Taliban as a movement that would restore law and order.[5] Richard Mackenzie argued that even before the Taliban marched to Kabul in 1996, the US drug enforcement officials based in Pakistan were optimistic that the Taliban would put an end to the booming drug trade in Afghanistan, serve as a bulwark against Iranian and Russian influence in Afghanistan, and restore order to the entire country, just as they did in Kandahar.[6]

It won't be a stretch to argue that the Bill Clinton administration seemed inadequately prepared to deal with the implications of the Taliban's takeover of Kabul in 1996. While some in that administration looked at the Taliban primarily as an anti-Iran group, a few even cheered the fact that the Taliban successfully restored order in a place that had turned into a violent struggle for power among warlords. Zalmay Khalilzad, for instance, presupposing that Osama Bin Laden had ceased to be welcomed in Afghanistan, wrote an opinion piece for the *Washington Post* in 1996, arguing for the US to re-engage Afghanistan.[7] The administration's ambivalence was most striking when Glyn Davies, the then acting spokesperson of the State Department, mentioned in September 1996 that the United States found nothing objectionable in the policy statements of the new government (Taliban), including its move to impose Islamic law.[8] In November 1996, the assistant secretary of state for South Asian affairs, Robin L. Raphel, mentioned that the Taliban had to be recognized as an indigenous movement that had demonstrated staying power.[9] Ahmed Rashid—a seasoned observer of Afghanistan—conjectured that the US supported the Taliban because Washington viewed the Taliban as anti-Iran and pro-Western.[10] Some also saw the first Clinton administration's interest in Afghanistan as limited largely to engaging UNOCAL and Delta oil companies who endeavored to build oil and gas pipelines linking Central Asia to international markets through Pakistan rather than through Iran. While such comments and speculations fuelled suspicions that the anti-Iranian zeal at the State Department orchestrated Taliban's meteoric rise, a more plausible conjecture is that the first Clinton administration misread Afghanistan's unfolding politics.

The Second Clinton Administration (1997–2000)

The Taliban's mistreatment of Afghan women began to attract the attention of prominent feminists in the second Clinton administration. For instance, on September 29, 1997, the Taliban detained Emma Bonino, the European Union commissioner for humanitarian affairs, during her visit to a women's hospital.[11] This invited widespread condemnation of the Taliban. The replacements of secretary of state Warren Christopher by Madeline Albright, and assistant secretary of state for South Asian affairs, Robin Raphael, with Karl Inderfurth, also brought new vocabulary in the US administration about the Taliban. The erstwhile vague references to Taliban's human rights violations soon became explicit condemnations. In a testimony to the Senate Foreign Relations sub-committee on Near East and South Asia in October 1997, the new assistant secretary of state for South Asia, Karl F. Inderfurth, identified Washington's objective in Afghanistan as a multi-ethnic, broad-based Afghan government that observes international norms. Then, in November 1997, Secretary of State Madeline Albright was the first cabinet-level official to strongly criticize the Taliban during a visit to an Afghan refugee camp in Pakistan.[12] She said:

> I think it is very clear why we are opposed to the Taliban—because of their approach to human rights, their despicable treatment of women and children, and their general lack of respect for human dignity.[13]

The Feminist Majority Foundation, under the leadership of Eleanor Smeal, joined hands with celebrities like Lionel Richie and Mavis Leno to criticize the Taliban.[14] First Lady Hillary Clinton soon gave a fillip to this momentum by giving several speeches condemning the Taliban. In a particular speech in April 1999, she said:

> When women are savagely beaten by so-called religious police for not being fully covered or for making noises while they walk, we know that is not just the physical beating that is the objective. It is the destruction of the spirit of these women.[15]

It was the first time either of the Clintons voiced condemnation of the Taliban.[16]

Senator of New York (2001–2009)

As a senator of New York, Hillary Clinton continued to champion the rights of Afghan women. In the aftermath of the September 2001 attacks on the US, and the subsequent US-led intervention in Afghanistan, she wrote a poignant piece about the US engagement as a new hope for Afghan women.[17]

> Thanks to the courage and bravery of America's military and our allies, hope is being restored to many women and families in much of Afghanistan. As

we continue the hard work of rooting out the vestiges of Taliban control and al-Qaeda terrorism, we must begin the hard work of nurturing that newfound hope and planting the seeds of a governing system that will respect human rights and allow all the people of that nation to dream of a better life for their children—girls and boys alike.

President and Mrs. Bush have properly highlighted the mistreatment of Afghan women by the Taliban and insist that women play a role in Afghanistan's future. We can help in Congress by completing our work on legislation to provide educational and health care assistance to Afghan women and children and promote the training of women to aid in the development of democracy and a civil society.

Senator Hillary Clinton visited Afghanistan thrice; in 2003 over Thanksgiving, and then in 2005 and 2007.[18] These trips enabled her to take stock of progress in Afghanistan, assess the needs of the engagement, and speak with the US troops deployed in Afghanistan. During the 2008 campaign, both Senator Obama and Senator Hillary Clinton called for a renewed attention on Afghanistan. Senator Clinton specifically pointed out the failure of the Bush administration in ignoring Pakistan's role in the conflict in Afghanistan, thereby putting on the table the idea of a regional solution to the Afghan conflict.

Secretary of State (2009–2012)

In 2009, Hillary Clinton joined President Obama's cabinet as the Secretary of State. In March that year, President Obama announced his military and political strategy for Afghanistan and Pakistan. He narrowed the goals of the war by focusing specifically on Al-Qaeda as opposed to Taliban. In doing so, he linked the war to its origins, that is, the attacks on September 11, 2001.[19] President Obama also invited the possibility of reconciliation with Taliban. To integrate these strategies into US diplomacy, Hillary Clinton took several decisions. Four of those decisions stand out: management of the challenging relationship with President Hamid Karzai; support for the troop-surge in 2009; endorsement of the peace process with the Taliban; and exploring a regional solution to the conflict.

Managing President Hamid Karzai

In August 2009, Hamid Karzai ran for re-election in an electoral process that was marred with fraud.[20] The vote count indicated that Karzai was ahead in the polls, but evidence of widespread irregularities propelled the UN to call for a run-off between Hamid Karzai and his closest rival, Abdullah Abdullah. Hamid Karzai refused to budge, and accused the US, in particular Richard Holbrooke, of trying to oust him.[21] To diffuse the crisis, Hillary intervened. She called Karzai to convey her concerns, communicating the stakes for both Afghanistan and the US in the election and the need to respect the process:

Think about the historical consequences both for yourself as the first democratically elected leader, and for your country. . . . You have an opportunity to emerge with a stronger government under your leadership, but that rests on the choices that you make going forward.[22]

Hillary explained to Karzai that if he accepted the run-off vote, he would gain the moral high ground and bolster his credibility with both the international community and his own citizens. Soon after Karzai relented and agreed for a run-off,[23] his rival Abdullah dropped out of the race. Karzai was declared a winner.[24] Speculations continue to abound on why Abdullah dropped out of the race, and whether he even considered the process fair enough to compete again.

On the eve of Karzai's inauguration, Hillary pressed Karzai to plan for a responsible, orderly transition from the US-led coalition forces to the Afghan National Army, about the prospects for a political settlement to bring war to an end, and to crack down on corruption.[25]

The US Troop Surge in 2009

As Karzai started his second term in Kabul, thousands of miles away in the White House, officials contemplated upon the request for more troops from General Stanley McChrystal. The White House was divided over the merits of sending additional troops to Afghanistan. For Vice President Joe Biden, the imperative of a troop surge was problematic. He argued that a large-scale effort at nation-building in Afghanistan was doomed to fail, given the weaknesses of the Afghan state. Biden proposed an alternative: instead of committing to a nation-building project in Afghanistan, the US could focus on counter-terrorism. Specifically, he argued that the US should direct its efforts to "disrupt the Taliban, improve the quality of the training of Afghan forces, and expand reconciliation efforts to peel off some Taliban fighters.[26]

Hillary opposed Joe Biden's light-footprint approach. Effective counter-terrorism, she argued, would require intelligence networks, which would not be possible without having substantial US military presence on the ground. Forcing the Taliban to the negotiating table required reversing their momentum, which necessitated a US troop surge. Even the diplomatic surge—which Richard Holbrooke pushed for—required a military surge. In the end, President Obama settled for the option to send in 30,000 troops with a clear mandate and articulated a time frame for their withdrawal.

The Peace Process with the Taliban

There is no contradiction between trying to defeat those who are determined to fight and opening the door to those who are willing to reintegrate and reconcile.[27]

Hillary Clinton put much greater emphasis on the peace process with the Taliban than did her predecessor, Dr. Condoleezza Rice. This was evident in her remarks during her visit to Islamabad in July 2010, and, subsequently, her talk at the Asia Society in New York in February 2011. One of the reasons behind her optimism in the process was that the war effort had gained significant momentum after the troop surge in 2009. There were more American boots on the ground that could potentially compel the Taliban to reconsider fighting the Afghan state. The Obama administration's approach to reconciliation had three key pillars that offered a stark departure from previous efforts.

First, the military would dismantle Taliban's infrastructure and make it more costly for the Taliban to continue fighting. Second, the civilian surge of diplomats and aid workers would enhance the capacity of the Afghan state to deliver services and thus enable it win the "hearts and minds" of the Afghan population. And, finally, the efforts to reconcile with the Taliban would weaken the alliance between the Taliban and Al-Qaeda.

The understanding that underscored this strategy was that the differences between the Al-Qaeda and Taliban were stark and discernible. As Hillary argued, the former were terrorists who launched the attacks on 9/11, while the latter were Afghan extremists fighting the Afghan state. In every conversation about reintegrating insurgents and reconciling with the Taliban, Hillary also underscored the primacy of respecting the rights of Afghan women. Borrowing from Bruce Reidel's assessment of Afghanistan in March 2009, she put forward three criteria for reconciliation; the insurgents would have to lay down their arms, reject Al-Qaeda, and accept the Afghan constitution. She was adamant that reconciliation with the Taliban must not lead to a return of reactionary social policies.

The Regional Solution to Afghan Conflict

The "regional solution" has meant different things to different people since General Petraeus put the concept on the table in 2009.[28] Some have understood it as expanding the operational theatre of the war to include Pakistan, others have framed it as an Af-Pak policy, while some have also viewed it as a general framework for neighborly cooperation.[29] Once the strategy played itself out, it seemed to draw elements from these three perspectives: more drone strikes in the tribal areas straddling Pakistan, developing a political strategy that would focus on reconciling the interests of Afghanistan and Pakistan toward building a regional strategy, and pushing for broader cooperation among all neighboring states to Afghanistan. As part of her regional strategy, Hillary put special emphasis on putting pressure on Pakistan to end its support to the Taliban.[30] In her book, she wrote, "I and others thought we could not trust Pakistan."[31] She adds, "I also knew elements in the Pakistani intelligence service, the ISI, maintained ties to the Taliban, al-Qaeda and other extremists."[32]

Getting Afghanistan Right

Can Hillary Clinton get Afghanistan right? Before attempting to answer this question, one must consider the fundamental challenges to Afghanistan's stability and political transition into a multi-ethnic, pluralistic democracy. Six challenges stand out. First, the ongoing insurgency led by the Taliban and allied groups to dismantle the Afghan state; second, internal fragmentation of the Afghan society initiated by ethnic cleavages and material interests; third, the interference, primarily from Pakistan, in Afghan politics through its support for the Taliban and allied groups; fourth, the absence of a system of governance that, by design, should be responsive and accountable to local, village-level needs; fifth, building a local economy; and sixth, human development.

Among these challenges, addressing the insurgency seems most crucial to consolidating Afghanistan's political gains. Unless the insurgency is quelled or negotiated with, making durable progress on other aspects seems a formidable challenge. The drawdown of the US forces by 2016 further complicates an already daring context. The sources of internal fragmentation in Afghanistan[33] aren't as extensively documented as the causes of external meddling,[34] but they intersect with the weaknesses of local economy in Afghanistan; the Afghan state is heavily dependent on international aid, which fuels an internal struggle for political rents. Yet, internal fragmentation points towards a fundamental issue that has been relegated to a lesser priority by the conflict, that is, the incomplete *nationalism project* that is necessary to unite the Afghan society.

The nationalism project for Afghanistan is an imperative that the Afghan government should put on its agenda. Neither the international community, nor the Afghan state has given this project the attention and priority that it deserves. *Nationalism project* implies implies the promise made by the Afghan state to the Afghan people. It entails broadening the Afghan state's engagement with all segments of the society. This is crucial because the end of the conflict, or the absence of violence, would not necessarily result into peace. Sustainable peace in Afghanistan would result from a sense of belonging to a national polity. This would entail concerted efforts by the Afghan state to accentuate a national identity relative to other identities. This would require the Afghan state to make a durable commitment to its citizenry, chart shared goals, and engage in broad outreach. Thus, this chapter does not advocate for subordination of all identities to the national identity. Rather, it advocates a process led by the Afghan state that increases the political salience of the Afghan identity relative to the political salience of other identities. The massive turnout in the Afghan presidential elections in 2004, 2009, and 2014 demonstrates that the Afghans believe in the notion of the state and are willing to give democracy a chance, despite circumstances pointing in the opposite direction. Afghanistan should harness this sentiment and engage in a decentralized outreach and engagement that is state-led.

If nationalism is a cultural solution to Afghanistan's instability, state building is an institutional counterpart of the same solution. Afghanistan needs to invest in durable political institutions that are responsive to local needs. The existing institutions, whether they are symbols of the state or patronage networks, have alienated and disenfranchised segments of the Afghan population. For stability in Afghanistan, both nation- and state-building need to be approached in tandem.

The international community has privileged the latter for the former and, in the process, undermined both.

Even a cursory glance at Hillary Clinton's engagement with Afghanistan would suggest that while she has sought to address these challenges, the one where she has had the most impact pertains to human development, specifically the rights of Afghan women. She is likely to continue championing the rights of Afghan women, explore prospects of peace talks with the Taliban, and refrain from abandoning the US engagement with Afghanistan. Yet, if we were to construct a report card for her outcomes in Afghanistan, we would be hard pressed to find much progress on the insurgency, peace talks, and regional solution. What is one, then, to make of Hillary's legacy for Afghanistan and the prospects for Ashraf Ghani's Afghanistan if she assumes the leadership in the US? This is not merely an academic puzzle; Afghanistan is the longest war in US history[35] and one of the largest multinational engagements for reconstruction. The outcome there would imprint itself on the prospects for similar engagements in the future.

Successes

In a nutshell, Hillary's success in Afghanistan pertains to bringing attention to the rights of Afghan women, supporting the raid that killed Osama Bin Laden, advocating for a civilian/diplomatic strategy in tandem with a military strategy, and pushing for sustaining the engagement with the country. Two of these are worth recounting. Hillary demonstrated tough leadership in moments of crisis, exhibiting clarity of character, sound judgment, and the vision to further the American core values. When the Obama administration contemplated killing Osama Bin Laden in Abbottbad, Hillary strongly supported the raid, against the now-contested indecision of Vice President Biden about the raid.[36] She has acquired a reputation for being resolute and is thus likely to argue for sustained engagement with Afghanistan. When it comes to defending the rights of Afghan women, she took the issue personally. One could thus argue that, without her involvement, the issue of the marginalization of Afghan women may perhaps not have acquired the salience that it did. As the secretary of state, she requested that all the US-led development and political projects in Afghanistan take into account the needs and concerns of Afghan women. She argued that creating opportunities for Afghan women wasn't just a moral issue; it was also a strategic decision that would enable *Afghanistan's* economic growth.

Missed Opportunities and Future Challenges

The three areas where Hillary Clinton and the Obama administration could be faulted for missing opportunities in Afghanistan are the 2009 presidential election in Kabul, the peace talks with the Taliban, and the regional solution for Afghanistan.

The 2009 election saga and the dysfunctional political structure

Few would contest the argument that the Afghan presidential election in 2009 severely undermined the legitimacy of the Afghan state as well as the credibility of the United Nations and the international community. If the scale of electoral fraud was not damning enough,[37] the alleged effort to cover it up[38] under the guise of political expediency sounded a death knell for the legitimacy project in Afghanistan. The circumstances under which Abdullah decided to pull out of the runoff[39] remain shrouded in mystery. While Hillary succeeded in convincing Hamid Karzai to contest the runoff, she and her colleagues apparently failed to convince Abdullah of the fairness of the election process. Many in Afghanistan would concede that despite massive amount of fraud, the logistics of a recount of the votes and the further delays that would have been caused by any measures to effectively deal with the situation was not something that they could afford. Yet, the fact that the US was seen as picking sides,[40] while the UN was tainted as allegedly covering up the electoral fraud,[41] meant that for many Afghans, the amount of risks that they took to go to the polling stations was questionable. One could assert that the election aftermath gave the Taliban precisely the invitation they were looking for. Emboldened by the erosion of credibility of the Karzai regime and its international partners, the Taliban gained greater political traction in the rural areas. Despite the subsequent troop surge in 2010, the frailties of the Afghan government fueled the perception among the masses that they could consider other alternatives both locally and nationally. To many Afghans, and especially in light of the presence of foreign forces in their country, the Taliban offered one such alternative. The Obama administration's inability or unwillingness to ensure a transparent electoral process in Afghanistan that would engender confidence of the political opposition and the masses was a missed opportunity.

Democracy is not a panacea that is endowed with the power to heal a country's past or to assure a stable future to a people. Instead, democracy provides an opportunity for people to be equal, be treated as equals, morally and intellectually, and be able to exercise political judgment. Theoretically, this situation accords privileges and rights that are unprecedented in Afghan history. This is thus a far better position to be in than having no right to vote at all, no concept of participation, and no contestation for political power. This counts as progress after having being ruled, not governed, by a one-eyed, self-proclaimed Emir of Afghanistan, a man called Mullah Omar, who had refused to be seen or be accounted for his barbarism and theocratic absolutism. But, for many Afghans, the difference between the current elites and their lamentable predecessors in the Taliban lies increasingly in style and diminishingly in substance. This has dangerous forebodings.

Democracy in Afghanistan has shown encouraging prospects, but the elections in 2009 and 2014 have deflated Afghans' optimism about the democratic process.

One cannot dismiss or disregard the unmistakable and widespread fraud in both the elections. Several Afghan elites, starting with Hamid Karzai, chose to define themselves by their irresponsibility and shortsightedness. In doing so, they represented everything that the new, post-2001 Afghanistan was not.

Confidence in the accountability of elected representatives and the process that leads to the elections is both a cause and a consequence of any well-functioning democracy. Elections provide a fluent indication of a direction where the country is headed. Across the democratic world, elections offer the best mechanism for transfer of power and a useful means to hold the government accountable. People can reward a responsible government by reelecting it. Conversely, they can punish an ineffectual government by voting for its competitor. Fraud tarnishes elections as opportunities for exercising such political preferences. But the ability of elections to produce responsible outcomes is contingent on the content of the electoral rules and the commitment of all actors to play by those rules. So, before we doubt the legitimacy of elections in Afghanistan, we need to look at issues that are more fundamental to the exercise of political power.

To prevent the election crises of 2009 and 2014 from repeating and becoming a norm in the Afghan electoral cycle, fundamental changes are warranted to make the political system more responsive to demands for accountability. An ideal system should institutionalize the rule of the majority that ensures the rights of the minorities. The centralized character of the current government overstates its ability to deliver and constrains its reach to the masses. A strong presidency may have been acceptable for the context in 2002; it is completely out of sync with the realities and expectations of Afghanistan in 2015. The emphasis of any restructuring should be on locally elected, accountable governments at the district level. The system should also institutionalize the practice of holding political leaders answerable to their constituencies.

These election experiences also provide an opportunity for the Afghans, for the US, and for the international community to consider whether it is good for Afghanistan to continue to rely on an arithmetic majority of votes as a means to decide electoral victory. Would it not be more useful for Afghanistan to aim for a broad-based, inclusive government that would strengthen national unity? Several other inconvenient questions warrant answers. How do we ensure independence and integrity of electoral institutions in a context that is perceivably hostile to the idea of neutrality? How shall we create a system that would institutionalize a level playing field for all candidates and make both candidates and voters more confident about the fairness of the process? One of the biggest risks going forward is not an under-emphasis on transparent process over the electoral outcomes or misallocating the share of responsibility between local and international actors; it is the US's endorsement of the wrong kind of compromises. And, finally, how do we prevent the elites from manipulating processes and induce them to become more accommodating of the changing realities in Afghanistan? None of these questions would respect an easy answer. But delaying or ignoring these questions would imperil the prospects of political transition in Afghanistan.

False narratives on Taliban and Al-Qaeda

The imposing memorial that stands in the Panjsher valley to commemorate Ahmed Shah Massoud is among the most visited sites in Afghanistan. Every day, busloads of Afghans arrive from across the country to pay tribute to their leader. Nearly fourteen years dead, Ahmed Shah Massoud stays vivid in popular memory. In the view of many Afghans, he remains the national hero, the best president that they never had. Massoud organized and led the domestic opposition against the Taliban, lobbied internationally against the Taliban, and demonstrated more openness and a gradualist approach for societal change than his contemporaries.

During the Taliban regime (1996–2001) in Kabul, the opposition led by Ahmed Shah Massoud correctly raised the issue repeatedly with the Western governments, especially the CIA, that the Taliban posed a serious threat not only to Afghanistan, but also to global security. He complained to the CIA that the US was too focused on Osama Bin Laden, and not interested in the root problems of Taliban, Saudi, and Pakistani support for terrorism that was propping him up.[42] Those complaints fell on deaf ears, and it was not until the attacks on 9/11 that the world paid attention to the threat of militant Islam mirrored in Taliban's violent fanaticism.

The evolving narratives about the Taliban that Hillary bought into suffer from the same misconceptions that the Bill Clinton administration fell for. Three of these narratives are worth highlighting.

First, the perception that the Taliban and Al-Qaeda can be neatly distinguished by their different motives and ideologies is largely correct. The Afghan Taliban's goals center on Afghanistan, while Al-Qaeda maintains ambitions of erecting a global caliphate. Yet, different political goals can seamlessly overlap. Even goals that conflict one another do not completely rule out prospects for collaboration between groups. The tribal networks that Al-Qaeda cultivated in Afghanistan and Pakistan take years of investment and cannot quickly be re-established elsewhere. Institutions like those are hard to change because of vested interests, but also because of high switching costs. Thus, even if one contends that these two groups are ideologically different, culturally distinct, and that they espouse different goals, those differences, in themselves, do not imply that these two groups would not find reasons to collaborate again in Afghanistan.

Another narrative that has recently gained traction is that the neo-Taliban, that is, the new *avatar* of the Taliban, is not the same breed of *Jihadists* that regressed Afghanistan back by a few decades when they reined over the country. The new Taliban are understood as more fragmented today in their command and control, more autonomous of Pakistani military than their previous incarnation, and can thus be negotiated with. The new Taliban, it is also argued, have learned their lessons and moderated their outlook. Yet, it is as hard to argue for this position as it is to argue against. The Taliban's relentless assault over progress continues; they shut down schools, maim teachers, injure students, assassinate politicians, shatter public gatherings, silence elders, challenge the state's authority, and undermine the legitimacy of the government. These actions do not signal much change in their policies.

One could argue that resistance to the Afghan state could not be seen as an indication of Taliban's imperative, and that their policies would truly moderate once they have acquired more power or unseated the Afghan government. But, that is a scenario we would not permit to play out. In absence of that, what is it about the neo-Taliban that we should consider to assess a shift in their priorities? The fragmentation in the group, the splits between the Peshawar *Shura* and Quetta *Shura*, are well documented, but how any of it translates into prospects for peace is shrouded in uncertainty.

A third problematic narrative relates to the criticism of the current system, the rampant corruption that bleeds the system, and the predatory nature of the state. These characterizations make many assume an apologist tone for the Taliban. Such criticisms of the contemporary Afghan state and its false comparison with the Taliban regime miss the point. Despite its obvious flaws, the current system is fairer for most Afghans than the Taliban regime. On many occasions, the Afghan elites, i.e., those who wield influence out of their traditional or bureaucratic authority or because of their proximity to those who are in power, flout basic rights of minorities and women; the Taliban entertain no concept of such rights. The Afghan elites machinate, partake and benefit from electoral fraud; the Taliban do not entertain the very idea of political contestation. The Afghan elites escape accountability, steal resources, and oppress those who would confront their influence; the Taliban oppress ideas as well as people, without prejudice to either. The Afghan elites monopolize economic as well as political opportunities, thus depriving Afghans basic access to means for upward mobility. They stifle masses with their excesses and underwhelm their constituencies with deceit and incompetence. The Taliban are the ne plus ultra of totalitarianism, the purveyors of ipsedixitism. They remain on standby to provide quick dispute-settlement and security in exchange for the surrender of one's ability to think. These are not distinctions without difference.

The illusion of regional solution

Among the many damning cables that Peter Tomsen sent as the US special envoy to the Afghan Resistance (1989–1992), several pertained to the sharp divergence in interests between the US and Pakistan in Afghanistan. For months, Tomsen sent cables detailing the extent of Pakistan's duplicity, the tactful employment of religious extremism as a tool to mobilize recruits and use them as a proxy against the Afghan state. These cables represented a blistering criticism of US policy in the region. Since then, Afghanistan has braved a civil war, the Taliban regime, and a Taliban insurgency. Yet, the prospect for a regional solution continues to elude Afghanistan.

While the logic of finding a regional solution to Afghanistan's instability is unassailable and faultless—and Hillary Clinton was correct, in principle, to put this on her agenda—states in the region have competing and non-negotiable interests in Afghanistan. Attempts to get countries in the region to agree on a framework have thus been more furtive than forthright. As a result, the proposed regional dialogues have been more talks but less follow-through, and have not addressed the conflict either militarily or politically. A more useful approach could have been an emphasis on strong bilateral frameworks and more assertive diplomacy from the US to stem Pakistan's support for the insurgency.

***

Hillary Clinton's relationship with Afghanistan evolved gradually. Her conversation with Afghanistan was almost "muted" during the first Clinton administration, which was content with continuing to outsource the US Afghanistan policy to Pakistan.[43] Hillary's engagement with Afghanistan took off in the second Clinton administration, directed primarily at the issue of mistreatment of Afghan women at the hands of the Taliban. Thus, the early relationship between Hillary and Afghanistan was centered on the role and the rights of Afghan women—an issue she cared deeply about. The scope of her relationship widened after the US intervention in Afghanistan in October 2001. As a senator and, subsequently, the secretary of state, she remained a champion of the rights of Afghan women, but she also got more involved in substantive policy debates on the scope of US engagement, the issue of US military surge, an impetus for civilian surge to complement military surge, reconciliation with the Taliban, the raid to kill Osama Bin Laden in Pakistan, and negotiating a sensitive relationship with President Hamid Karzai. As we anticipate her run for the White House, three questions merit particular attention. First, Can Hillary sustain US engagement in Afghanistan in the face of mixed results and unfavorable domestic public opinion for such engagement? Second, can she ensure a role for the United States in bringing a negotiated end to the Afghan war? And, third, can she develop and implement a regional framework for stability in Afghanistan?

Even the most ardent interventionist would concede that sustaining Afghan engagement would not be politically desirable domestically in the US. Despite a spike in violence in Afghanistan and increasing demand from segments of the Afghan population to the US to not abandon them, the domestic public opinion in the US is unfavorable to the prospect of an extended engagement. One could speculate that the activities of the ISIS bring home the necessity of "being on the ground," but more Americans view the Afghan war as a mistake today than anytime before.[44] Thus, Hillary may push for continued engagement, but that may be severely limited in its scope and objectives, and lean heavily toward economic assistance and military training.

A negotiated end to the Afghan war is not outside the realm of possibility, and the US would certainly need to spearhead such initiative. But, for a peace deal to work out with the Taliban, the US would need to get Pakistan on board in total sincerity. For that to materialize, the US would need to address Pakistani interests in Afghanistan, some of which would not only contradict the interests of other regional players, but also undermine the goals of US policy in Afghanistan. Thus, short of Pakistan altering its strategic calculus, and the US incentivizing such change, the peace talks would remain a chimera.

Finally, durable peace in Afghanistan necessitates internal as well as regional agreement on the distribution of power. Internally, the merits of any framework for stability, such as reconciliation with the insurgents, needs to be sold broadly, not just to the different Pashtun tribes but also to all major ethnic groups. Only then can one expect most Afghans to buy into the implications of any deal on future power sharing. Regionally, the impetus for getting all relevant stakeholders—Iran, Pakistan, India, China, Russia, and Turkey—on board is still alive. However, their interests seem less reconcilable than those of the internal stakeholders. Whether bilateral frameworks of cooperation between countries in the region is the way forward seem, ironically, both an open question and a tempting consideration at this stage. Afghanistan's geography, however, wasn't always hostile to peace. There were phases in Afghanistan's history that were punctuated with stability, albeit also with isolation. Leaders look into the future to make decisions, but Afghanistan's history may offer a reason for Hillary Clinton to look into its past and search for answers there.

References

1 Saad Lydia, "Hillary Clinton Favorable Near Her All-Time High." Gallup Poll, March 30, 2011.
2 One could contend that the situation in Iraq also continues to pose a formative challenge to US national security interests. It undoubtedly does. But what makes Afghanistan unique is the bi-partisan support for US intervention in the country; the realization, from the outset, that it was the "right" war. Both Democrats and Republicans would concede that Afghanistan was the state and the society to which the US owed better prospects after abandoning it after the US objectives—withdrawal of the Soviet Union from Afghanistan—were accomplished in 1990. Stark disagreements tend to animate policy conversations in Washington, DC, about the outcome of the US engagement in Afghanistan, but not so much about the merits of US intervention in Afghanistan in October 2001.
3 Barnett Rubin, "U.S policy in Afghanistan." *Muslim Politics Report*, no. 11, January–February 1997.
4 During the *Jihad* against the Soviets, seven politico-military parties were based out of Peshawar. They constituted the alliance of the seven Sunni parties, including Hezb-e Islami, led by Gulbuddin Hekmatyar; Jamiat-e Islami, led by Burhanuddin Rabbani; Hezb-e Islami-Khales, faction led by Younos Khales; Mahaz-e Milli-ye Islami-ye Afghanistan, led by Pir Sayed Ahmad Gaylani; Jabha-ye Nejat-e Milli-ye Afghanistan, led by Pir Sebghatullah Modjadedi; Harakat-e Inqelab-e Islami-ye Afghanistan, led by Mawlawi Mohammad Nabi Mohammadi; and Ettehad-e Islami-ye baraye Azadi-ye Afghanistan, led by Abdul Rab Rasul Sayyaf.
5 Steve Levine, "Helping Hand." *Newsweek,* October 14, 1997.
6 Richard Mackenzie, "The United States and the Taliban" in *Fundamentalism Reborn: Afghanistan and the Taliban,* William Maley (ed.). NYU Press, 1998.

7　Zalmay Khalilzad, "Afghanistan: Time to Reengage." *Washington Post*, October 7, 1996.

8　Richard Mackenzie, "The United States and the Taliban" in *Fundamentalism Reborn: Afghanistan and the Taliban*, William Maley (ed.). NYU Press, 1998.

9　Statement by Robin L. Raphel, Head of the US delegation at a UN meeting on Afghanistan. November 18, 1996.

10　Ahmed Rashid, *Taliban and Militant Islam*, 2000. New Haven, CT: Yale University Press.

11　"Taliban Briefly Detains European Aid Official Visiting Hospital." *New York Times*, September 30, 1997.

12　Steven Erlanger, "In Afghan Refugee Camp, Albright Hammers Taliban." *New York Times*, November 19, 1997.

13　Ian Brodie, "Albright Attacks Taliban Oppression of Women." *The Times*, November 19, 1997.

14　William Maley, *The Afghanistan Wars*, 2002. New York, NY: Palgrave Macmillan.

15　Ahmed Rashid, *Taliban: Militant Islam, Oil and Fundamentalism in Central Asia*. Yale University Press, 2001.

16　Steve Coll, *Ghost Wars: The Secret History of the CIA, Afghanistan and Bin Laden*. Penguin Press, 2004.

17　Hillary Clinton, "New Hope For Afghanistan's Women." *Time*, November 24, 2001.

18　Hillary Clinton, *Hard Choices*. Simon & Schuster, June 2014.

19　Ibid.

20　Ghaith Abdul-Ahad, "New Evidence of Widespread Fraud in Afghanistan Election uncovered." *Guardian*, September 28, 2009.

21　Jacob Siegel, "Afghan Leader Hamid Karzai Feels Betrayed by His U.S. Allies." *Daily Beast*, January 15, 2014.

22　Hillary Clinton, *Hard Choices*. Simon & Schuster, 2014.

23　Jon Boone, Ewen MacAskill and Patrick Wintour, "Karzai Bows to Calls for Afghanistan Poll Runoff." *Guardian*, October 19, 2009.

24　Pamela Constable and Joshua Partlow, "Karzai Declared Winner of Afghan Election a Day after Rival Quits." *Washington Post*, November 3, 2009.

25　Duncan Gardham and Thomas Harding, "Hillary Clinton Calls for Hamid Karzai to Halt Afghan Corruption." *The Telegraph*, November 16, 2009.

26　Peter Baker, "How Obama Came to Plan for 'Surge' in Afghanistan." *New York Times*, December 5, 2009.

27　Hillary Clinton, *Hard Choices*. Simon & Schuster, June 2014.

28　Remarks by General David Petraeus at *Passing the Baton: Foreign Policy Challenges and Opportunities Facing the New Administration*. United States Institute of Peace, January 8, 2009.

29　Ashley Tellis, "Implementing a Regional Approach to Afghanistan: Multiple Alternatives, Modest Possibilities" in *Is a Regional Strategy Viable in Afghanistan?* Carnegie Endowment for International Peace, 2010.

30　Declan Walsh, "Hillary Clinton Visits Pakistan to Urge Action against Taliban Militants." *Guardian*, October 21, 2011.

31　Bruce Riedel, "Hillary Clinton's New Book Shows Deep Distrust of Pakistan in the Hunt for Bin Laden." *Daily Beast*, June 18, 2014.

32　Ibid.

33　Amrullah Saleh, "The crisis and politics of ethnicity in Afghanistan." *Al Jazeera*, June 26, 2012.

34 Jonathon Burch, "RPT-Report Slams Pakistan for Meddling in Afghanistan." *Reuters*, June 13, 2010.

35 Scott Neuman, "Ceremony In Afghanistan Officially Ends America's Longest War." NPR New Blogs. Retrieved from www.npr.org/sections/thetwo-way/2014/12/28/373597845/ceremony-in-afghanistan-officially-ends-americas-longest-war.

36 Jordan Fabian and Amie Parnes, "Biden Contradicts Clinton's Account of bin Laden Raid Decision." *The Hill*, October 20, 2015.

37 Alex Strick Van Linschoten, "Go Tell the World about Our Fake Election." *Foreign Policy*, August 21, 2009.

38 Peter Galbraith, "U.N. Isn't Addressing Fraud in Afghan Election." *Washington Post*, October 4, 2009.

39 Jon Boone, "Afghanistan Election Challenger Abdullah Abdullah Pulls Out of Runoff." *Guardian*, November 1, 2009.

40 Yochi Dreazen, "Gates: U.S. Tried to Oust Karzai in 'Failed Putsch.'" *Foreign Policy*, January 9, 2014.

41 Ben Farmer, "US Diplomat Claims UN Tried to Gag Him." *Telegraph*, October 4, 2009.

42 Steve Coll, *Ghost Wars*. Penguin Press, 2004.

43 Ted Galen Carpenter, "The Unintended Consequences of Afghanistan." *World Policy Journal*, Vol 1, No. 1. Spring 1994.

44 Gallup Poll, "Americans view Afghanistan War as a Mistake." Retrieved from www.gallup.com/poll/167471/americans-view-afghanistan-war-mistake.aspx.

9

HILLARY CLINTON

Soft Power, Hard Rhetoric and US Foreign Policy

Kenneth Christie

Hillary Clinton's role as secretary of state under the first Obama administration has recently come under intense scrutiny, particularly so in light of her running for the Democratic presidential nominee in the 2016 elections just around the corner. The questions surrounding her actions and tenure in this office remain unanswered but certainly add up to a deal of controversy and debate. The Clinton family has been a major player in US politics and look set to continue to be, so it's important to understand the roles and actions of the elites here. Hillary has been simultaneously criticized and praised like any secretary of state, and it's important to understand the different sides in the debate.

This chapter sets out to achieve three things. The main objective is to assess US foreign policy and identity in relation to Hillary Clinton's role and in particular how and why she is perceived by the Arab world following the Arab Spring and the controversial intervention in Libya and the Benghazi incident. The next step is to see how she is perceived on the larger world stage and what her foreign policy doctrine is, and lastly this chapter will assess the challenges and prospects of US foreign policy and its identity following her role. Hillary Clinton is first and foremost a fairly controversial politician in US politics, and the answers to these kinds of questions are fairly complex and not always straightforward, particularly so because she is tied in with the Obama administration in its first term.

Identifying the Project of US Foreign Policy

To begin with, it's important to say a few words about foreign policy. It's a subject that is becoming absent from standard international relations textbooks and rarely do we see its mention in these kinds of texts anymore. There are good reasons for this. The end of the Cold War saw a shift in the way the major actors in international relations viewed the world. There was a great deal of emphasis on "soft" power and soft diplomacy. This emphasized the rebranding of the American image as one concerned with diplomacy and development over hard firepower. They wanted the world to see they had real values that were worth emulating, particularly as hard power had achieved so little. The US, and with Hillary as secretary of state, emphasized this by talking about human rights, Internet freedom, and public health among an entire raft of issues that were determined to be "soft." Hillary Clinton was seen as exemplifying the soft power in her tenure at the State Department. The security threats in the post–Cold War period and post-9/11 period have also significantly changed as we are dealing with the rise of different global actors (essentially non-state groups) who rely on complex networks and new, different techniques in technology and methods in promoting and exacerbating conflict. Indeed, some of these groups are defined as much by the term "network" or "movement" as by anything else. The USA and its Western allies redefined the theater of war after 9 November 2001, with the attacks on the Twin Trade Towers in New York. So the actors in foreign policy have shifted to some extent, as have the issues. Foreign policy also rarely acts in a separate context from domestic policy. Following 9/11, the US gained an appetite for military adventures, but there is little of that in the post–Iraq invasion period as public opinion started to criticize the goals and means of the war and questioned its necessity.

We can also argue that in the post–Cold War period, the meaning of the state underwent a period of redefinition, one which led it away from the traditional realist perspective as the superpowers' predominance was challenged by intrastate and external-state actors. For instance, human security, human rights issues, refugees, ethnicity, gender issues and the environment, among others, have emerged as crucial global themes in international politics at the close of the 20th century. Democratization and globalization have become key elements for many social scientists in explaining these global changes. The collapse of the Soviet Union and authoritarian regimes in Eastern Europe, Latin America and elsewhere has seen the process of democratization carried further. Democracy has also emerged as the legitimate form of government in Southern Europe (Spain and Portugal only became democracies in the mid 1970s) and in part East Asia. The development of the Arab Spring in 2011 in a region known to be reluctant to democratic overtures is also beginning to produce political and social change. It will be far more difficult now to reverse these trends. Political change has forced these issues out into the open in a way that is difficult to ignore. Again it was within the context of these changes that Hillary Clinton had to work.

End of Cold War

With the end of the Cold War, many people had hoped that an era of peace and tranquility might develop. Francis Fukuyama declared the "end of history" had arrived with the ascendance of liberal democracy. The major power blocks no longer threatened mutual and global annihilation, international governmental organizations were strengthened, and free trade was supposed to bring nations together in mutual self-interest. The USA emerged unchallenged as the sole super-power to dominate political and economic life. However, internal power struggles and ethnic and separatist movements flourished, using violence to achieve state and non-state objectives. The world was much more complex after the Cold War; it was no longer a black-and-white power struggle between two major superpowers. As much as the triumphalism of the USA following the collapse of the Soviet Union and Eastern Bloc was highlighted, it unleashed a great many new tensions and problems the US would have to try and deal with. And in many respects it was not incapable of dealing with this new complexity. Again it was within the context of these changes that Hillary Clinton had to work.

As we have seen, the end of the of the Cold War created confusion over foreign policy, and it helps to look at traditional ideas of what foreign policy is perceived as to understand this. An example of a definition of foreign policy is that it

> involves goals, strategies, measures, methods, guidelines, directives, under-standings, agreements and so on, by which national governments conduct international relations with each other and other international organiza-tions and non-governmental actors. (Jackson and Sorenson, 2007, p. 223)

Immediately we can see the problem with this. We have so many non-state actors playing a role in international relations, from the environmental movement to private security armies to the Islamic state and many more. All of these actors are competing for power and many of them in untraditional forms. So foreign policy and its goals become confused and difficult to measure at times. The American state has struggled with these changes. Walter Russell Mead has argued that gaug-ing the performance of a secretary of state is actually very difficult. "The conven-tional indicators—landmark treaties, a new doctrine, signature deals—are actually poor guides to assessing the caliber of American diplomats" (Mead, 2015, p. 1).

The entire question of US national identity, for one thing, and its relationship to foreign policy has become ever more important following the end of the Cold War. Americans appear reluctant to think of themselves as belonging to an impe-rial power and yet at the same time the American state acts as the global hegemon, using preemptive measures to secure national interests. Such reluctance (on the public's part) is particularly so when the connotations of empire and imperialism are generally construed as negative influences, with a history of misdeeds and atrocities. Americans, however, have long seen themselves as unwilling to become involved, even though the record of their government's actions differs with this assessment. It is clear today that the United States has used instruments of foreign policy as a tool to secure these interests. Rather than resorting to diplomacy, the US has aggressively sought to take control. The fact that Americans belong to the most powerful nation-state the world has ever seen is an important one; many see the US as having carte blanche to intervene and interfere at will.

These themes—the promulgation of democracy and freedom (or even "wars" on specific threats)—are not new aspects to American foreign policy, but rather should be viewed as part and parcel of US identity. Woodrow Wilson, first put them into a practical bent after the First World War, but there is a fairly long continuity made explicit from the presidency of Jimmy Carter in the 1970s through Ronald Reagan and the George H. W. Bush presidencies, continuing through President Clinton to George W. Bush and under the Obama administration. To some extent, the US has seen itself as an "exceptional" nation not bound by the rules of normal nation-states, and this has provided a certain justification for its actions. What is new, in its latest incarnation, is the extent of the missionary zeal in promoting it, coupled with the visceral military power to enforce it. The US sees itself as having a civilizing, democratic mission to project its image. And despite its proclaimed reluctance (Americans don't like to think of themselves as imperialists), the US perceives itself as capable of transforming the world in its own image. This transformation appears to have gone awry, both in practical and ideological connotations. The USA has been viewed as a hegemonic power which has resorted to imperial strategy to achieve its ends, and that's the view of supporters as well as critics. As Hans Kohn pointed out in the 1950s, "American national identity has been based in the belief that the nations binding principles are rooted in qualities and capacities shared by all people everywhere." Several neo-conservatives reinforced this missionary framework in the late 1990s, arguing that "the US must discourage advanced industrial nations from challenging our leadership or even aspiring to a larger regional or global role." This is a powerful signature for expanding its remit. However, the US does not like to think of itself as "imperialist," a negative, pejorative term in a world where self-determination is an accepted international norm. It holds this role in a state of ambiguity and confusion. This new meta-narrative means that the "power" to "narrate" is vested in the USA as the only global superpower. Contemporary criticisms of US imperialism take for granted the idea that a non-imperial United States would consume only its share of global resources, would respect the sovereignty and popular will of other nations, and would pursue multilateral solutions to international problems. And yet America has struggled to define its role and where exactly it can play a concrete role in the post–Cold War.

Hillary under the Obama Administration

After a fierce and failed attempt for the Democratic presidential nominee in the run-up to the 2009 election, Hillary Clinton was given the role of secretary of state in the first Barack Obama administration between 2009 and 2013. This was a reward, and she was quickly turned into a loyal member of the Obama administration, putting aside all political differences. During her tenure, she visited more countries than any other previous secretary of state (Garber, 2013), and she was at the center of the American response to the Arab Spring and played a large part in the US intervention in Libya, which has been criticized in various parts. Clinton also took responsibility for different security errors and lapses during the 2012 Benghazi attack, which resulted in the deaths of personnel in the US consulate in Libya, but this proved to be the shadow that would haunt her for the remainder of her term in office and continues to this day to be controversial. Clinton's belief was that "smart power" would win the day for US foreign policy: diplomacy and American firepower were essential ingredients to convince the rest of the world of American stature and purpose. This was a two-edged sword, as Americans in some ways were tired of foreign wars and conflicts that seemed far away, reflecting the isolationist strand in US foreign policy, whereas Hillary was assertive and wanted to do more to preempt such conflicts. The results are therefore a mixed bag.

Obama Barack's Appeal in the Muslim World

One of the special features of the 2008 presidential election campaign was the unprecedented appeal of one candidate in the Islamic world, Obama. Large sections of Muslim populations on a global basis were fascinated by the campaign and hoped that Obama would achieve his goals. And the fact that this level of support came at a time when the Muslim world displayed a likewise unprecedented degree of anger and indignation over US foreign policy toward the Middle East is just as striking. This "Obama phenomenon" really seemed to be encapsulated by the new president's willingness to open and talk to "America's enemies," a marked contrast from the Bush administration. The Obama government was keen to reach out to the Muslim world; he was keen to promote diplomacy after years of failure in the Middle East to achieve a settlement between the Israelis and the Palestinians. In terms of the 2008 presidential elections, it seemed that Obama represented change; that is, change from what was widely seen as disastrous policies. It would be a fresh beginning, and there was little stomach in the region for a continuation of US foreign policy seen as intervention and destructive.

Within the UAE, for instance, Obama came across as a very popular candidate. The fact that he lived for some time in a Muslim country (Indonesia) when he grew up, that as an African-American he came from a minority background in the US, and that he appeared to have a radically different set of policies and ideas than that of the Bush administration certainly helped. In this context, one must remember that Obama's predecessor in the White House was very unpopular in the UAE in particular and the Middle East in general. This support for Obama evinced itself in a generalized degree of support, even though it would be fair to say that many Emiratis are generally apathetic about politics.

It would also be fair to say that eight years of the Bush administration has tarnished America's reputation around the world and has been a cause of anti-Americanism at a very serious level. The radical change in leadership, which would have been unthinkable 50 years ago, has given people a kind of fresh impetus to become involved and be interested in politics. This has had a kind of knock-on effect (effect by association), where the UAE has paid a keener than usual interest in the US election. Moreover, the hype in the media and the interest generated by the primaries and the candidates in terms of this being seen as a landmark election has made people more interested.

Obama's declarations and policy positions also make him popular in the UAE. On the campaign trail he spoke out against the war in Iraq and called for a phased withdrawal of troops from there, as well as the need to offer incentives and negotiate with Iran over its nuclear program.

The Context of the Arab Spring

The Arab Spring, which emerged piece by piece and country by country in early 2011, was a tremendous period of social and political change throughout the world of the Middle East and North Africa. In all of these conflicts, upheavals, the dismantling of old regimes, and not long after, the counterreaction, several questions came to the fore. These include, what went wrong, and why did it go wrong? Moreover, the process of why and how many of these systems failed (or have held together) in the face of the forces of political and social change is crucial to the conflicts. Spring appears to have turned into winter: the initial optimism of widespread social and political change has all but evaporated, and the chilly winds of authoritarian and military rule have been reasserted. This has had major policy implications for US foreign policy and how the US perceived the region and in turn was perceived. These implications and consequences continue until today, and Hillary Clinton was US secretary of state when the Spring started and when the world saw the failure of the much promised and heralded political and social change.

The Arab Spring and Political and Social Change

Leaders in the USA described the Arab Spring as historical in terms of the opportunities it presented and its being transformative in political nature. It signaled hope for a region which had seemed mired in political and social stagnation. Certainly in the early days of the Spring, the Obama government held very idealistic views that this was the beginning of real change in a region that was mired in stagnation and undemocratic governments incapable of change. There was a great deal of positive belief that the time had come for one of the last great democratic revolutions.

And it appeared to shake some of the foundational cores of the region's democratic recalcitrance, starting with the self-immolation of a young Tunisian fruit and vegetable vendor who was protesting against heavy-handed police intervention that disallowed him to sell his produce. Midway through December 2010, the police in the small town of Sidi Bouzid decided to take Mohamed Bouazizi's vegetable cart, claiming he was unlicensed to sell. The vendor, who was unable to get redress, set himself alight (he died from the burns on January 4, 2011), and the country was engulfed in political and social protest. Broad-based uprisings closely followed. The Tunisian president, Zine el-Abidine, was removed from power. Hosni Mubarak was forced to step down in Egypt and Muammar Qaddafi was ousted in Libya. More than two years later, the initial promise of the Arab Spring is difficult to ascertain, as the region again seems to have slipped back into its typical patterns and in some cases has actually exacerbated authoritarian tendencies. In Syria we are witnessing a vicious sectarian form of civil war that appears intractable, while Iraq and Yemen exhibit high levels of political violence and chaos. Even Libya, where humanitarian intervention was invoked to get rid of the long-standing dictator, has had its difficulties, failing to rein in local militias and warlords in the countryside who appear to act with impunity. The ongoing governance crisis in Egypt continues apace, and a return to military government has undermined what could have been the foundational stone for democracy in the region.

The Arab Spring over the last six years has basically failed in its promises. It promised democracy to the one of the last places in the world which appeared to be holding out. It promised a better relationship with the West, a relationship strained to the brink in the quagmire of Middle Eastern politics. None of its revolutions have been successful; the experiments have by and large failed. In Libya, despite intervention under a humanitarian guise and the removal of Gaddafi, the result has been chaos and ethnic tribal warfare, where Islamic factions and warlords compete for power and insecurity reigns. The indecisiveness of what to actually do in Egypt created power vacuums and in turn the army generals stepped back into power. Syria went from bad to worse with massive humanitarian disasters that have completely destabilized parts of the Middle East and that are now spreading to Europe. There has been a revival of Sunni-Shia hatred in Iraq and Syria as well as other states that are now perceived as proxies for this ethno-religious battle, such as Yemen. The government of the US continues to sell Saudi Arabia weapons, while Saudi Arabia continues to spread its extreme form of Islam, which some have compared to ISIS. It's in Iraq, however, that the total failure of this policy and the Arab Spring have come full circle. Iraq, like Syria, is essentially a failed state with little or no hope of regaining the central control that Saddam Hussein once exercised. Saddam was a terrible dictator, but the slaughter of religious minorities now continues apace in the Middle East and there seems no end in sight. In a speech in early 2011 in Qatar, Clinton had stressed the need for Arab leaders to take action, admonishing them for failing to "build a future that your young people will believe in, stay for and defend" and arguing also that the people of the Arab world had "grown tired of corrupt institutions and a stagnant political order."

The Benghazi Incident

Perhaps the defining moment of Hillary Clinton's job as secretary of state was the Benghazi incident. The attack on Benghazi in September 11, 2012, was an attack by Islamic militants in the heart of Libya. The attacks were specifically targeted at the American diplomatic compound in Benghazi, Libya, and managed to kill the American ambassador, J. Christopher Stevens, and an information officer, Dean Smith. The Benghazi attack took place on the evening of September 11, 2012. Stevens was the first American ambassador killed in a conflict since 1979. The attack has also been viewed as the Battle of Benghazi. Shortly afterward a second assault hit another compound about a mile away, killing two CIA contractors and injuring many more.

Most ordinary Libyans condemned the brutality of the attacks and were supportive of the late ambassador. They staged public demonstrations condemning the militias (formed to oppose leader Colonel Muammar Gaddafi) which were suspected of the attacks.

Following the Benghazi attack, the United States increased security worldwide at different diplomatic and military facilities and initiated an investigation of the attack. Following the tragedy, the State Department was criticized for denying requests for additional security at the consulate prior to the attack. As secretary of state, Hillary Clinton subsequently took responsibility for the security lapses.

It's hard to know what to make of the security lapse and whether Hillary can really be to blame for the Benghazi incident. In a high-profile interview with *Atlantic* magazine, she stated that America contributed to the overthrow of Libyan leader Muammar. But the interviewer pushed her on the notion that the US did not stick around for the aftermath which she rebuts.

> [E]ither we should have helped the people of Libya try to overthrow a dictator [. . .] or we should have been on the sidelines. In this case we helped, but that didn't make the the road any easier in Syria, where we said, "It's messy, it's complicated, we're not sure what the outcome will be." So what I'm hoping for is that we sort out what we have learned because we've tried a bunch of different approaches." (Goldberg, 2014, p. 19.)

Part of the problem in judging Hillary on this matter is the fact that the Arab Spring had different outcomes across the board, from Egypt to Tunisia to Libya and so on. Ultimately it was a mess and continues to be a difficult, complicated mess, which any secretary of state in an American administration would find difficult to deal with. This is not to forget the terrible conflicts raging in Syria and Iraq, which in part the West helped to create.

In Syria

No one knows how Syria's war will end. Four years of violence, destruction and instability have had a terrible impact on millions of people, both in Syria and the wider Middle East. But it is already clear that international divisions over the greatest crisis of the 21st century have contributed to its severity and longevity.

Americans, Europeans, Russians, Iranians and Arabs all played their part. Competing interests, misreadings and indecision were on display when the uprising began in March 2011. Western governments were still dazzled by the speed and drama of the early Arab Spring. Dictators had been overthrown in Tunisia and Egypt, protests were shaking Bahrain, and NATO was poised to intervene in support of rebels in Libya fighting Muammar Gaddafi.

Initially Hillary Clinton called Bashar al-Assad a "reformer" but then decided he had "lost legitimacy." In August, Barack Obama fatefully called on Assad to step aside "for the sake of the Syrian people." Eight years after (2011) the US-led invasion of Iraq, that statement meant Western support for regime change in another Arab capital. But the Arab Spring was poorly managed and only succeeded in damaging much of the solid, though of course, undemocratic, structure of the Middle East.

The Global Stage

The questions remain whether Hillary Clinton was a great secretary of state or simply a competent one, or even, as some of her critics maintain, a poor and indecisive leader shackled by the whims of the West Wing. There is evidence to support a very mixed picture of her role on the world stage. In an interview shortly after his inauguration, President Obama praised Hillary Clinton, stating that she would "go down as on of the finest secretaries of state we've had" (Hirsh, 2013, p. 1). Clinton, who had challenged Obama in the 2009 primaries, was given a leading role and turned into a leading advocate and campaigner for the Obama way of doing things.

However, it's unlikely that anyone will remember her as a "great" secretary of state, which is reserved for the likes of George Marshall or Dean Acheson, among others. Rather, the legacy that Clinton left might come to be seen as that of a highly competent and, to some extent, effective strategist and leader. The jury is out. Clinton is still dealing with the fallout from the Benghazi incident (which she did claim responsibility for and which resulted in the deaths of several Americans).

To start with, was there a Hillary doctrine or policy that she might be assessed by? The fact is that Hillary departed office after 4 years without a doctrine that could be readily attributable to her, without much of a strategy and with no real diplomatic success. She was certainly competent but not in the style of previous great secretaries of state. If anything characterizes a grand strategy that Hillary might have aspired to, it would have to place her in the "exceptionalism" category, meaning that she saw the US as having unique role and that the idea and practice of the USA in the world as having a viable future.

Conclusion: Future Challenges

Hillary Clinton has come across as a fairly divisive and difficult figure in the run-up to the US presidential campaign. The next election in 2016 will be fascinating to watch, particularly if Donald Trump succeeds in taking the Republican nomination. What is even more interesting is the veiled and not so veiled criticism of her former boss, Barack Obama. In her bid for the Democratic presidential nominee, Hillary publicly condemned Barack Obama's foreign policy record in an attempt to distance herself from any criticism of her time in office. This is the politics of the presidential campaign, of course, but Barack's initial attempts to reach out to the Islamic world have by and large proved a failure. The war on terror has continued, and his use of drones in conflict has been widely criticized by friends and foes alike. Hillary wants to provide some distance from the share of the blame. And the world (in particular the Middle East) is the sight of humanitarian disasters that affect US policy on a daily basis. This has become more explicit in nature. Her view of the US's role in the world and that of Obama were sharply contrasted in an interview she conducted for the *Atlantic* magazine. In the same interview she also mentioned significant disagreements between Obama and herself over the continuing crises in the Middle East.

Citing the Obama administration's characterization of foreign policy as "don't do stupid stuff," Hillary castigated this, saying, "Great nations need organizing principles and 'don't do stupid stuff' is not an organizing principle." Clinton, in her book *Hard Choices* (2014), also stated that during the Arab Spring she wanted to see Hosni Mubarak, the Egyptian president, make way for his successor, but she was overruled by the Obama administration.

Her proposed foreign policy doctrine certainly sees a much more assertive voice for the US and its role in the world, an action plan, if you like, to make decisions more quickly and respond to situations in a more timely fashion. She clearly criticized the Obama administration when it failed to take action to arm the Syrian rebels in the early stage of the civil war, which then left open the door for ISIS and other groups to step in.

It must be remembered that secretaries of state don't necessarily hold sway over US foreign policy. Clinton's lack of a grand strategy in many ways could be attributed to her job. And that was to implement Barack Obama' ideas. In some ways her hands were tied and she was constrained. Her soft power approach focusing on gender issues in the developing world, empowering women, public health and opening doors in Burma, among other concerns, were examples of good, solid success. Her lack of strategy and insight into the Arab uprisings, however, were problematic and may have exacerbated the situation. Clinton was a realist who wanted more but was frustrated because of the administration's control over policy.

However, in recent events it is clear that some of that realist strategy has paid off. The USA has now signed an historic agreement with Iran on nuclear policy, and much of the credit can be given over to Hillary Clinton. In the 2008 battle for the Democratic nomination, Barack Obama and Hillary Clinton argued with some animosity about Iran and what to do with it. Hillary thought that Obama's policy was naïve and reckless, too full of idealistic virtues. When Clinton, as the hawk, threatened to destroy Iran if it used nuclear weapons against Israel, Obama made her out to be like George W. Bush in terms of bellicosity and rhetoric. However, it was Hillary Clinton who won the say on this deal, which was negotiated between 26 March and 2 April 2015, and has had far-ranging consequences for US foreign policy and the Middle East. Obama has been touting the success widely, and the International Atomic Energy Agency certified in January 2016 that Iran has complied with its agreement to scale back its nuclear program. Nuclear-related sanctions have been lifted, and in different side agreements, Iran has released five Americans who were held captive, and the US, using the constitutional pardon powers, has granted clemency to seven Iranians held in the United States.

In addition, it was announced that the United States and Iran had settled a long-standing dispute over Iranian assets frozen during the 1979 Tehran hostage crisis, when Iranian students stormed the United States embassy in Tehran, taking 66 hostages; President Carter froze $400 million in Iranian assets that was going to fund military equipment. These funds are already being returned with $1.3 billion in interest, leading to the settling of claims at the Iran–United States Claims Tribunal in The Hague.

Therefore, Clinton and Obama are completely linked with these deals. If Clinton becomes the next president of the USA, the success of these deals will depend on how much Clinton is committed to making these deals work, the ones she initiated as secretary of state.

The fact remains that Hillary continues to be fairly hard-lined on the issue of Iran, so it will be interesting to see if she reverses some of the US foreign policy deals signed under Obama if she takes the presidency in 2016. Some commentators have seen these kinds of views and her work in foreign policy as a liability for Hillary Clinton. The fact that she has had more foreign policy experience than any of the other potential candidates in the 2016 presidential race has also meant that the risks have become higher. Crises, such as the Arab Spring, have not gone away, and ISIS remains a powerful threat in Syria and Iraq to US foreign policy.

The fight against ISIS has demonstrated great confusion within the Obama administration, and again Clinton was clearly more hawkish over the tactics, while Obama has racked up the rhetoric without much of the firepower to support it. Pledges to "destroy ISIS" are all very well, but without "boots on the ground" it's unlikely that bombing will work. US foreign policy seems in the last stages of the Obama administration to be limited and against any increase in forces or operations. Spending nearly $11.5 million a day on an unsuccessful war is increasingly unpopular, and so far the US has spent over $5.5 billion without any real results. For Hillary and Obama, the fight against ISIS militants, indeed the entire policy in Syria, has been a failure which has seen no resolution and an increasing quagmire in which ISIS appears to have gotten stronger at the expense of their enemies.

Moreover, the blunders over the Benghazi raid may return to haunt Hillary Clinton as her critics start to find flaws in her actions. The Arab Spring has certainly not met any stated goals of US foreign policy, such as the promotion of democracy, human rights and the empowerment of women in the Middle East. In fact, it appears to have been the opposite. Jihadism is clearly on the rise, democracy has taken several steps backward and the Arab Spring has turned to winter along with massive human displacement all over the Middle East.

However, Hillary Clinton has clear views on American power and its limitations. In her recent interview in the *Atlantic*, she stated that Iraq taught America both the limits and importance of its power to spread democracy, freedom, and other American values (Goldberg, 2014, p. 24). Seeking a more assertive strategy and goals while being constrained by a reluctant White House meant that Clinton's legacy will be a moderate one, winning small battles and being consistent but ultimately not changing the rules of the game—a game that may be ultimately beyond the scope and ability of any foreign policy to change.

References

Books

Allen, Jonathan and Aimee Parnes, *HRC: State Secrets and the Rebirth of Hillary Clinton* (London: Hutchinson, 2014).

Bacevich, A. J., *American Empire: The Realities and Consequences of American Diplomacy* (Cambridge, MA: Harvard University Press, 2002).

Bender, Thomas, *A Nation Among Nations: America's Place in World History* (New York: Hill and Wang, 2006).

Borgwardt, Elizabeth, *A New Deal for the World: America's Vision for Human Rights* (Cambridge: Harvard University Press, 2005).

Campbell, David, *Writing Security: United States Foreign Policy and the Politics of Identity*, Revised Ed. (Manchester: Manchester University Press, 1998).

Chomsky, Noam, *Deterring Democracy* (London: Vintage, 1992).

Christie, Kenneth (Ed.), *US Foreign Policy and National Identity in the Twenty-First Century* (New York: Routledge, 2008).

Christie, Kenneth and Mohammad Masad (Eds.), *State Formation and Identity in the Middle East and North Africa* (New York: Palgrave MacMillan, 2013).

Clinton, Hillary, *Hard Choices* (New York: Simon and Schuster, 2014).

Ferguson, Niall, *Colossus: The Rise and Fall of the American Empire* (London: Penguin, 2004).

Fukuyama, Francis, *Democracy, Power, and the Neoconservative Legacy* (New Haven: Yale University Press, 2006).

Fukuyama, Francis, *The End of History and the Last Man* (London: Penguin, 1992).

Garber, M. (2014). Hillary Clinton Traveled 956,733 Miles During Her Time as Secretary of State, Atlantic, Jan 29; www.theatlantic.com/politics/archive/2013/01/hillary-clinton-traveled-956-733-miles-during-her-time-as-secretary-of-state/272656/; last accessed on March 28, 2016.

Gardner, Lloyd C. and Marilyn B. Young (Eds.), *The New American Empire: A 21st Century Teach-In on US Foreign Policy* (New York: New Press, 2005).

Hollis, Martin and Steve Smith, *Explaining and Understanding International Relations* (Oxford: Clarendon Press, 1991).

Hunt, Michael H., *Ideology and US Foreign Policy* (New Haven: Yale University Press, 1987).

Huntingdon, Samuel P., *Who Are We? America's Great Debate* (London: Simon & Schuster, 2004).

Huntington, Samuel P., *Who Are We? The Challenges to America's National Identity* (New York: Simon & Schuster, 2004).

Jackson, Robert and Georg Sorenson, *Introduction to International Relations: Theories and Approaches* (Oxford: Oxford University Press, 2007).

Kagan, R., *Paradise and Power: America and Europe in the New World Order* (London: Atlantic, 2003).

Kaplan, Robert F. and William Kristol, *The War over Iraq: Saddam's Tyranny and America's Mission* (San Francisco: Encounter Books, 2003).

Kohn, Hans, *American Nationalism: An Interpretive Essay* (New York: MacMillan 1957).

Lieven, Anatol, *America Right or Wrong: An Anatomy of American Nationalism* (Oxford: Oxford University Press, 2004).

Maas, Matthias (Ed.), *The World Views of the U.S. Presidential Election 2008* (New York: Palgrave MacMillan, 2009).

McEvoy-Levy, Siobhan, *American Exceptionalism and US Foreign Policy* (New York: Palgrave, 2001).

Mead, Walter Russell, Was Hillary Clinton a good secretary of state? *The Washington Post*, May 30, 2015, p. 1.

Mead, Walter Russell, *Power, Terror, Peace, and War: America's Grand Strategy in a World at Risk* (New York: Vintage, 2004).

Mead, Walter Russell, *Special Providence: American Foreign Policy and How It Changed the World* (New York: Routledge, 2002).

Morgenthau, Hans J., *Politics Among Nations: The Struggle for Power and Peace, Brief Ed.* (Boston: McGraw-Hill, 1993).

Nau, Henry R., *At Home Abroad: Identity and Power in American Foreign Policy* (Ithaca: Cornell University Press, 2002).

Noonan, Peggy, *When Character Was King: A Story of Ronald Reagan* (New York: Penguin Books, 2001).

Nye, Joseph S. Jr, *The Paradox of American Power: Why the World's Only Superpower Can't Go It Alone* (New York: Oxford University Press, 2002).

Journal Articles

Goldberg, Jeffrey (2104), "Hillary Clinton: 'Failure' to Help Syrian Rebels Led the the Rise of ISIS," *Atlantic.* See www.theatlantic.com/international/archive/2014/08/hillary-clinton-failure-to-help-syrian-rebels-led-to-the-rise-of-isis/375832/; last accessed on March 28, 2016.

Hirsh, Michael, "The Clinton Legacy" (2013), *Foreign Affairs.* See www.foreignaffairs.com/articles/united-states/2013-04-03/clinton-legacy; last accessed on March 28, 2016.

Ikenberry, John G., "American Power and the Empire of Capitalist Democracy," *Review of International Studies*, 27, (2001), pp. 191–212.

Lexington's Notebook, (2012). "An Interview with Hillary Clinton." *Economist*, March 22, 2012; www.economist.com/node/21550643; last accessed on March 28, 2016.

Kristol, Irving, "My Cold War," *National Interest* (22 March 1993).

McCormick, James M., "Domestic Factors and the Bush Administration: Constraints on Foreign Policymaking?" Paper presented at the BISA US Foreign Policy Working Group Conference, University of Leicester, UK, 21 September 2006.

Nye, Joseph S. Jr., "Redefining the National Interest," *Foreign Affairs*, 78(4), (1999), pp. 22–35.

Ryn, Claes G., "The Ideology of American Empire," *Orbis* 47(3), (Summer 2003): 385–397.

Smith, David, "Niall Ferguson: The Empire Rebuilder," *Observer*, (June 18, 2006), 35.

10

HILLARY CLINTON AND ISRAEL

American Jewish and Israeli Perceptions

Ellen Fleishman

I have a vested interest in the peace and security of Israel and the Middle East, as does any world citizen, but as an American Jew with family there, my interest is more personal.

I want my grandchildren to survive, and not be killed in a terrorist attack, or during their military service. I want my daughter to remain alive while she visits the supermarket for groceries. I want my son-in-law to return from work, whole and unharmed.

The current Israeli–Palestinian conflict can be said to have begun in 1896 with the publication of Herzl's *The Jewish State*. For Israelis and Jews around the world, the establishment of the state of Israel by UN resolution on November 29, 1947, was cause for great celebration and dancing in the streets. For Palestinians living in that part of the world, it was the Nakba, the catastrophe, the disaster.

More often than not those belonging to each side refuse to step into each other's shoes to understand the differences in their points of view, or show empathy. The ability to empathize is one of the hallmarks of emotional maturity and is the basis of mercy and forgiveness, aspects of holiness in most major world religions, including Judaism, Christianity and Islam.

This lack of empathy may be the basis for the intractability of the Israeli–Palestinian conflict. If each side could allow themselves to see the issues from the other side's perspective, it might be more difficult for them to adhere so narrowly to their own self-interest.

In the 1960s, as an eight-year-old child growing up in a largely Catholic Jersey City, New Jersey, my girlfriend's grandmother literally pushed her toward me while we all stood in her kitchen, to tell me she hated me because I am Jewish. My neighbors shouted from their windows that the Jews killed Christ.

While living in Germany in 1978, one of my neighbors told me Germans were Aryans while Jews had hooked noses.

Those small but painful incidents of anti-Semitism pale in comparison to that experienced by contemporary Jews in Russia, Eastern Europe and the Middle East, even after World War II and the Holocaust. On July 4, 1946, 42 of the 200 Jews who had returned to Kielce, Poland, were killed in a pogrom (Kielce Pogrom, n.d.). On November 14, 2013, George Bush, a long-time staunch supporter of Israel, nonetheless provoked irate Jewish responses when he spoke at the Messianic Jewish Bible Institute, a Christian group that aims to convert Jews to Christianity. Mick Huckabee, Oliver North and Glenn Beck did the same in prior years (Jewish Israel, November 26, 2013). These evangelical Christians support Israel not to allow Judaism to flourish and for Jewish people to experience life free from religious persecution, but to permit the possibility of Jewish conversion to Christianity and an in-gathering of Christians to Israel which will herald the second coming of the messiah.

Hence, many American Jews find any criticism of Israel intolerable. To them, any negative assessment of Israeli policies, actions or words is a flat-out indication of anti-Semitism. As a tiny minority of 14.2 million in a world population of 7 billion, (0.2%; 2014 estimates) (Jewish population by country, n.d.), Jews feel extremely vulnerable and insecure. They believe their safety is dependent upon the continued existence of Israel. That, in fact, was Herzl's argument for bringing Israel into existence, as throughout history, Jews worldwide suffered intense persecution, discrimination and death, while living elsewhere.

There is probably a direct correlation between the degree of rancor of many Israeli and American Jews toward Hillary Clinton and the perceiver's degree of empathy with the Palestinians. The degree of Palestinian empathy directly correlates with some Jews' condemnation of the empathizer—whether the empathizer is Jewish, Christian or Muslim—in the Jewish mind that is restricted to its own perspective. Therefore, as a Jew, if I espouse the Palestinian point of view as valuable to consider in weighing the issues, I am judged to be anti-Semitic and anti-Israel. In this way of thinking, you are either with Israel or you are not. There is no room for seeing issues from the other's point of view.

Hence Israelis and many American Jews deeply distrust Barack Obama and Hillary Clinton. Hillary recently published an article in the *Forward* (Clinton, November 4, 2015) detailing her love and support for Israel which, to the Israel-only perspective, contradicts many of her actions during her tenure as secretary of state.

The current Israeli Prime minister, Benjamin Netanyahu, believes in "greater Israel" and wishes to incorporate the West Bank into Israel proper. With the exception of a ten-month hiatus in 2009 (Bronner and Landler, 2009), he refuses to cease settlement building in the West Bank, despite continued pressure from the Obama administration, which earned Obama and Hillary, as Obama's secretary of state, great right-wing America Jewish and Israeli opprobrium (Dunetz, 2015).

Hillary now indicates she wholeheartedly supports Netanyahu's position (Clinton, November 4, 2015), but many Israelis do not believe her and others, who can empathize with the Palestinian perspective, believe that ultimately the Netanyahu position will in fact destroy Israel with its inability to compromise and make room for a Palestinian state living side by side with Israel. These leftist Israelis say Hillary is no friend to Israel (Levy, 2015) due to her very avowal of Netanyahu's policies.

Contrast this with a September 2015 article lambasting Hillary for emails between her and Sidney Blumenthal, a leftist who argues for a two-state solution (Shapiro, 2015). Shapiro's view is that email exchanges between Hillary and Blumenthal reveal deep anti-Israel sentiment, since Blumenthal takes the position that ignoring the Palestinian position is not only unfair to them, but represents a public relations nightmare for Israel. Blumenthal objects to the one-sidedness of American Jewish leadership who unquestioningly support Bibi Netanyahu's policies.

It is important to note that Americans are increasingly examining the Israeli-Palestinian conflict through the lens of human rights—especially younger Americans, African Americans and Hispanic Americans. These groups are, through their own historical and current position in American society, more able to empathize with Palestinian suffering and are less sympathetic to heavy-handed Israeli counterterrorism policies. These groups are also growing segments of the American population and the Democratic Party (Wittes-Coffman, 2015). Their views will make it more difficult for American-Israeli policy to ignore the Palestinian position, and will force the American Congress and president to take empathy with Palestinians seriously.

History

Understanding the current situation and the current Israeli attitude toward Hillary Clinton requires knowledge of basic history leading to this moment. According to legend, Jews and Arabs have a common ancestor. Both groups view themselves as descendants of Abraham, with Jews derived from Isaac, the son of Sarah, and Arabs from Ishmael, the son of Hagar, Sarah's handmaiden, who Sarah gave to Abraham as his concubine. Arabs are described as a nomadic, tribal people of central and Northern Arabian Peninsula who developed customs and codes to survive in the harsh desert (Bickerton and Klausner, 2002). They eventually embraced Islam in the seventh century and went on to conquer the Middle East in the seventh and eighth centuries, making Islam the region's religion and Arabic its language. Today Arabs constitute the majority of 22 nation-states from Morocco to Iraq and number approximately 390 million (List of Arab countries by population, n.d.).

Currently there are two major Islamic groups, the Sunnis and the Shiites. The major difference between them is political in terms of how Muhammed's successor was determined. Muhammed was the acknowledged religious, political and military leader of his new community of believers in one God. When Muhammed died in 632, his successors, or caliphs, were responsible for political and military leadership as well, but not for revelation, though perhaps for interpretation of the hadiths, or written compilations of oral testimony by Muhammed. The caliph also stifled revolts by recalcitrant tribes and extended Islam beyond Arabia (Bickerton and Klausner, 2002).

Sunnis believe the first rightful caliph was Muhammed's father-in-law, and that caliphs may be selected in some fashion. Shiites believe caliphs should descend from Ali, Muhammed's son-in-law and cousin, and the position is inherited from one generation to the next (Bickerton and Klausner, 2002). There are approximately 1.6 billion Muslims in the world (Islam by country, n.d.) with approximately 85% being Sunni, 12% Shiite, and a smattering of other sects.

Jews claim descent from Abraham's son Isaac, and Isaac's twelve sons, who formed twelve tribes. Jews constitute an ethnic, religious and/or cultural group and number approximately 14.2 million, or approximately 0.2% of the world population. Judaism is the world's oldest monotheistic religion and is the forerunner to Christianity and Islam. Unlike Christianity and Islam, however, Judaism does not seek converts, but rather is particularistic, adhering to the view that God chose Jews to enter into a covenant with God and save all humankind through obedience to God's teachings, such as the Ten Commandments. God also promised the Jews the land of Israel, the borders of which vary (e.g., Genesis 15:18–21; Numbers 34:1–12; Deuteronomy 1: 7–8). (Bickerton and Klausner, 2002).

Following the exodus from Egypt in approximately the 13th century BCE, the twelve tribes first inhabited the land east of the Jordan River. The kingdoms of Israel and Judah were established in the subsequent centuries. These lands were conquered by Babylonia in 586 BCE, and later ruled by the Greeks, Romans, Arabs, Crusaders, Mamluks, Ottomans and British, (Reiner and Reiner, 2015) prior to returning to Jewish rule on May 14, 1948, when David Ben Gurion proclaimed Israel to be independent (Israel, n.d.).

Hillary Clinton and Israel

Hillary Clinton is no stranger to controversy. Her early avid promotion of national health care reform during her husband's first presidential term made her a darling of the Democratic left and feminists, and a demon of the Republican right. That dichotomized perception applies to Israelis as well. The Israeli left believes she is not as hard on Netanyahu's settlement policies as she should be, especially since she began campaigning for president (Levy, 2015). The Israeli right demonizes her for not supporting further settlements and putting forth requests for compromise on a two-state solution (Dunetz, 2015).

Palestinians, including women, believe she has abandoned them in her quest for the presidency (Awwad, 2015; Weiss and Robbins, 2015). In October 2015 Hillary issued a statement very sympathetic to Israeli Jews regarding the recent wave of stabbing attacks by Palestinians, referring to how the Jewish citizens must always look over their shoulder when praying or visiting the supermarket.

Weiss and Robbins (2015) comment on how this excludes empathy with Palestinians and their plight, who have lived under occupation for 50 years, and seems to deny the Palestinian right to resist. They further expound this is pandering to the American Jewish donor, particularly Haim Saban.

Ms. Awwad (2015) writes an open letter to Secretary Clinton in the *Huffington Post*. She expresses how Hillary once inspired her with feminist declarations such as "women's rights are human rights." Ms. Awwad is, however, very disappointed in Hillary's *Forward* article. Not once does Hillary refer to Israel's human rights violations against Palestinian women and children, and she also describes Palestinians as lurking terrorists motivated by "incitement." Ms. Awwad further describes the constant everyday humiliations of having to be searched at checkpoints to go to school. During one incident Israeli soldiers released dogs to chase her and her family, and shot their guns at them. In other incidents pregnant women stopped at checkpoints have given birth there. Isra' Abed, a young Palestinian mother who posed no threat, was gunned down by Israeli police in Afula, and later cleared of any wrongdoing (ThirdIntifada, 2015).

Palestinian and Israeli textbooks have been analyzed by various academic and governmental bodies to determine their degree of bias, distortion, inaccuracy and incitement to violence and hatred (Textbooks in the Israeli–Palestinian conflict, n.d.). In a 2001 press conference, Hillary stated that the Palestinian textbooks contained anti-Semitic rhetoric and taught Palestinian children hatred (Newman, 2008). More recently, a 2009 US State Department report indicates that after the 2006 textbook revision by the Palestinian Authority's Ministry of Education, international academics concluded the books did not incite violence against Jews, but did show imbalance, bias and inaccuracy. Some maps did not depict the current political reality. They showed neither Israel nor the settlements, and some were inconsistent in defining the 1967 borders.

It is also true that maps produced by the Jewish Agency (2006) do not show Gaza or the West Bank, but portray the entire region as Israel. In addition, under Netanyahu, the word "Nakba," or catastrophe, to describe the establishment of the State of Israel, was banned from Israeli textbooks (Textbooks in the Israeli–Palestinian conflict, n.d.).

The Palestinian Ministry of Education (2005) observes that Hillary has criticized Palestinian textbooks since her first senate campaign, and stated that "All future aid to the Palestinian Authority must be contingent on their obligation to change textbooks in all grades." From the Palestinian Authority point of view, however, Hillary's campaign against "a new generation of terrorists" is itself an act of incitement to hate and racism (Palestinian Ministry of Education, 2005).

On Thursday, November 11, 1999, while First Lady, Hillary visited a school in the West Bank and sat in a classroom alongside Suha Arafat. Suha falsely alleged that Israel Defense Forces used poisoned gas to contaminate Palestinian land and drinking water. Rather than condemning Ms. Arafat's false statements, Hillary kissed her on both cheeks upon leaving, provoking a furor of condemnation in the American and Israeli Jewish communities (Jewish Telegraphic Agency, April 20, 2015). However, on Friday, November 12, 1999, while in Jordan and after learning exactly what Ms. Arafat had said, Hillary strongly condemned Suha's inflammatory rhetoric, stating that it interfered with the peace process (Associated Press, 1999).

Hillary explained later that the simultaneous translation she heard in her ears on November 11, 1999, communicated something much less problematic. Therefore she was unaware Suha had made those false statements, and she behaved towards her as befitted a First Lady of the United States (Lueck, 2000). Despite this, there remain Jewish detractors who point to this misunderstanding as evidence Hillary is anti-Semitic (Jewish Telegraph Agency, April 20, 2015).

Haim Saban, a billionaire dual American and Israeli citizen, wholly supports Hillary and has donated from $10 to $25 million to the Clinton Foundation. Saban and his wife slept in the Lincoln bedroom several times, as a reward for his donations to the Democratic Party, while Bill was president. Currently, Saban is viewed as Hillary's major financial backer, and Saban's donor circle constitutes a significant part of her financial base. Saban also created a Middle East Policy think tank at the Brookings Institution (Sniegoski, June 15, 2015).

In typical Clinton fashion, Hillary's most recent speech to the 2015 Saban Forum takes ideas from both the left and right to fashion a cross-partisan alternative, to appeal to the center (Maloney, December 12, 2015). This has long been a Clinton strategy adopted after Bill failed to win a 1980 second term as Arkansas governor. Bill lost that term because he did not deliver a promise to chicken processor tycoon Tyson to increase the limit that trucks could carry from 73,000 to 80,000 pounds, which would make Arkansas chicken farmers competitive with other states (Kelly, 1994).

Bill regained the governorship in 1982, but he never again adopted a position challenging his financial backers, nor one far from center on any issue (Kelly, 1994). Hillary religiously follows this strategy herself.

Dunetz (2015) presents as anti-Israel the fact that in 1998 Hillary called for the establishment of a Palestinian state. However, many contemporary analysts view two states as the wisest possible solution to the conflict (J Street, 2015; Beinart, 2014). At the same time, however, observers believe the current density and number of Israeli settlers in the West Bank preclude this possibility, much to Israel's detriment (Beinart, 2014). Incorporating the West Bank into Israel proper will greatly increase the number of Palestinian Arabs in the Israeli population. The Arab population will exceed the Jewish one, and if Israel remains a democracy the nature of Israel will change dramatically.

Hillary, however, warned that the alternative to the current Palestinian Authority could be the black flag of ISIS (Maloney, 2015), indicating that how important it is to work with the current Palestinian administration to negotiate an acceptable resolution of the conflict.

The 1993 Oslo Declaration allowed for a shared American-Israeli approach to solving the conflict—direct, bilateral negotiations led by the US. Current Israeli leadership embraces anti-solutionism as a strategy. Netanyahu emphasizes there will be no Palestinian State under his watch (Coffman, 2015). Hence, it would seem that Israeli-Palestinian talks are at a standstill until the next cycle of violence prompts various forces to reconsider their intransigency.

J Street believes that reaching a sustainable two-state solution to the Israeli-Palestinian conflict is both a fundamental American interest and essential to the survival and security of Israel. In the seventh decade following its establishment, Israel and most of her neighbors have yet to secure internationally recognized borders or to make peace. With the Jewish and Arab populations between the Jordan River and Mediterranean Sea at near-parity, demographic trends preclude Israel from maintaining control over all of Greater Israel while remaining a democratic state and a homeland for the Jewish people. As then Israeli prime minister Ehud Olmert said in November 2007, "If the day comes when the two-state solution collapses, and we face a South African–style struggle for equal voting rights, then, as soon as that happens, the State of Israel is finished" (J Street, December 25, 2015).

Iran Nuclear Deal

In a September 2015 speech at the Brookings Institution, Hillary clarified that while she supported the Iran nuclear agreement, she would be very tough on Iran's nonnuclear activities. She plans to boost military aid to Israel to maintain Israel's military superiority in the region. Hillary also called for increased cooperation with US allies in the Gulf to counter Iran's backing of militant proxy groups in Lebanon, Syria, Yemen and the occupied Palestinian territories. She called for putting more troops in the Middle East and for blocking Iran's efforts to prop up Assad in Syria. As a result of sanctions relief, monies bound for Iran may go to arming Iran's military proxies. Iran has funded Hezbollah, its proxy in Lebanon, which is fighting with Assad. Hillary seeks to block this funding, and to block Iranian planes from entering Syrian air space. A greater American military presence will also help to ensure the Strait of Hormuz remains open as a passageway for the flow of international oil off the Iranian coast (Schulberg, 2015a).

Hillary was noncommittal on whether or not she would permit Israel to have the Massive Ordinance penetrator, a 30,000-pound bunker-buster bomb which could theoretically be used against Iranian nuclear facilities (Schulberg, 2015b).

***

The Israeli-Palestinian conflict would seem to be intractable. Most Israelis and Palestinians themselves, as well as worldwide observers, anecdotally report they believe the problem will never end.

Yet the British left India, and India became an independent democracy, with a continually growing middle class. The Soviet Union fell, as did the Berlin Wall. Peace came to Northern Ireland. Apartheid ended in South Africa. Sadat signed a peace agreement with Begin through Jimmy Carter's mediation. The outcome of that extended Camp David retreat was uncertain to the last minute, however (Wright, 2014). The talks were about to break down many times during those days. It was only through sheer persistence and luck that the agreement was realized.

Closer to home, I would never have predicted that the United States would have a black president in my lifetime. Yet not only was one elected to two terms, currently one of the leading candidates for Republican nomination is also black.

But what lessons can we learn from these unpredictable events and how they led up to peace? And one can often see causal relationships in retrospect that could not have foretold what was to come. But in most of these extremely important world events, there appears to have been a confluence of events which came together to create the right moment for change to occur. Often, there was an economic underpinning. American strategies to weaken the Soviet Union economically worked. The Soviets could not keep up the arms race and also build their civil economy. Economic sanctions against South Africa contributed to forcing its people and their government to overturn its repressive policies. Perhaps the situation in Northern Ireland is more analogous to the Israeli–Palestinian situation than the others. In Northern Ireland many factors came together to permit an agreement between Catholics and Protestants, an important one being an improved economy and high-tech jobs coming to the region.

So must we wait for some yet little understood and unpredictable chain of events in Israel/Palestine to come together to have the two peoples lay aside the grudges, enmities, hatred and mistrust accumulated since 1896 to reach a peaceful resolution of some kind? Are we powerless to influence those events with our research?

Perhaps the most important psychological research to influence American policy was that of Kenneth and Mamie Clark. The Clarks studied the effect of segregation on black children's self-esteem. Their research involved each child being presented with two dolls. The dolls were identical except for their skin and hair color. One doll was white with yellow hair, while the other was brown with black hair. The child was then asked questions inquiring as to which one is the doll they would play with, which one is the nice doll, which one looks bad, which one has the nicer color, etc. (*Brown vs. Board of Education*).

The responses of black children in segregated schools were compared with black children in integrated schools in New York. The experiment showed a clear preference for the white doll among all children in the study. These findings exposed internalized racism in African-American children, self-hatred that was more acute among children attending segregated schools (*Brown v. Board of Education*).

This research is said to have greatly influenced the Supreme Court's decision to strike down school segregation. Chief Justice Earl Warren wrote in the *Brown vs. Board* opinion, "To separate black children from others of similar age and qualifications solely because of their race generates a feeling of inferiority as to their status in the community that may affect their hearts and minds in a way unlikely to ever be undone" (*Brown v. Board of Education*).

The court used this research to bolster its decision. Perhaps the court was happy to find evidence to support the decision it wanted to make anyway. It is also of interest to note that the justices made a special effort to make the decision unanimous, that unanimity lending it a moral weight that a single dissenting vote would have detracted from (*Brown v. Board of Education*).

But would the court have been similarly persuaded in 1939 or 1944? I think it unlikely. The world was embroiled in a world war and the Supreme Court would not have wanted to create even more unrest with its decision. But in 1954 the horrors of the Holocaust, a clear result of racism brought to its most extreme expression, had been exposed to the world. The United States was ready to end its own repression and expression of racist policies. The right confluence of events occurred to bring about the *Brown* decision.

I believe peaceful resolution of the Israeli-Palestinian conflict will occur when that happy confluence of factors arises and the conflict will become history, rather than current events. The horror of war is not visited only upon the victims, but also the perpetrators. Post-traumatic stress disorder can last a lifetime. Suicide rates among veterans are astronomically high, as we have heard in the news media (Zarembo, 2015). People will lay aside their enmity for the benefit of their children.

At that time we may look back at Hillary Clinton's approach as persuading the opposing parties to step into each other's shoes. We will herald her, and Obama before her, as having foresight and perspicacity. It will have been nothing more than encouraging the development of empathy for the neighbor, for a person once believed to be the enemy, but who was after all no different from oneself, with the same desires for a decent, peaceful, ordinary life for oneself and one's children.

References

Associated Press (1999, November 13). Hillary Clinton Rebukes Arafat's Wife. *LA Times*. Retrieved from http://articles.latimes.com/1999/nov/13/news/mn-33069.

Awwad, Layali (2015, November 9). Open Letter to Hillary Clinton from a Young Palestinian Feminist. *Huffington Post*. Retrieved from www.huffingtonpost.com/layali-awwad/hillary-clinton-palestine_b_8513966.html.

Beinart, Peter (2012). *The Crisis of Zionism*. Henry Holt and Co., New York.

Beinart, Peter (2014, August 11). Israel's New Lawyer: Hillary Clinton. *Haaretz*. Retrieved from www.haaretz.com/opinion/.premium-1.610007?date=1449362204384.

Bickerton, Ian, and Klausner, Carla (2002). *A Concise History of the Arab-Israeli Conflict*, 4th edition. PrenticeHall, Upper Saddle River, NJ.

Bronner, Ethan, and Landler, Mark (2009, November 25). Israel Offers a Pause in Settlement Building. *New York Times*. Retrieved from www.nytimes.com/2009/11/26/world/middleeast/26israel.html?_r=0.

Brown v. Board of Education. (n.d.). *Wikipedia*, Retrieved December 12, 2015, from https://en.wikipedia.org/wiki/Brown_v._Board_of_Education.

Charen, Mona (2104, July 29). Israel Supporters: Beware of Hilllary Clinton. *Washington Examiner*. Retrieved from www.washingtonexaminer.com/israel-supporters-beware-of-hillary-clinton/article/2551389.

Clinton, Hillary (2015, November 4). How I Would Reaffirm Unbreakable Bond with Israel — and Benjamin Netanyahu. *Forward*. Retrieved from http://forward.com/opinion/national/324013/how-i-would-rebuild-ties-to-israel-and-benjamin-neta/.

Costa, Robert, and Gold, Matea (2015, December 5). One of Jeb Bush's Top Advisers on Israel: George W. Bush. *Washington Post*. Retrieved from www.washingtonpost.com/politics/one-of-jeb-bushs-top-advisers-on-israel-george-w-bush/2015/05/07/920fec8e-f4da-11e4-bcc4-e8141e5eb0c9_story.html.

Dunetz, Jeff (2015, November 9). Hillary Clinton's Latest Lie: She's a Friend of Israel. *The Lid*. Retrieved from http://lidblog.com/hillary-clintons-latest-lie-shes-a-friend-of-israel/#.

Herzl, Theodore (1896/1997). *The Jewish State*, first printing edition. Henk Overberg (trans.) Northvale, NJ: Jason Aronson, Inc.

Hunter, F. Robert (1993). *The Palestinian Uprising: A War by Other Means*, revised edition. University of California Press (Berkeley and Los Angeles, California).

"Islam by country" (n.d.). *Wikipedia*. Retrieved December 12, 2015, from https://en.wikipedia.org/wiki/Islam_by_country.

"Israel" (n.d.). *Wikipedia*. Retrieved December 12, 2015, from https://en.wikipedia.org/wiki/Israel.

J Street Policy (n.d.). *J Street*. Retrieved December 26, 2015, from http://jstreet.org/policy/pages/twostate-solution.

Jewish Agency (2006). Map of Israel. *Jewish Agency for Israel Publications Section*, Jerusalem, Israel.

Jewish Israel. (2013, November 26). George Bush Joins the Lineup of Illustrious Christian "Friends of Israel" Who Support Efforts to Convert Jews. Retrieved from http://jewishisrael.ning.com/profiles/blogs/george-bush-joins-the-lineup-of-illustrious-christian-friends-of-.

"Jewish population by country" (n.d.). *Wikipedia*. Retrieved December 12, 2015, from https://en.wikipedia.org/wiki/Jewish_population_by_country.

Jewish Telegraphic Agency (2015, April 20). As First Lady, Hillary Was a Prized Jewish Keynoter—Until She Kissed Suha Arafat. *Jerusalem Post*. Retrieved from: www.jpost.com/International/As-first-lady-Hillary-was-a-prized-Jewish-keynoter-until-she-kissed-Suha-Arafat-398658.

Kelly, Michael (1994, July 31). The President's Past. *New York Times Magazine*. Retrieved from www.nytimes.com/1994/07/31/magazine/the-president-s-past.html?pagewanted=2.

"Kielce Pogrom" (n.d.) *Wikipedia*. Retrieved December 13, 2015, from https://en.wikipedia.org/wiki/Kielce_pogrom.

Levy, Gideon (2015, November 10). Hillary Clinton Is No Friend of Israel. *Haaretz*. Retrieved from www.haaretz.com/opinion/1.684711.

"List of Arab countries by population" (n.d.) *Wikipedia*. Retrieved December 13, 2015, from https://en.wikipedia.org/wiki/List_of_Arab_countries_by_population.

Lueck, Thomas J. (2000, July 14). Mrs. Clinton Explains Kiss in Middle East *New York Times*. Retrieved from www.nytimes.com/2000/07/14/nyregion/mrs-clinton-explains-kiss-in-middle-east.html

Maloney, S. (2015). Toughness triangulated: Hillary Clinton's policy on the Middle East, Brookings Institute, Dec 12, at www.brookings.edu/blogs/markaz/posts/2015/12/12-hillary-clinton-trump-terrorism-tough-triangulate-maloney; last accessed on March 28, 2016.

Newman, Marcy (2008, December). Will Palestinians Hit Hillary's Glass Ceiling? *Electronic Intifada*. Retrieved from https://electronicintifada.net/content/will-palestinians-hit-hillarys-glass-ceiling/7836.

"Palestinian Declaration of Independence" (n d.) *Wikipedia*. Retrieved December 26, 2015, from https://en.wikipedia.org/wiki/Palestinian_Declaration_of_Independence.

Palestinian Ministry of Education. The Myth of Incitement in Palestinian Textbooks (2005, June 13). Retrieved from https://electronicintifada.net/content/myth-incitement-palestinian-textbooks/5626.

Plessy v. Ferguson (n.d.). *Wikipedia*. Retrieved December 25, 2015, from https://en.wikipedia.org/wiki/Plessy_v._Ferguson.

Reiner, Ilan, and Reiner, Amir (2015). *Israel History Maps Atlas*. Self-published, Tel Aviv, Israel.

Rosen, Steven J. (2010, April 1). Obama's Foolish Settlements Ultimatum. *Middle East Forum*. Retrieved from www.meforum.org/2630/obama-settlements-ultimatum.

Schulberg, Jessica (2015a, September 9). Hillary Clinton Promises a More Muscular Foreign Policy as President. *Huffington Post*. Retrieved from www.huffingtonpost.com/entry/hillary-clinton-iran-foreign-policy_55f05c2ae4b002d5c07786b2.

Schulberg, Jessica (2015b, September 9). Hillary Clinton Gives Speech on Countering Iran after the Nuclear Deal. *Huffington Post*. Retrieved from www.huffingtonpost.com/entry/hillary-clinton-iran-israel_55efb2fbe4b093be51bcbb6f.

Schutz, Marisa (2015, November 6). Hillary Clinton Says She'll Meet with Netanyahu "In Office." *New York Post*. Retrieved from http://nypost.com/2015/11/06/hillary-clinton-will-invite-bibi-to-the-white-house-if-elected/.

Seigel, David (2015, December 6). Clinton Projects Cautious Optimism on Israeli-Palestinian Conflict. *CNN.com*. Retrieved from www.cnn.com/2015/12/06/politics/hillary-clinton-israeli-palestinian-saban/.

Shapiro, Ben (2015, September 2). Hillary Clinton Emails Show Rabid Anti-Israel Correspondence with Sidney Blumenthal. *Breitbart*. Retrieved from www.breitbart.com/big-government/2015/09/02/hillary-clinton-emails-show-rabid-anti-israel-correspondence-with-sidney-blumenthal/.

Sniegoski, Stephen (2015, June 14). Hawkish Hillary Clinton and Her Israel-First Political Sugar Daddy Haim Saban, *The Council for the National Interest*. Retrieved from www.councilforthenationalinterest.org/new/hawkish-hillary-clinton-and-her-israel-first-political-sugar-daddy-haim-saban/#.Vn2rCv9IjIV.

"Textbooks in the Israeli–Palestinian conflict." (n.d.) *Wikipedia*. Retrieved December 26, 2015, from https://en.wikipedia.org/wiki/Textbooks_in_the_Israeli%E2%80%93Palestinian_conflict.

ThirdIntifada (2015, 29 October). Israel Clears Palestinian Woman of Stabbing Charges. Retrieved from www.middleeasteye.net/news/israel-clears-palestinian-woman-stabbing-charges-1415394768#sthash.pWSryCQs.dpuf.

Weiss, Phil, and Robbins, Annie Hillary (2015, October 13). Clinton Expresses Alarm for Israeli Jews, and Not One Word about Palestinian Victims. *Mondoweiss.net*.

Retrieved from http://mondoweiss.net/2015/10/hillary-clinton-palestinians#sthash .UaXgWZCn.dpuf.

Wittes-Coffman, T. (2015). Israel's inertia on the Palestinian conflict has a price: American support, Brookings Institute, Dec 9, www.brookings.edu/blogs/markaz/ posts/2015/12/09-israeli-inertia-has-a-price-wittes; last accessed on March 28, 2016.

Wright, Lawrence (2014). *13 Days in September: Carter, Begin, and Sadat at Camp David.* Vintage Books, New York.

Zarembo, Alan (2015, December 30). Detailed study confirms high suicide rate among recent veterans. *Los Angeles Times.* Retrieved from www.latimes.com/nation/ la-na-veteran-suicide-20150115-story.html.

11

A TRANSLATION OF HER OWN

Hillary, Japan and the Pivot to Asia

Eijun Senaha

Living History, Hillary Rodham Clinton's first memoir, is one of the most controversial autobiographies in literary history. Even before the book was completed in 2000, it was already of public interest because of the phenomenally lucrative book deal she received. On June 9, 2003, when the book came out, it became an immediate success. It sold over a million copies and enjoyed diverse feedback. In 2004, the audiobook version was awarded the Best Spoken Word Album at the 46th Grammy Awards.

On the contrary, the Japanese translation, published later in 2003, did not experience the same outcome. Despite the publisher's early effort to create a Hillary Boom, the book did not do well at all. It was unranked among the top 50 in Japan's 2004 book market, with Bob Woodward's *Bush at War* ranked 16th and Michael Moore's *Stupid White Men*, originally published in 2001 in the US, at 24th. It was Clinton's imprudence in describing Japan and its people and the publisher's opportunistic commercialism that turned Japanese readers away from purchasing the book. In *Living History* there was very little mention of Japan, reminding Japanese of their national trauma of "Japan Passing" suffered at the hands of President Bill Clinton, along with his First Lady, when in 1998 the two decided against a state visit to Japan, but rather stayed in China for nine days. Simply put, Clinton's autobiography was not designed in a way to adequately appeal to Japanese readers.

Clinton's latest memoir, *Hard Choices*, published in June 2014, did not make the sensation impact that *Living History* did in the US, as reviewers did not find much that was particularly new in the book, calling it a political campaign piece for her 2016 presidential ambitions. However, the new book does contain more accounts about Japan, which may please Japanese readers. The Japanese translation came out in May 2015, and there has been some cautious optimism for this book's Japanese version with the change in publisher, allowing more time for a proper translation and the willingness to wait for the ideal moment of release. Although it is likely Japanese will appreciate Clinton's effort to play to the Japanese audience, it is unknown yet how the publication strategy and translation will mesh with Clinton's own narratives.

Text and Contexts

The publisher of *Living History* is Simon & Schuster, founded in 1924 and one of the four major English-language publishers and publishing houses.[1] In 2000, it agreed to pay Clinton an eight-million-dollar advance for her autobiography. It was a near-record figure for an advance to an author at that time.[2] Critics charged that the book deal, coming soon after her election to the U.S. Senate but before being sworn into office, was not in adherence to the ethical standards required for members of the U.S. Senate.[3] However, in February 2001, the Senate Ethics Committee gave Clinton approval for the deal.[4] When it became available to the public, people rushed to the bookstore. Its sales during its first week set a record for a nonfiction book.[5] In the first month, she sold more than one million copies.[6] In fact, Clinton, after signing an estimated 20,000 copies during the book's sales promotions, suffered tendonitis in her wrist and required treatment.[7] According to Nielsen, she sold over 1.4 million copies (excepting the e-book version) by 2004 in the US alone.[8]

Text

Both hardcover and paperback editions were made available. On the book's front cover, with her sepia-toned black-and-white photograph, Clinton smiles with short-cut blond hair, wearing a black turtleneck sweater and resting her chin on her right knuckles. In the lower portion of the cover, there are, in what appears to be Clinton's handwriting, the title and her name in gold. The back cover is filled with nine personal pictures (both black-and-white and colored) of her with people in her respective life stages: childhood, college life, marriage, childbearing, First Lady, and senator.

The text of the paperback edition, after a one-page abstract and a page advertising her three previously published books, consists of a title page; verso of the title page; a page for seven lines of "Dedication" to her parents, husband, daughter, and "all the good souls around the world"; two pages of "Contents"; a five-page "Author's Note"; 786 pages of content divided by 38 chapters; a six-page "Afterword," which was added for the paperback edition in 2004; an eight-page "Acknowledgements"; a page of "Key to Photographs" of seventy-five pictures which were chronologically arranged in two separate sections of the text; 44 pages of a two-column "Index" that consists of approximately 1,700 primary keywords, almost 1,000 of which are persons; and finally a page for "Permissions Acknowledgments."[9]

Contexts

Living History is an encyclopedic autobiography. The anonymously written abstract on its first page, "About Living History," introduces its coverage as follows: "In *Living History*, Hillary Rodham Clinton writes with candor, humor, and passion about coming-of-age during a time of tumultuous social and political change in America and about the White House years" (n.p.). The abstract goes on to sell the book based on her thirty years in public life, her life with Bill Clinton and how she persevered through betrayal, investigations and living in the public eye. It claims that in the book she clearly shares her ideas on all the important issues of the day, from health care to international relations to women's rights and more. The abstract ends by professing that the book reveals much about this important public figure and allows Clinton to speak sincerely "as a wife, a mother, and as one of the most formidable figures in the history of American politics" (n.p.).

As comprehensive as it is, *Living History* deals with extensive subjects and issues in the form of autobiography. The term "autobiography" obtains from Greek root words: *autos* denotes "self," *bios* "life," and *graphe* "writing," according to the analysis of Sidonie Smith and Julia Watson, and taken together in this order, the words *self life writing* offer a brief definition of *autobiography*, providing as many as sixty genres in this literary term.[10] Clinton's work can arguably belong to at least 20 genres as defined and applied below:

Apology:

A manner of presenting and defending oneself in the face of accusations and criticism. One uses an apology to rationalize one's actions, values and lifestyle. Within this genre, one typically concedes faults and mistakes or shows contrition in order to absolve oneself.[11]

The Clintons' involvement with Whitewater Development Company is one of the major issues written in this book, with a whole chapter, "Whitewater," devoted to the subject and further references throughout the rest of the book. Though she eventually proves herself not guilty, she is clearly affected by this series of tenacious allegations as her "self-defense" runs from the chapter "Little Rock" to "Impeachment."

Auto/Biography:

This term indicates the marriage of the two genres: autobiographical narrative and biography. The slash symbolizes separation between these two different, contradictory genres. The use of this term either signals an autobiographical approach that contains elements of biography/ies, or a personal narrative in a larger biography form. Modern writers create a "relational" story by blending biography and autobiographical narrating.[12]

Because Clinton not only tells her own story but the stories of others, like her family and relatives, this slashed term may well apply to the entire work. This explains why the book has eight hundred pages and an extensive index of nearly 2,000 items.

Bildungsroman:

The conventional use of the bildungsroman has been in the form of a novel about a young man's personal and social growth and maturing. Even so, modern female authors, and other underrepresented people, have adopted this genre to show a synthesis of their emerging identities and their more pronounced public profiles.[13]

Smith applies this definition in her literary criticism of *Living History*, focusing on the ways in which the book attempts to demonstrate the ability of a woman to act as the U.S. president.[14] Smith indicates that Clinton uses the book in order to bolster her 2008 U.S. presidential campaign by authenticating her political persona, thereby evaluating the book as a sort of feminist bildungsroman.

Collaborative Life Writing:

When an autobiographical text is produced by more than one author, it is called collaborative life writing. Such a text is created in one of these three manners: when the subject of a life story is interviewed and the text takes the form of a story as related to the interviewer; when the interviewer is also the ghostwriter who documents, edits and even adds to an autobiography of a celebrity or political figure; when a text is co-written or group-written and individual voices are not identified or where one voice is deemed to represent the group. Both the interviewer and editor facilitate a collaborative narrative, and in fact, two or more individuals are often included in the production of the story, especially when it needs to be translated.[15]

Clinton asked three women, as she admits in "Acknowledgments": "The smartest decision I made was to ask Lissa Muscatine, Maryanne Vollers and Ruby Shamir to spend two years of their lives working with me" (794). Muscatine was a natural choice since she was Clinton's speech writer when she was First Lady. Clinton saw Vollers as someone with the ability to help Clinton's voice surface in the book. Shamir was tasked with researching and collating everything written about Clinton.

Confession:

The confession, either oral or written, targets the audience to listen, judge, and forgive. Rita Felski sees feminist confession as a text that presents the author publically, creating a feminist community based on the knowledge derived from personal experience.[16]

In "Author's Note," Clinton does not make it clear whether the book is a confession or to whom this book is addressed as she says, "I have done my best to convey my observations, thoughts and feelings as I experienced them. This is not meant to be a comprehensive history, but a personal memoire that offers an inside look at an extraordinary time in my life and in the life of America" (xv). However, in the added "Afterword," she appears to understand to whom she has been talking: "I am grateful for the many kindnesses *Living History* readers have shown me" (792). She goes on to write how she finds it exciting that the readers find inspiration in her narrative, and she hopes that continues. As defined above, Clinton assumes the readers to be her interlocutors for her confession.

Filiation Narrative:

Oftentimes, life-based narratives look to venerate a long-term relationship to a relative or family member. Such texts are usually written by the grown children of a man who was exacting, despotic and inattentive. The exception to this is when the writer attempts to recapture the relationship with a deceased mother.[17]

One of the characteristics of this book is its maternal filiation. Clinton affectionately refers to her mother, Dorothy Howell Rodham, at least thirty times, recalling how exceptional it was that her mother turned out to be such a stable, caring person despite the dearth of nurturing attention she experienced in her early life. Clinton's affection is also directed to her daughter, Chelsea Victoria, about whom she writes more than her husband. Clinton writes, "I believed that being a mother was the most important job I had ever had" (166). Clearly one of Clinton's purposes in writing this book is to express maternal filiation.

Genealogical Stories:

"A method for charting family history, genealogy locates, charts, and authenticates identity by constructing a family tree of descent" (271, Smith and Watson), it uses accepted forms of family trees and charts based on ancestral evidence, documents and family history to establish one's origins. Efforts in this field focus on reconstituting and authenticating the past. The motivation is to establish and document relationships rather family stories.

Early in the book, Clinton uses the whole chapter "American Family" to introduce her "pedigree" as American. Though she does not show a family tree or documents, she carefully illustrates her genealogy. Clinton's hybridity goes back to English, Welsh, Scotch, Native American, and French families. She takes obvious pride: "I was born an American in the middle of the twentieth century, a fortunate time and place" (1).

Life Narrative and Life Writing:

Smith and Watson explain that *life writing* is the use of someone's life story, either the writer's or someone else's, as the topic of the writing. They contrast that with a *life narrative*, a text that takes the producer's life as the subject with the form taking one of a myriad of media. It can be written, performed, visual, in the form of a film or a digital recording. Smith and Watson declare that these two terms are indicative of the diversity of self-referential works. "We employ the term *life writing* for written forms of autobiographical, and *life narrative* to refer to autobiographical acts of any sort" (4).

According to this definition, her hardcopy editions are life writing, and the audio-recording edition belongs to life narrative. One might be concerned that the difference between vocal and literary expressions may create different impressions to the listener and reader even if they share the same text. However, others may argue that the difference is unimportant, especially for people who have physical or medical conditions that make reading difficult or who are learning English as a second language.

Memoir:

Rather than focus on just the life and actions of the narrator, a memoir tends to spotlight the travails of others. Although "autobiography" and "memoir" are popularly used synonymously, there are important differences. Lee Quinby describes how the autobiography elucidates an "I" that is both confessional and self-revealing, while the memoir illuminates an "I" that reports on the words and actions of other people. In memoirs, the bias is more interactive and focused on outside of self.[18]

After relating her first experience of writing an autobiography in the sixth grade in "Author's Note," Clinton comments on how, forty years later, she found herself writing another memoir, this time an account of her time in the White House with Bill Clinton. Not only does Clinton call the book a memoir, but many reviewers characterize it as such as well. Thus Clinton consciously writes "a memoir," a subjective report, in relation to others.

Periautography:

The term is used by James Olney to mean "writing about or around self" as one mode of life writing he takes up in *Memory and Narratives*.[19]

As "peri" is a prefix that means "around" and "surrounding." *Living History* introduces many lives who constructed her history. Almost one thousand people are mentioned in this autobiography, and Clinton also thanks about 500 people in her "Acknowledgments." They are, in addition to her own family, royal families, politicians, businesspeople, artists and athletes, young and old, somebody and nobody, and others.

Personal Essay:
A personal essay is a form of writing where the author explores his or her reactions to a specific subject.[20]

Clinton regards the product as a personal one when she conveys that she attempted to show the ebb and flow of events and relationships and how they shaped her. This clearly indicates that the book is more of a personal than public revelation. However, her public careers, especially as First Lady and senator, may not allow the book to be read as a personal essay because her personal life is public as much as her private one is political.

Prosopography:
This is a mode of writing that captures the communally shared experiences and patterns of a group undergoing the same event or period of time. Each member cannot necessarily be cited but the shared undertaking can be described.[21]

Clinton's descriptions of over twenty people of the so-called Hillaryland family well describe this genre, as she appreciates their presence and dedication throughout her White House days: "Soon, my staff became known around the White House as 'Hillaryland'" (197). She recounts how her staff had its own "subculture" in the White House that valued discretion and camaraderie. She commented on how Hillaryland was never the source of leaks although the West Wing was. They even had lapel buttons that read "Hillaryland" and they handed them out to the family members of the overworked staff. They became honorary members to Hillaryland, which allowed them to visit anytime and attend all parties.

Relational Life Writing:
The term was coined by Susan Friedman to portray when women reveal an identity of selfhood in autobiographical writing. She describes how such female writings have a "sense of shared identity with other women, as aspect of identification that exists in tension with a sense of their own uniqueness."[22]

The book constructs a network of women as Clinton creates a unique maternal family of her own. This matrilineal way of relating appears to extend to the whole of society as she travels and meets women.

Eleanor Roosevelt is Clinton's spiritual mother figure. Though she died in 1962, Clinton creates a fictional chapter, "Conversations with Eleanor," in which she enjoys conversation with and seeks advice from Eleanor, addressing a photograph of her in the Oval Office. In this chapter, after a defeat in the midterm election, she imagines a conversation with her and recollects that "Eleanor Roosevelt once said, 'If I feel depressed, I go to work.' That sounded like good advice to me" (389). This constitutes the most literarily creative chapter for Clinton as a writer.

Clinton then shares identity with another figure, Jacqueline Kennedy Onassis, her spiritual sister, who, as an experienced wife and mother at the White House, became her living mentor as well as a role model in both her private and public careers: "She was a transcendent public figure, someone I had admired and respected for as long as I could remember" (199). Clinton continues by describing how Jackie Kennedy was a stylish and intelligent First Lady and a great mother to her children. At the time Clinton wrote this part, she was waiting for Jackie Kennedy to answer her question on how to raise children in the public eye during her next visit to the White House. When she died in 1994, Clinton recalls the condolence she expressed at the Jacqueline Kennedy Garden in the White House: Clinton spoke on Jacqueline Kennedy's devotion to her children and grandchildren, quoting Jacqueline as saying, "'If you bungle raising your children, I don't think whatever else you do matters very much'" (350). Clinton expressed total agreement.

Another Clinton sororal relation could have been developed with Princess Diana as her little sister. Clinton remembers well when they first met in June of 1994 (Diana at 33, Clinton at 47). Clinton writes that on this visit, she came to like Diana despite the brief time they had together. She felt that Diana was being torn by competing forces, but she still wanted to make a difference. Clinton found her a devoted mother, and they often talked about how to raise children under public scrutiny.

In *Living History*, Clinton develops sisterhood with so many women, dead and alive, including friends, queens and princesses, mothers, wives and daughters of noted and unnoted people all over the world. Clinton does not forget to mention Mother Theresa, but laments that there were "more people to include than could be named" (xi).

Self-Help Narrative:

In this mode of narrative, the writer must reveal a negative behavior pattern or destructive habit and how they are trying to or have already overcome it. Typically this genre involves a fall from grace, followed by a recognition of the problem and ending with recovery and enlightenment.[23]

After Bill Clinton's public apology over an affair with Monica Lewinsky, Clinton mentions how she sought salvation: "By the time we returned to the White House, there were several challenges on my mind, personal and political" (704). She recalls how she and Bill Clinton began marriage counseling to see if they were going to save their marriage. Although she felt hurt and shaken, she still felt that her husband was a good person and a good president. At this point, she resolved to defend her husband against the increasing assaults by the independent counsel.

Near the end of the book, when Clinton decides to run for Senate from New York, she reveals a code that she learned from Sofia Totti, the captain of the girls' basketball team: "Dare to compete." Clinton writes how she was "caught off guard" by this challenge. After the event, Clinton started to question herself and whether she was afraid or unsure to take the challenge, even though she had encouraged other women to face challenges. She writes how she said to herself, "Maybe I should 'dare to compete'" (746). This moves her forward. Clinton comes to think that perhaps she should run. Though Clinton says Maggie Williams helped her think through why she should run, it is obviously Clinton's positivism that helped her at this turning point. She writes that staying with Bill and running for the Senate seat were the two toughest decisions she has ever had to make. This self-help narrative becomes a record of "an act of self-promotion, designed to be truthful but selective" (Whitt, 2010, p. 874), by which Clinton performs for readers so they understand her in a positive light.

Testimonio:

This genre suggests the writer will give a testimonial of an injustice he or she has witnessed so readers can both judge and act on the situation. As John Beverley explains, the intent of the writer is to show a purity of motive rather literary art.[24]

Clinton was never arrested or found guilty of anything, but she was the constant target of allegations of wrongdoing by her and her husband. This book therefore takes the form of a public arena for her testimony. Not surprisingly, readers were most drawn to read what she says about the Whitewater and Monica Lewinsky scandals. Her husband's affair with Monica Lewinsky particularly interested readers because Clinton could have been the first First Lady to divorce a sitting US president: "I could hardly breathe. Gulping for air, I started crying and yelling at him. . . . This was the most devastating, shocking and hurtful experience of my life" (693). However, a public opinion poll puts a period to her outrage: She comments on how the president's job approval remained strong through the affair, which heartened the First Lady. Sixty percent of Americans felt that the president should not resign, that Congress should not move to impeach and that the salacious details of the Star report were "inappropriate." She was further encouraged by her own soaring approval rate, hitting 70 percent, making her appreciate the compassion of the American public. Clinton eventually succeeds at this testimony, and at the same time, wins the people over to her side.

Trauma Narrative:

This narrative form is used to relate a shocking and unspeakable experience that the writer is unable to relegate to long-term, fading memory.

Leigh Gilmore comments on how this form is used by a writer who is attempting to come to terms with this devastating event and the event's inexplicableness.[25]

There seems to be no traumatic experience in which Clinton herself was victimized. However, her childhood memory of her mother appears to have created in her an indirect trauma that was to remain long in her mind. Dorothy Rodham's early life without proper parenting was recalled earlier in the book: Clinton comments on how her mother's parents were in no position to be proper parents, leaving Della, her then three-year-old mother, home alone. Della was abandoned at home with meal tickets for a restaurant near their apartment in Chicago's South Side. With her sister Isabelle, Della was sent from one relative to another. They never stayed in a school long enough to make friends. The parents had a scandalous divorce in 1927, with neither parent wanting the children. The small children were put on a train and sent to California to be raised by their paternal grand-parents in Alhambra, near Los Angeles. This "inherited" trauma of divorce must have weighed heavily on Clinton when she faced a potential divorce with her own husband, thinking that this trauma would then be passed on to her daughter Chelsea.

Travel Narrative:
This genre entails all forms of travel-related writing, whether travelogues, journals, adventures narratives, letters home, etc.[26]

In *Living History*, Clinton recounts visiting at least 80 nations and areas outside the US and introduces her impressions and their issues. In the chapter "Vital Voices," she mentions how she was prepared, writing that the State Department provided information on the countries they were visit-ing and the various protocols and cultural issues to look out for. She writes that she would be warned about how she might be served exotic food and advised on face-saving ways to avoid eating it.

In many of her visits abroad, Clinton was involved with various political crises and faced critical decisions. On the other hand, there were "humor-ous" episodes Clinton recalls, bringing about needed comic relief to this book. Such "ridiculous" experiences include how, at Nelson Mandela's inauguration in 1994, she avoided meeting Fidel Castro at all cost, since "Even if I accidentally bumped into him, the anti-Castro factions in Florida would go wild" (347–378). She was also urged to try moose lips at a dinner hosted by Boris Yeltsin at the Kremlin's St. Catherine Hall.[27]

Acts of Witnessing:
In acts of witnessing, the narrator can either be an actual witness who records the event and raises awareness, or someone responding to the

account of an actual witness. This form shows how the subject deals with and reacts to trauma.[28]

It is noteworthy that, looking back at her success in this publication, Clinton writes in the "Afterword" of the 2004 paperback edition, that "I believe in the promise of America because I am a product of America's steady progress toward realizing its ideals of equality and justice, freedom and opportunity" (790) and "I have been fortunate to be part of this extraordinary human experience known as America" (791). Clinton recognizes that her life has been the witness of America.

These genres categorically illuminate many, but not all, literary aspects in Clinton's autobiography. One more essential autobiographical element that deserves examination is her book as feminist narrative, or autogynography. In the first edition of *Reading Autobiography*, Smith and Watson introduce this term in their appendix of "Fifty-Two Genres of Life Narrative," quoting Donna C. Stanton:

> [Stanton] proposed this term to suggest the centrality of gendered subjectivity to the literary production of self-referential acts. Although Stanton offers a postmodern critique of the unexamined belief in referentiality, she argues that the textuality of the psychic splitting of woman's subjectivity must be located in her "different status in the symbol of order." And she concludes that women's "gendered narrative involved a different plotting and configuration of split subject" (16). Stanton notes that, at the moment of second-wave feminism in which she was writing, "the gender of the author" "did make a difference" because the refusal of the referential status of the signature threatened to perpetuate "female anonymity" (18–19).[29]

This may be one of the reasons the book reviews were varied. Her "gendered narrative" of split subjectivity provides miscellaneous information that is often inconsistent and contradictory, causing readers to react differently. Clinton's public and private portraits compose her multitudinous "selves," including her anxieties over gender in her conscious and unconscious minds. Therefore, Clinton's writing becomes a representation of women's ambivalence and paradox, and the book becomes a confusingly controversial autogynography.

Regardless of her split subjectivity, Clinton's feminist ideology is consistent throughout the book. Clinton's feminist debut goes back to her Wellesley days, and the climax came when she delivered a graduation speech as president of college government. She says she "spoke about awareness of the gap between the expectations my class brought to college and the reality we experienced" (61). Clinton admits that the speech was an attempt to define and understand the world in which the young women found themselves. The speech tried to express their desire to create something within those limitations and to reflect the many conversations and concerns that the graduates, and all American women, had. This was the generation of women who would face the coming changes.

Right after the speech, Clinton was invited to a local TV show, and *Life* magazine featured her along with another female student activist from Brown University. Twenty-five years later, *Frontline*, the PBS television series, produced the documentary "Class of '69," calling it "Hillary's Class," in which the producer, Rachel Dretzin, explained that *Frontline* chose this class because their generation has been active in a moment of unique and significant change for women (40).

Clinton built her credentials internationally when she attended the 1995 Fourth World Conference on Women in Beijing. She wrote about how the conference was a great platform for countries to face the myriad problems from maternal and child health care to women's suffrage, property and legal rights, and all issues in between. In "Women's Rights Are Human Rights," Clinton delivers the most memorable speech at the conference by stating, "This is truly a celebration—a celebration of the contributions women make in every aspect of life" (452), and by concluding, "I believe that on the eve of a new millennium, it is time to break our silence. It is time for us to say here in Beijing, and the world to hear, that it is no longer acceptable to discuss women's rights as separate from human rights. . . . and women's rights are human rights, once and for all" (454–455). She received an enthusiastic standing ovation, and the *New York Times* reported that the speech "may have been her finest moment in public life" (455).

American Literary Responses

American reviews were mixed, and most regarded the book as politically motivated. Hilary Hammell analyzes the reviews also as "mixed, with a typical evaluation commending the chapters describing her early life, decrying the overly lengthy later treatments of relatively mundane events as First Lady, and criticizing the lack of candor in the sections covering controversial episodes, including those surrounding her husband and the Lewinsky scandal" (n.p.). Observers later noted the difference in how Clinton portrayed her upbringing and Carl Bernstein's biographical take on her demanding father.[30] Writing an autobiography becomes a political act, especially when the politician-author is aiming for the presidency of the United States. Clinton did have this in mind and strategically carried out this project: one for idolization of self and another for fundraising purposes. Therefore, American critics were more interested in Clinton's political qualifications than her feminist portraits. Peter Stothard says, "Hillary Clinton's autobiography reads like a manifesto of a presidential campaign not yet fought" (1).

In his criticism of *Living History*, Jan Witt comments on Clinton's purpose behind writing the book, stating that Clinton wished to "explain herself to the electorate" (857) in her bid to run for president of the United States. He writes that Clinton also wished to address her relationship with her husband, Bill Clinton, and to outline her history of public service given the climate of increasing sexism. Witt also laments the confusing genre of memoir, with its tendency to allow exaggeration and egotism. Witt repeat that Clinton wrote *Living History* in order to attract voters, defend herself, and lay out her past and her current political goals before the media and historians could add more to the already large collection of Clinton reportage.

Through *Living History*, Clinton gained direct access to the readers, showing them the different ways they could understand her roles as activist, lawyer, First Lady and senator. By availing herself of the opportunity for to speak directly to the electorate, she added to the genre, allowing readers yet another, albeit filtered, way to understand important world figures.

Another reason that Clinton's writing effort was harshly criticized by some in the media was for being an obvious fund-raising tool, in effect, a literary political campaign. Clinton's advance with the publisher was only the beginning: *USA Today* reported that "Clinton received $8 million from Simon & Schuster to write *Living History* and didn't take long to earn back her advance. Nearly 1.7 million copies of the hardcover are in print and a 525,000 first printing is planned for the paperback" (n.p.). *BBC* in its 2008 article found that "Clinton's earnings exceed $100m," stating ironically that "Mrs. Clinton made more than $10m from her book *Living History*. She donated all the proceeds from another work, *It Takes a Village*, to charity. Although the New York senator revealed highlights of tax returns from 2007, she requested an extension for their full disclosure, citing the need for more information on a blind trust dissolved last year" (n.p.).

Nevertheless, feminist critics welcomed the book. Elaine Showalter, a renowned literary scholar, writes that *Living History* is a valuable feminist document in her review "The Throne behind the Power":

> To Michiko Kakutani, the powerful book critic of the *New York Times*, Clinton's analysis of this role seems grandiose and self-regarding; others have argued that Clinton abjures responsibility by discussing abstractions of identity or celebrity. But her gradual understanding of the vicariousness of her life, despite its visibility, is the true narrative of her memoir. That discovery makes the book a valuable feminist document. (n.p.)

Clinton's encyclopedic autobiography is open to both positive and negative interpretations. Whatever the opinion may be, the book did generate a debate about what Clinton actually is and what the future of the US can be. The book enabled various literary interpretations. Eventually, though the opinions are still varied and divided, this campaign book was a remarkable success as a political revelation and a fund-raising bonanza for Clinton.

Japanese *Living History*

In translating *Living History* into Japanese, the publisher made poor strategic decisions. In principle, any publisher that holds translation copyrights for a book needs to make careful decisions about who is qualified to translate the work and when to publish. The appointed translator should translate the material with enough accuracy and knowledge to allow the Japanese reader to understand what the author describes. A publisher should find the best timing for release: It can publish almost simultaneously with the original, or wait and observe the market response of the original before deciding on a Japanese strategy. However, the publisher's awkward responses, both hasty and slow, in publishing two versions of one book in the same translation, produced a poor consumer response in Japan to what was a best-selling autobiography in America.

The Japanese translation was first hurriedly released in late December 2003, only six months after the original US edition was published.[31] In the rush to publish, the title was not translated and was written *ribingu hisutorii*, a phonetic approximation of *Living History* in Japanese. The US paperback edition came out in April 2004, ten months after the hardcover edition, but the Japanese counterpart spent more than three years in waiting. It finally hit Japanese bookstore shelves on November 17, 2007, but this time it was divided into two volumes. By this time, Clinton was already running for the Democrat's US presidential nomination. Several bookstores confirmed that the publisher aborted further printing and promoting of *Living History* after only the first printing of both hardcover and paperback editions.

Prepublication

The publishing of *Living History* in Japan was to be a challenge. Neither the publishing house nor the translator had a background in the "autobiography business." They were obviously not qualified when they ambitiously seized the "opportunity" to translate, promote and publish an overwhelmingly complex work by a foreign political headliner.

Publisher

Hayakawa Shobo, or Hayakawa Publishing Corporation, published the Japanese translation of *Living History*, both hardcover and paperback editions.[32] It was founded in 1945 and first specialized in dramas and plays. In the 1950s, it started the *Hayakawa's Mystery* (1953) and *SF Magazine* (1959) series, translating American mystery and science fiction into Japanese. Hayakawa is now mainly known for its long contribution in introducing SF-mystery stories to Japanese readers. It also conducts the Hayakawa SF Contest to recruit new Japanese writers to this field.

In an email interview with Hayakawa Publishing Corporation, a secretary of the company president's office responded on behalf of President Hiroshi Hayakawa.[33] Questions and answers to this interview are as follows:

Q1. Please tell me about Hayakawa's acquisition process regarding the copyright of *Living History*, including the reason for pursuing this contract, the contract fee, any special conditions, and any interesting episodes during the negotiations for this contract.

Hillary had already accomplished herself as first lady and later senator, and was such a person of the hour that she was much talked about as becoming the first woman President in the near future. It is our policy as well to keep good connections with overseas companies of long-established history in translating publications, and one of the reasons for the decision was that Simon & Schuster enthusiastically recommended the project to President Hayakawa when he was visiting New York on a business trip.

I briefly read a part of the manuscript before the acquisition in a room where a copyright agent was closely watching me. My impression was that her story was not the politician's propaganda common in Japan but a dramatic narrative of a woman whose life is still underway and whose future is attractive. These are the reasons I wanted to acquire the copyright by all means. I cannot tell the copyright fee and its conditions.

Q2. The hardcover edition was published in 2003 and paperback in 2007. Will you tell me why you waited more than three years between the two editions? Was it a company policy, a sales consideration or any other reason for this decision?

It was because it had been a while since the hardcover was released, and it was time to publish it in paperback. Furthermore, she was regarded as the most likely presidential prospect for the 2008 election, and that was the reason we decided to publish the paperback edition in 2007.

Q3. Please tell me the number of copies sold and any impressions of each edition and version.

I cannot tell you.

Q4. What do you think of the sales? Did you have any particular expectations for the sales of this book whose author, Hillary Clinton, would possibly be elected the next US president?

Hillary is now being talked about as running for the 2016 Presidential election. Then, this book will be the most suitable book to know the character of the future "President Hillary."

The interview implies that Hayakawa's motive was to reap ambitiously high sales. By not commenting on the contract details and the sales numbers, the publisher hesitates to reveal the literally unspeakable consequences of the project. It seems Hayakawa overly relied on the established reputation of Clinton and the recommendation of Simon & Schuster, without thinking twice. It was unfortunate as well that Hayakawa missed two opportunities. First, Clinton was expected to visit Japan for the book campaign in 2003, but she did not come. Second, when Clinton ran for the presidential election in 2008, Clinton did draw the attention of Japanese readers, but much less than another candidate, Barack Obama. In the same year, Obama published a translation of his autobiography *Dreams from My Father: A Story of Race and Inheritance* and successfully sold over 30,000 copies between December 2007 and February 2009.[34]

Translator

Hayakawa's project falters in translation as well. Yoko Sakai was in charge of translation, but her specialty was not autobiography.[35] She studied drama at college and started her career as a drama director. Her translations were mainly literary works, including such works by Neil Simon, Brian Jacques, and Louanne Johnson. *Living History* was her first and only autobiography until she published Diane Keaton's 2011 autobiography, *Then Again*, in 2014. Furthermore, with the fact that almost all of Sakai's translations are published by Hayakawa, there seems to be a cozy relationship between Sakai and Hayakawa since the 1980s.

Unfortunately, Sakai is an unreliable translator. She acknowledged four people in her "Translator's Afterword." There was one who helped her translate parts of the book; one who is an oceanographer familiar with translation culture; a professor of international politics who, according to her, was actually the supervisor of this translation project; and a woman who taught her the English nuance. Her acknowledgments may be more than diplomatic, because several mistakes are found in translation, such as writing "President Kennedy" for "Robert Kennedy," "experiment" for "experience." It is doubtful how well this "translation team" helped Sakai complete her first mission of translating a politician's autobiography in the limited time.

Campaign

Hayakawa Publishing recruited *AERA*, a weekly magazine published by Asahi Shimbun Publications, to create interest in the eventual Japanese publication of *Living History* one month after the US version of *Living History* was published.[36] *AERA* featured an exclusive preview in its July 14, 2003, issue, months before the Japanese translation of *Living History* was released. This article, however, was quite untimely for Hayakawa. Hayakawa must have expected that an *AERA* article on an early draft of the translation would create a Hillary Boom that would peak in time for the publication of the Japanese translation. In the end, however, this setup for the book campaign was premature and only revealed how flustered Hayakawa was.

Kaori Ara, a member of *AERA*'s editorial department, wrote this five-page article, entitled "Exclusive Abridged Translation of *Living History*: Hillary Inscribes

Love, Conflicts, and Decisions." Ara emphasizes that the article is a scoop and blatantly publicizes the book's Japanese translation by Yoko Sakai from Hayakawa Publishing, writing that the book will come out "in the spring" (27) of 2004. This concedes that the book was, as of July of 2003, originally scheduled to be published in the spring of 2004, spending at least another nine months in preparation. It was actually published in December of 2003: Hayakawa advanced the publication by four months. Hayakawa will not supply the reason for this change, but this obviously was to generate serious mistakes in translation and contradictions in dating.[37]

Ara reviews the book melodramatically. She says the book is filled with love for her husband. Ara introduces the setting of the book as private and emotional as follows:

> She seems to be very pretty in the scene of the first encounter with Bill. Regarding "the inappropriate relationship," she cries, shouts and grieves. (27)

Ara does not forget to mention the political reasons for publishing the memoire and says, "And she moves on, as a Senator. A story of the first half of her life. You may also hear her say, 'See me as one politician.' She is talked about as a presidential candidate" (27). Then Ara picks up five of Clinton's eventful episodes: 1970 at Yale where they made each other's acquaintance, the 1998 Monica Lewinsky scandal, her maternal love for Chelsea, and the 1999 decision to run for a Senate seat. Still, Ara stays focused on Clinton's human side, saying Clinton wanted to straighten herself up by writing. Ara concludes the article romantically:

> Quite a few journalists have written about Hillary, and there may be no surprising news in this memoire. But it is meaningful for her to tell him about herself. She may have wanted Bill to recall the enchantment he experienced when they first met. (31)

Ara interviews two Japanese who know Clinton personally, and they are both supportive of this article. Reiko Kinoshita, a journalist, says this is as if Clinton is challenging the reader about her decision not to divorce her husband after the Lewinsky scandal by saying, "Have you ever loved a man as much as I love him?" (28). Masahito Watanabe, a former staff member of Clinton's 2000 Senate campaign, interprets the work as a book about "Mother Hillary" (30) who always took great care of her daughter.

The book campaign by *AERA* magazine may have succeeded in drawing the attention of Japanese readers to an exaggerated version of Clinton. However, this effort did not translate into high sales numbers for Hayakawa. The campaign by *AERA* was too tendentiously written and hurriedly issued.

Text and Contexts

The Japanese *Living History* came out in December 2003. At a glance, the front cover is not much different from the original. The background photograph of the author is the same, and the handwritten title and author's name remain.[38] The Japanese title is vertically printed on the right side of the book along with the subtitle, "Autobiography of Hillary Rodham Clinton," and the translator's name. The publisher's name appears at the bottom with "Exclusive Translation Copyright." One of the visual differences one can notice may be the ink colors used in the handwritten title and the author's name, both of which are gold in English versions. The Japanese hardcover edition has a gold title but the signature is in white, with the two lines of the paperback's first volume all in salmon pink and the second volume in baby blue.[39] Clinton's sophisticated image in the English version is replaced by these immature colors.

The structure of the text is nearly the same, except it does not have an index, and two essays by Japanese have been added. The index is a critical source, but it appears the Japanese translator/publisher has elected to omit this cross-reference tool. Instead, two articles are added: "Afterword by Translator," a reprint from the paperback written by Yoko Sakai in December 2003; and "Explanation: The First Woman President?: Preview of the 2008 US Presidential Election" by Kazuo Minato.[40]

Sakai believes that the "translator has to be an actor," saying, "Especially in translating autobiography, the translator needs to have an ability to perform every stage of the author's life." She admits, however, "it was too big of a job for me as a mere translator" (468). In this "Afterword," with her unique modesty, she divides Clinton's life stages into a five-act play representing the lives of "all of us," dramatizing the work as a lesson the readers of the twenty-first century have to learn in order to be responsible for the future.[41] Then she thanks the four who helped her complete this translation.

Minato, whom Sakai acknowledges for his advice as a supervisor in her "Translator's Afterword," has his own column here, where he introduces the US election system and schedule, analyzes both Republican and Democrat candidates, compares Clinton to Barack Obama, and reveals his concerns with Clinton's politics of "Japan Passing." His sources, however, are unreliable. He refers to a *FOX TV* survey conducted in October 2008, and Clinton's essay from *Foreign Affairs* published on October 15, 2007, but neither was available when he was writing the "Explanation." Because the Japanese paperback edition was supposed to have been printed on November 10, 2007, these references did not yet exist. The publisher and/or Minato either deceived the reading public or made a series of mistakes in dating.[42]

As for the context, it is undeniable that Japanese readers will be disappointed to find that Clinton mentions very little of Japan. In fact, "Japan" and "Japanese Americans" are the only two items listed in the index of over 2,000 keywords.

Although "Japan(ese)" is referred fifteen times and four Japanese names appear in the text, these references are made in passing or as data points rather than descriptions of actual experiences with Japan of the Japanese. For example, she recalls that her parents were married in 1942 after the *Japanese* attacked Pearl Harbor and describes *Japan* as one the industrialized nations. These general references do not make Japanese feel they are paid enough respect.

The only reference that the Japanese reader may find satisfying is the recollection of her first visit as First Lady to the 1993 G7 Summit in Tokyo. She briefly mentions the meeting with the Emperor and Empress during their US visit in 1994: "Gentle, artistic and intelligent, this engaging couple employ the grace of their nation's art as well as the serenity of the peaceful gardens I finally visited while at the Palace" (258). Japanese may be bewildered by her comparison of the Emperor and Empress with Japanese gardens. She also mentions Prime Minister Ryutaro Hashimoto and his wife Kumiko, misspelling her name as "Kamiko," at the 1997 G8 Denver Summit. Altogether, Clinton spends less than a page out of 800 pages on Japan. Due to the omission of the index, many Japanese may not notice how little they were considered. However, there were some Japanese readers who quickly noticed and pointed this out in their reviews.

Japanese Critical Responses

Japanese reviews were also mixed. Professional critics and reviewers wrote about the abstract and the sales history, and evaluated it as a politically motivated campaign book, as US critics did. These responses are roughly divided into three viewpoints: those with a general and/or near-neutral description, those with interest in US-Japan relations, and those with feminist perspectives. Most of them are positive, but feminist reviewers are divided, and there are many reviewers who are negative toward the US-Japan future.

Descriptive Reviews

Nikkei BP, an Internet journal, is one of typical professional reviewers which only introduce the book summary and history. It simply says, "The memoirs of the author who is the former first lady and a member of the Senate from New York. It became a topic and sold 200,000 copies on first day in the United States. It illustrates the first half of her life, including her childhood in a suburban middle-class family, an encounter with Bill Clinton, various scandals in the White House, and running for senator, the details accounting for more than 700 pages" (n.p.). This type of book description provides fundamental information and is seen in both the US and Japan. This seemingly neutral description, however, does shed light on her public career and makes the book a political product.

American Studies

For those who are interested in learning American politics and culture in the post–World War II era, Clinton is the living history and her autobiography becomes a textbook. They think that she is the front-runner for the 2016 presidential election in the United States, and read the autobiography because they felt that they must know her. Katsuyuki Namba, a blogger, gives a positive review:

> Though it was a thick book of more than 700 pages, I finished reading at a stretch. Awfully interesting.
>
>   . . .
>
> For anyone interested in modern American society, this is a must book. It is a good work to understand the history and psychology of an American woman in mid-career, who may become the President; and the social history of the US in the second half of 20th century. There are plenty of other ways to enjoy the book. (n.p.)

Thus, as a narrative of postmodern American history, the book is easy to understand and fun to read. Because it is written in a simple narrative form, the first person, with her own personal point of view, about both public and private stages in and around the White House, this autobiography becomes a political gossip. Furthermore, this can be read as suspense because Clinton's life is ongoing, and this book may enable the reader to witness and predict the US future.

Masato Watanabe introduces the US perception of the book and examines its liability. In *America Now*, Watanabe calls it a campaign book, writing that the presidential election lasts so long that the book can become a weapon of the proxy war:

> It was [*Living History*] that made her a "name brand" as "politician Hillary," not a mere autobiography. In fact, it is in this book when published in 2003 that people concerned became able to figure out her intention of becoming the president. Otherwise, the publication of the autobiography could have increased the risk of becoming a target of political attack just after she became a senator. In addition, her intention was so obviously found that she spends a considerable amount of pages in showing off her passion for politics and revealing in the form of an autobiography the sequence of events that led to her running for the Senate. (n.p.)

This helps the Japanese reader understand the circumstances of the book and learn that it is a politically tendentious product more than an entertaining study of US history in general. Likewise, it has to be mentioned that there are many Clinton books published in Japan, by Japanese and in translation, many of which are written with their own political points of view.[43] Therefore, readers need to be critical and aware of political bias, whichever book they may choose to read.

US-Japan Relations

For those who are interested in US-Japan relations under a possible Clinton administration, this book does not offer optimism. They question why Clinton writes only a few lines on the visit to the Imperial Palace and says the Emperor and Empress are elegant and full of intelligence. This indicates that her interest in Japan is very low. They wonder what will happen to US-Japan relations if she becomes the president and are worried about Clinton's second "Japan Passing" as President Bill Clinton passed Japan in 1998 and visited China, making "Japan Passing" a topic.

Hillary Rodham Clinton refers to Japan three times: when the Emperor and Empress visited the White House; a G7 dinner at the Imperial Palace in Tokyo; and in reference to Mrs. Kumiko Hashimoto, wife of then prime minister Ryutaro Hashimoto, at the G8 Denver summit. Clinton was impressed with Empress Michiko, but she wrote one line only out of consideration for Mrs. Hashimoto. There are no Japanese women in the Hillary network, no politicians, no businesswomen, no women of culture. They are concerned with the future of the US-Japan relationship without any Japanese woman who can make friends with her.

Thus, there is little optimism in US-Japan relations in a future Clinton administration. Traditionally, critics agree that the Japanese government under the Liberal Democratic Party has kept closer relation with Republican presidents. This does not necessarily mean that Democrats are difficult partners, but a President Clinton could be challenging.

Feminist Reading

Japanese readers of the book as a feminist narrative are divided. Some see Clinton as a role model for Japanese women as many American feminists locate her, while others see her as representing an unattainable goal for Japanese women, which can actually be harmful. In short, a wide spectrum of views on Clinton, from extremely critical to very positive, is as pervasive in Japan as in the US.

Many, particularly of Clinton's generation, admire her autobiography because they regard Clinton as someone who represents women who experienced difficulties when they tried to develop their careers in society. They know very well how she has paved her own way in politics. A younger generation also shows their respect to Clinton, blogging that they see her so positively and are amazed that Bill Clinton gave up his dream for Hillary. They also enjoy learning her responses to her scandals. They think she boasts about what she achieved but will not admit when she did something wrong. Others, who have a conservative view toward marriage and the role of women, value Clinton as a hero of perseverance and optimism. In a world where divorce is so easy to choose, they believe she is the woman who overcame her husband's affair. They admire how Clinton finds something meaningful in a tiny comment others may overlook as she positively gets over difficulties or obstacles.

Professional reviewers also praise the book as an autobiography of the American feminist canon. Yuko Iguchi, in her book review in *Sankei Shimbun Newspaper* in 2004, identifies in the closing chapter a farewell party just before leaving the White House as actually the beginning of Clinton's bright political future:

> [T]he 1992 campaign song "Don't Stop Thinking About Tomorrow" was played, and everybody's mind fermented and everyone started to sing together, a song that best expressed her political philosophy.
>
> The ending of the book, in which she raises her head up against the worst case of the Monica scandal and brings the reader to elation, is filled with the enthusiasm and power to give birth to the first woman president of the United States four years later. (n.p.)

Clinton succeeds in winning the hearts and minds of both conservatives and liberals across generations. The presumed intention of the book as a political campaign seems well achieved.

However, the book also received negative responses. They appear to be annoyed by the presence of such an active feminist as Clinton that they become pessimistic about the future of Japanese women. Daisuke Inoue is a frank blogger who reveals that he simply does not feel comfortable with Clinton's book:

> Honestly speaking, I didn't like the book personally. I like the story based on Hillary's personal experiences, including her childhood memories and days as first lady, but I wasn't interested in the slightest in the episodes of the Clinton Administration because I felt like I was forced to read the Democrats' PR book. Well, in short, it is propaganda. Because I am Japanese and don't support either Democrats nor Republicans, I sure don't feel comfortable when she boasts how good her party is and criticizes how Republicans are off point. Therefore, unless you like the Clinton Administration, you don't have to buy this book. (n.p.)

This misogynistic attitude also comes from a professional woman critic. Yukari Nukumizu writes a book review, "Conduct Book for the Young Ladies: Hillarian Married Life?" for *Weekly Asahi*, a journal known for its liberalism:

> This book is so appropriate that it lacks reality, such as an appropriate angry "punch" on her inappropriate husband. Maybe she is a lady like that by birth. I was once stunned to see her, on a TV program, vigorously tell

everything about the scandal with an oily face while clenching her husband's hands. She is a commander, or a female "white knight." [. . .] Young ladies, what do you think about making her your role model? (n.p.)

Nukumizu challenges Japanese women with a provocative statement on Clinton's egoistical pursuit of happiness over her unfaithful husband. She asks if Japanese women can put up with a traditional lifestyle in order to achieve something bigger, something more public than private. This anti-feminist way of living, exemplified by Clinton's decision, may be the transcendental choice of the post-liberal feminists.

***

Japanese may feel pleased when they read Clinton's newest effort, *Hard Choices*, out in translation in May 2015, right after Clinton announced her presidential candidacy in April. The publisher must have carefully calculated the timing for a commercial reason, as it has been postponed several times since the previous year, so Japanese would pay most attention to the book. Their feelings of being slighted in *Living History* have been mostly compensated for in this new book. Clinton describes Japan and its people as if they were her first priority, with special memories that she denotes with confidence and intimacy. Not only the context but the preparation of the translation and publication of the book soothe the hopeful reader. The original publisher, Simon & Schuster, has sold its translation copyright to another company, The Nikkei, which is more experienced and savvy in the publication industry.[44] The assigned translator is not disclosed, but the publisher spent more time than what was spent on *Living History*.

Clinton's revision of Japan and its people appears personal more than political. She does mention the importance of Japan as an ally in various senses and levels, but expresses its presence like a good old friend she has known for a long time and someone she still counts on. She introduces more specific episodes she experienced personally. This may unleash the Japanese from the trauma of "Japan Passing," as she succeeds in showing how much she cares. There are sixteen pages and eight topics spent in describing Japan in *Hard Choices*: her first visit to the country with her husband in 1993, the economy of "Lost Decade" and thereafter, its relation with other countries, and its role in climate change since the Kyoto Accord. Clinton also remembers her official visit as the US secretary of state in 2009, when she held her first town hall meeting at the University of Tokyo and introduced the story of the university president's daughter who, inspired by Clinton's speech, joined Japan's Foreign Service. Clinton expressed her heartfelt condolences during another official visit to Japan in April 2011, immediately after the "Triple Disaster" of earthquake, tsunami, and meltdown at the Fukushima Nuclear Power Plant. She does not forget to mention meeting then with Empress Michiko, who Clinton says developed the warm personal relationship they had enjoyed since she was First Lady.[45] As a feminist politician, Clinton expresses her gratitude of meeting with Japanese women, including the first women astronauts Chiaki Mukai and Naoko Yamazaki, and praises Prime Minister Shinzo Abe's announcement of increasing women's economic participation, "womenomics," by saying, "We need more far-sighted leadership like that at home and around the world" (571).

In Chapter 3, "Asia: The Pivot" of Part Two, "Across the Pacific," Clinton confesses she had a choice of three approaches in the region: broadening the relationship with China, strengthening the US treaty alliances in order to provide a counterbalance to China's growing power, or harmonizing the regional multilateral organizations.[46] She decided that the "smart power choice was to meld all three approaches" (45) and choose Japan as the first destination. Clinton writes about when she and Bill first visited Japan with a trade delegation when he was governor of Arkansas. She comments on how Japan's "Economic Miracle" caused anxiety and fear of US stagnation. When Emperor Akihito and Empress Michiko of Japan visited in 1993 when Bill was president, the US had recovered its economic stature, while Japan was facing a "Lost Decade." Its previously envied economy had slowed to a snail's pace, which meant a different set of problems for the relationship. Even so, Japan was still one of the world's great economies and one of the America's closest partners. She writes that she made Japan her first stop as secretary of state to show how the new administration values the relationship in view of US strategy in the region.

Living History might have entertained American readers with abundant names of actual people they are already familiar with and a series of scandals they are already exposed to but not fully disclosed politically and privately. In short, the book resonates with her own people who shared the history Clinton wrote. However, this exclusive relation between Clinton and American readers, whether or not they liked Clinton, raised Japanese suspicion of being taken for granted, ignored, and neglected, much like the 1998 Japan Passing. Though Japanese reviews were mixed, much like they were in the US, sales of *Living History* were low. It was not only because of Clinton's contextual problems that went against Japanese expectations but also because of the poor performance of the publisher and translator: they were not able to overcome the challenges of the project, and in fact, compounded the challenges.

On the contrary, all indications point to more success for *Hard Choices*, even though it has received a low profile in the US, as *Wikipedia* analyzes: "The book was seen partly in the light of a possible Clinton bid in the 2016 presidential election" (n.p.). The Wikipedia entry describes how the book tour felt like a political campaign, with protesters and supports showing up at book-signing events. Although *Hard Choices* reached the top of the New York Times Best Seller List, it sold less than her earlier book, *Living History*.

Clinton's second memoir may become one of the harder choices in her literary career in the US, but the very same book may regain Japanese trust. It is ironic after all that her adjustment for Japanese readers may mean a bad fit for American readers. *Living History* was once one of the hard choices for Japanese to pick and read, but *Hard Choices* may now become a Japanese living history of their own. Meanwhile, Clinton has developed into a unique autobiographer whose writing style, in an excitable language with her multilateral visions and actions, remains skillfully out of joint. Hillary Rodham Clinton's writing style reveals a proud woman standing at the crosswords of how to express her own personal history and identity. Does she sentimentalize it or politicize it? In her two biographies she both rejects and justifies her unique identity in a translation of her own to connect with her readers.

Notes

1 The information of the company is from its own homepage and Amazon. According to the Simon & Schuster, it was founded in 1924 by Richard L. Simon and M. Lincoln Schuster and is now a part of CBS Corporation. The homepage says "Simon & Schuster is a major force in today's consumer publishing industry, dedicated to bringing an extensive cross section of first class information and entertainment in all printed, digital and audio formats to a worldwide audience of readers" (n.p.).

2 David D. Kirkpatrick's "Hillary Clinton Book Advance, $8 Million, Is Near Record."

3 n.p., Anthony York.

4 n.p., Associated Press.

5 n.p., Deirdre Donahue.

6 n.p., Michael Wilson.

7 n.p., David D. Kirkpatrick's "Author Clinton Shakes Many Hands and Sells Many Books."

8 Nielsen BookData responded to an email inquiry on the sales of this book on September 11, 2014.

9 The text referred to in this chapter is Scribner's first mass market paperback export edition published in April, 2004.

10 Along with the etymology of "autobiography" in "Life Narrative: Definitions and Distinctions" (1), Smith and Watson offer the revised glossary of sixty genres in "Appendix A" (253–286) of the second edition of *Reading Autobiography* as the entries are listed below: "Academic Life Writing," "Addiction Narrative," "Adoption Life Stories," "Apology," "Autie Biography," "Auto/Biography," "Autobiography in Second Person," "Autobiography in Third Person," "Autoethnography," "Autofiction," "Autographics," "Autohagiography," "Autosomatography/Autopathography," "Authothanatography," "Autotopography," "Bildungsroman," "Biomythography," "Captivity Narrative," "Case Study," "Collaborative Life Writing," "Confession," "Conversion Narrative," "Diary," "Digital Life Stories," "Ecobiography," "Ethnic Life Narrative," "Ethnocriticism," "Filiation Narrative," "Gastrography," "Genealogical Stories," "Heterobiography," "Jockography," "Journal," "Letters," "Life Narrative," "Life Writing," "Meditation," "Memoir," "Nobody Memoir," "Oral History," "Otobiography," "Periautography," "Personal Essay," "Poetic Autobiography," "Prison Narratives," "Prosopography," "Relational Life Writing," "Scriptotherapy," "Self-Help Narrative," "Self-Portrait," "Serial Autobiography," "Slave Narrative," "Spiritual Life Narrative," "Sports Memoir," "Survivor Narrative," "Testimonio," "Trauma Narrative," "Travel Narrative," "War

Memoir" and "Acts of Witnessing." Each discussion of the following twenty genres in this section of "Context" consists first of the definition by Smith and Watson and then its application to *Living History*.

11 255–256, Sidonie Smith and Julia Watson, 2010.

12 Ibid., p. 256.

13 Ibid., pp. 262–263.

14 20, Sidonie Smith.

15 Smith & Watson, 2010, pp. 264–265.

16 86–88, Rita Felski.

17 270, Sidonie Smith and Julia Watson, 2010.

18 299, Lee Quinby.

19 xv, James Olney.

20 276, Sidonie Smith and Julia Watson, 2010.

21 Ibid., p. 278.

22 44, Susan Friedman.

23 279, Sidonie Smith and Julia Watson, 2010.

24 94, John Beverley.

25 46, Lee Gilmore.

26 284, Sidonie Smith and Julia Watson, 2010.

27 613–614, *Living History*.

28 285, Sidonie Smith and Julia Watson, 2010.

29 187, Smith and Watson's *Reading Autobiography: A Guide for Interpreting Life Narratives*, 1st ed. Stanton's quotes are from "Autogynography: Is the Subject Different?"

30 n.p., Rachael Combe.

31 The exact publication date of the first edition has two sources: December 23rd, according to Amazon, and the 31st, according to publication record of the hardcover edition. References in Japanese in this chapter are paraphrased and/or translated into English by the author.

32 *Hayakawa Online* and *Wikipedia*'s "Hayakawa Shobo." Hayakawa Shobo is a family company, founded by Kiyoshi Hayakawa (1912–1993), who started the publishing business in 1935. Ayako Hayakawa is currently chairperson; Hiroshi Hayakawa, having worked as the company's fifth editorialist, became president in 1989. He received the Ellery Queen Award by Mystery Writers of America (MWA) in 1998 for his contribution to this field. Atsushi Hayakawa is the vice-president. According to *E-Partner*'s 2008 and 2013 "Amazon Japan's Best Publishers," Hayakawa is ranked 44th in 2008 and 39th in 2013 in total sales among Japanese publishers.

33 The email inquiry with the following four questions was sent on July 30, 2014, and responded to on August 5, 2014. I am grateful that the contents of the email are allowed to be used in this chapter.

34 279, Eijun Senaha.

35 Her biographical sources are from home pages of *Bungakuza* and *WebcatPlus*.

36 According to its home page, *AERA*, originally Latin meaning "era," stands for "Asahi Shimnbun Extra Report and Analysis."

37 Translation mistakes are discussed in the previous section, and dating contradictions in the next, when Yoko Sakai and Kazuo Minato are examined.

38 The Japanese text referred to in this chapter is a paperback edition published in November 15, 2007.

39 The paperback's first volume is 477 pages long, and the second volume 478 pages.

40 A specially appointed professor of Jumonji University, Saitama, and a former editorialist and Washington, D.C., branch manager of *Yomiuri Newspaper*, as of the publication date.

41 238. This is Clinton's answer to Lee Atwater's poignant question: "Who will lead us out of this 'spiritual vacuum?'" in the chapter "The End of Something," where Clinton deals with her father's death.

42 Minato is probably referring to the November issue of *Foreign Affairs Report*, a Japanese translation of the English *Foreign Affairs* that appeared as November/December issue. Clinton's English essay appears as "Security and Opportunity for the Twentieth-first Century" and the translation as "Campaign 2008: If I Were to Be Elected President."

43 Some of Clinton's biographies written by Japanese authors are Reiko Kinoshita's *First Team* (1993); Takashi Kakuma's *The Day When Hillary Becomes President: Scandals and American Political Conscious* (2001); and Yukiko Kishimoto's *Hillary and Rice: Faces of Women Who Move America* (2006). Some of the translations published in Japan are Norman King's *Hillary: Her True Story* (1993) by Keiko Musha in 1994; Judith Warner's *First Lady* (1993) by Shin Kawai in 1993; Richard Kozar's *Hillary Rodham Clinton* (1998) by Reiko Kinoshita in 1999; Gail Sheehy's *Hillary's Choice* (1999) by Yoshiko Sakurai in 2000; George Stephanopoulos's *All Too Human: A Political Education* (2000) by Shun Daichi 2001; Christine Ockrent's *La Double vie de Hillary Clinton* (2001) by Kinuko Tottori in 2003; and Jeff Gerth and Don Van Natta, Jr's *Her Way: The Hopes and Ambitions of Hillary Rodham Clinton* (2007) by Makoto Naruke in 2008. More negative criticism of Clinton is translated into Japanese, and only a few Japanese biographers write of her bright sides, as Watanabe says in *America NOW* that more than 80 % of books on Clinton are against her in the US.

44 It was founded in 1876 and is said to be one of the major publishing houses in Japan ("Amazon Japan's Best 100 Publishers"). The Nikkei is known for its nonfiction publications, including economics newspapers and broadcasting business. According to its home page (www.nikkei.com), the company creed is "Fair and Impartial," and it is based on unbiased, comprehensive journalism of quality and reliability. It has 36 bases with more than 230 staff all over the world. Its core is newspaper, but the group business consists of more than 40 affiliated companies. Despite its high reputation as the largest Japanese newspaper company, its overall sales ranking among all Japanese publishers is 23rd in 2013.

45 Clinton reveals intimacy with the Imperial family: "We greeted each other with a smile and hug. Then she welcomed me into her private quarters. The emperor joined us for tea and a conversation about my travels and theirs" (pp. 48–49).

46 44, *Hard Choices*. All references to *Hard Choices* are from this text, a hardcover edition published in 2014.

References

2004 Shuppan Nennkan [Publication Yearbook 2004]. Tokyo: Shuppan News, 2004. Print.

2004 Shuppan Shihyo Nenpo [Almanac of 2004 Publication Index]. Tokyo: All Japan Magazine and Book Publisher's and Editor's Association, 2004. Print.

AERA. HP (http://en.wikipedia.org/wiki/Aera_(magazine)). Dec. 1, 2014. Web.

"Amazon Japan's Best 100 Publishers." *E-Partner*. (www.1book.co.jp/002667.html). Feb. 13, 2009. Web.

Anderson, Linda. *Autobiography*. 2001. London: Routledge, 2007. Print.

Ara, Kaori. "Exclusive Summary of *Living History*: Hillary Inscribes Love, Conflicts, and Decisions." *AERA*. 16.29 (Jul. 14, 2003): 27–31. Print.

Associated P. "Hillary Deal Clears Ethics Pane." *CBS News*. (www.cbsnews.com/ stories/2001/02/15/politics/main272221.shtml). Feb. 15, 2001. Web.

BBC News. "Clintons' Earnings Exceed $100m." *BBC* (http://news.bbc.co.uk/2/ hi/7331834.stm). Apr. 5, 2008. Web.

Beverley, John. "The Margin at the Center: On 'Testimonio' (Testimonial Narrative)." *De/Colonizing the Subject: The Politics of Gender in Women's Autobiography*. Ed. Sidonie Smith and Julia Watson. Minneapolis: U of Minnesota P, 1992. 91–114. Print.

Brockmeier, Jens, Donal Carbaugh, eds. *Narrative and Identity: Studies in Autobiography, Self and Culture*. John Benjamins, 2001. Print.

Clinton, Hillary Rodham. *Hard Choices*. New York: Simon & Schuster, 2014. Print. Trans. ann. 2 vols. Tokyo: The Nikkei, 2015. Print.

——. *Living History*. New York: Simon & Schuster, 2003. Trans. Yoko Sakai. Tokyo: Hayakawa, 2003 (Hardcover) and 2007 (2 vols. Paperbacks). Print.

——. "Security and Opportunity for the Twentieth-first Century." *Foreign Affairs* 86.6 (November/December issue, 2007 (www.foreignaffairs.com/articles/63005/ hillary-rodham-clinton/security-and-opportunity-for-the-twenty-first-century)). Dec. 20, 2014. Web. Trans.

—— "Campaign 2008: If I Were to Be Elected to President." *Foreign Affairs Report* (www .foreignaffairsj.co.jp/archive/yoshi/2007_11.htm#1). Dec. 20, 2014. Web.

Combe, Rachael. "At the Pinnacle of Hillary Clinton's Career." *Elle* (www.elle .com/Life-Love/Society-Career-Power/At-the-Pinnacle-of-Hillary-Clinton-s-Career). Apr. 5, 2012. Web.

Donahue, Deirdre. "Clinton Memoir Tops Best-Selling Books List." *USA Today* (www .usatoday.com/life/books/news/2003-06-17-hillary-list_x.htm). Jun. 17, 2013. Web.

Felski, Rita. *Beyond Feminist Aesthetics: Feminist Literature and Social Change*. Boston: Harvard UP, 1989. Print.

Friedman, Susan Stanford. "Women's Autobiographical Selves: Theory and Practice." *The Private Self: Theory and Practice of Women's Autobiographical Writings*. Ed. Shari Benstock. Chapel Hill: U of North Carolina P, 1988. 34–62. Print.

Gerth, Jeff and Don Van Natta, Jr. *Her Way: The Hopes and Ambitions of Hillary Rodham Clinton*. 2007. Trans. Makoto Naruke. Tokyo: basilico, 2008. Print.

Gilmore, Lee. *The Limits of Autobiography: Trauma and Testimony*. Ithaca: Cornell UP, 2001. Print.

Hammell, Hilary. "Hillary's Turn." *Yale Review of Books* (Spring, 2004). (www .yalereviewofbooks.com/archive/summer03/review14.shtml.htm). Oct. 20, 2014. Web.

"*Hard Choices*." *Wikipedia* (http://en.wikipedia.org/wiki/Hard_Choices). Jan. 14, 2015. Web.

Hayakawa Online. (www.hayakawa-online.co.jp/html/company.html?code=HOL 2014BtoC) Jan. 6, 2015. Web.

"Hayakawa Shobo." *Wikipedia* (http://ja.wikipedia.org/wiki/早川書房). Jan. 6, 2015. Web.

Iguchi, Yuko. Review. *Living History: An Autobiography of Hillary Rodham Clinton*. Tokyo Morning Ed. *Sankei Shimbun* (www.yukoiguchi.net/2004/02/post_d614.html). Feb. 8, 2004. Web.

Inoue, Daisuke. Review. *Living History: An Autobiography of Hillary Rodham Clinton.* Blog. (http://ameblo.jp/inouedaisuke324/entry-11610741544.html). Jul. 22, 2004. Web.

Kakuma, Takashi. *The Day When Hillary Becomes President: Scandals and American Political Conscious.* Tokyo: Shogakukan Bunko, 2001. Print.

King, Norman. *Hillary: Her True Story.* 1993. Trans. Keiko Musha. Tokyo: Shogakukan, 1994. Print.

Kinoshita, Reiko. *First Team.* Tokyo: Shueisha, 1993. Print.

Kirkpatrick, David D. "Author Clinton Shakes Many Hands and Sells Many Books." *New York Times.* (http://query.nytimes.com/gst/fullpage.html?res=9C02E6D8103FF9 35A15754C0A9659C8B6). Jul. 26, 2003. Web.

———. "Hillary Clinton Book Advance, $8 Million, Is Near Record." *New York Times.* (http://query.nytimes.com/gst/fullpage.html?res=9C0DE2DD1739F935A257 51C1A9669C8B63). Dec. 16, 2000. Web.

Kishimoto, Yukiko. *Hillary and Rice: Portraits of Women Who Move America.* Tokyo: PHP Shinsho, 2006. Print.

Kozar, Richard. *Hillary Rodham Clinton.* 1998. Trans. Reiko Kinoshita. Tokyo: Toyo Shorin, 1999. Print.

"*Living History.*" *Wikipedia* (https://en.wikipedia.org/wiki/Living_History). Web. Dec. 10, 2014.

Moore, Michael. *Stupid White Men . . . and Other Sorry Excuses for the State of the Nation!* New York: Harper, 2001. Trans. Iwan Fushimi. Tokyo: Nikkei Publishing, 2003. Print.

Namba, Katsuyuki. Review. *Living History: An Autobiography of Hillary Rodham Clinton.* Blog (www.geocities.jp/nanbaincidents/livinghistory.htm). Jul. 17, 2004. Web.

Nikkei BP. Review. *Living History: An Autobiography of Hillary Rodham Clinton. Amazon .co.jp* (www.amazon.co.jp/Living-History-Hillary-Rodham-Clinton/dp/0755312619). Jan. 12, 2004. Web.

Nikkei, The. *HP* (www.nikkei.co.jp/nikkeiinfo/en/). Jan. 13, 2015. Web.

Nukamizu, Yukari. Review. *Living History: An Autobiography of Hillary Rodham Clinton. Weekly Asahi* (http://book.asahi.com/bunko/TKY200801210217.html). Jan. 25, 2008. Web.

Obama, Barack. *Dreams from My Father: A Story of Race and Inheritance.* 1995. New York: Crown, 2004. Print.

———. *My Dream: Autobiography of Barack Obama [Mai Doriimu: Baraku Obama Jiden].* Tokyo: Diamond, 2007. Print.

Ockrent, Christine. *La Double vie de Hillary Clinton.* 2001. Trans. Kinuko Tottori. Tokyo: KK Best Sellers, 2003. Print.

Olney, James. *Autobiography: Essays Theoretical and Critical.* Princeton: Princeton UP, 2014. Print.

———. *Memory and Narrative: The Weave of Life-Writing.* Chicago: U of Chicago P, 1998. Print.

Quinby, Lee. "The Subject of Memoires: Women Warrior's Technology of Ideographic Selfhood." *De/Colonizing the Subject: The Politics of Gender in Women's Autobiography.* Ed. Sidonie Smith and Julia Watson. Minneapolis: U of Minnesota P, 1992. 297–320. Print.

"Sakai, Yoko." *Bungakuza* (www.bungakuza.com/hikage08/translator.html). Dec. 1, 2014. Web.

——— *Webcat Plus* (http://webcatplus.nii.ac.jp/webcatplus/details/creator/157869.html). Dec. 1, 2014. Web.

Senaha, Eijun. "Radical Masculinity and Traditional Manhood: Japanese Acknowledgments for Literary Obama." *The Global Obama: Crossroads of Leadership in the 21st Century.* Eds. Dinesh Sharma and Uwe P. Gielen New York: Routledge, 2014. Print.

Sheehy Gail. *Hillary's Choice.* 1999. Trans. Yoshiko Sakurai. Tokyo: Asuka Shinsha, 2000. Print.

Showalter, Elaine. "The Throne behind the Power." *The Guardian* (www .theguardian.com/profile/elaineshowalter). Jun. 14, 2003. Web.

Simon & Shuster. *HP* (www.simonandschuster.com). Oct. 15, 2014. Web.

Smith, Sidonie. "'America's Exhibit A': Hillary Rodham Clinton's *Living History* and the Genres of Authenticity." *American Literary History.* 24.3 (Fall, 2012): 523–42. Print.

—— and Julia Watson, eds. *De/Colonizing the Subject: The Politics of Gender in Women's Autobiography.* Minneapolis: U of Minnesota P, 1992. Print.

——. *Reading Autobiography: A Guide for Interpreting Life Narratives,* 1st ed. Minneapolis: U of Minnesota P, 2001. Print.

——. *Reading Autobiography: A Guide for Interpreting Life Narratives,* 2nd ed. Minneapolis: U of Minnesota P, 2010. Print.

——. *Women, Autobiography, Theory: A Reader.* Madison: U of Wisconsin P, 1998. Print.

Stanton, Donna C. "Autogynography: Is the Subject Different?" *The Female Autograph.* Ed. Donna C. Stanton. New York: New York Literary Forum, 1984. 3–20. Print.

Stephanopoulos, George. *All Too Human: A Political Education.* 2000. Trans. Shun Daichi. Tokyo: Kodansha, 2001. Print.

Stothard, Peter. "Schooled in Scandal." *Times Literary Supplement* 5230 (June 27, 2003): 1. Print.

USA Today. "Hillary Clinton Writes New Afterword for Paperback of 'Living History.'" *Associated P* (http://usatoday30.usatoday.com/life/books/news/2004-04-06-living-history-addition_x.htm). Apr. 6, 2004. Web.

Warner, Judith. *First Lady.* 1993. Trans. Shin Kawai. Tokyo: Asahi Shimbunsha, 1993. Print.

Watanabe, Masato. "On Presidential Election and Book Campaign." *America NOW.* 27. Tokyo Foundation (www.tkfd.or.jp/research/project/sub1.php?id=209). Oct. 29, 2008. Web.

Wilson, Michael. "Senator Clinton Offers a Cure For Foot-in-Mouth Disease." *New York Times* (http://query.nytimes.com/gst/fullpage.html?res=9C05E3D8133D F933A25754C0A9659C8B63). Jul. 10, 2003. Web.

Whitt, Jan. "'The Gray Zone': Hillary Clinton and the Ways We Live (and Tell) History." *Women's Studies* 39.8 (December, 2010): 851–876. Print.

Woodward, Bob. *Bush at War.* New York: Simon & Schuster, 2002. Trans. Kazuya Matsuda. Tokyo: Kashiwa Shobo, 2003. Print.

York, Anthony. "Hillary's Book Deal Blues." *Salon.com* (http://archive.salon.com/politics/feature/2000/12/19/clinton/index.html). Dec. 19, 2000. Web.

BIOGRAPHICAL NOTES

N'Dri Thérèse Assié-Lumumba, president of the Comparative and International Education Society (CIES), is a professor of African and diaspora education, comparative and international education, social institutions, African social history, and the study of gender in the Africana Studies and Research Center at Cornell University.

Kenneth Christie is a political scientist, author and editor who has taught and conducted research at universities in the U.S., Singapore, South Africa, Norway, and Dubai. He is widely published as an author and editor, with eight books to his credit. He is head of the Human Security and Peacebuilding program at Royal Roads University, Canada.

Florence L. Denmark is the Robert Scott Pace Distinguished Research Professor at Pace University. She served as president of the American Psychological Association, the International Council of Psychologists, Eastern Psychological Association, New York State Psychological Association and Psi Chi. She was also a vice-president of the New York Academy of Sciences.

Ellen Fleishman is a supervisor of school psychologists at the NYC Department of Education for 23 years, a position she currently holds, and has taught at both the graduate and undergraduate levels. Dr. Fleishman has published in psychological journals and has presented research at conferences in the US and Europe.

Hillary I. Goldstein is a graduate student in psychology at Pace University, working on her doctorate in clinical and school psychology.

Robynn Kuhlmann earned her PhD in political science from the University of New Orleans. Her fields of study are American political institutions and political behavior. She is an assistant professor in political science at University of Central Missouri Warrensburg, Missouri.

Donald Morrison is an author, journalist and educator. At *TIME*, he was editor of its Asian edition in Hong Kong and its European edition in London. He has taught at New York University in London, Tsinghua University in Beijing, and the Institut d'etudes politiques (Sciences Po) in Paris.

Grant J. Rich is an international psychologist, recently moving from Juneau, Alaska, to Cambodia and finally to India, where he is associate professor at the Ashoka University, New Delhi. His interests in cross-cultural and international psychology were shaped at the University of Chicago, where he received a PhD in interdisciplinary human development and psychology.

Eijun Senaha is an associate professor of English literature and film studies at Hokkaido University, Japan. He received a doctorate in English literature from the University of South Carolina, with a special focus on gender relations, women's studies and queer studies.

Prakhar Sharma is a program manager at the Political Violence Field Lab, Yale University. He is completing a PhD in Political Science at Syracuse University and is a contributing editor to the *Fair Observer*. He has worked as a consultant at the World Bank, the American University of Afghanistan and the UNICEF in Afghanistan.

Gregory W. Streich currently serves as professor of political science at the University of Central Missouri, Warrensburg, Missouri. He is the author of many articles on topics such as justice, democracy and national identity. He is the author of *US Foreign Policy: A Documentary and Reference Guide*.

Kristin Thies is a graduate student in psychology at Pace University, working on her doctorate in clinical and school psychology.

Adrian Tworecke is currently pursuing her doctoral degree in child clinical and school psychology at Pace University. Her research interests include the psychological and cultural influences on women's development and identity; how social media effects women's self-esteem and body image; and issues concerning sex, gender and sexuality.

INDEX